Giving Credit to Dictatorship

This edited volume explores the interplay between [illegible]al, economic, and financial development in twentieth-century European authoritarian regimes.

The book features case studies that explore the impact of domestic and international finance on the rise, stabilization, and decline of various European dictatorships of the twentieth century, such as Italy, Germany, Yugoslavia, Portugal, Spain, Greece, and Turkey. The chapters delve into the role that the regimes played in shaping and transforming the financial system, exploring their international interconnections as well as the influence of economic theory and ideological constructs in dictatorial environments. Applying the methodological framework of the history of capitalism to the analysis of the relationship between authoritarian regimes and financial systems, the book provides new insights into the relationships between politics and economics, and it offers a fresh perspective on contemporary political issues and their interaction with the global financial system.

This collection is an ideal resource for postgraduate students and researchers in history, economics, political economy, and political sciences.

Valerio Torreggiani is Research Fellow at the Institute of Social Sciences, University of Lisbon. He is the author of several works on the history of capitalism, organized interests, and corporatism in the nineteenth and twentieth centuries, such as *Corporatism in Early Twentieth-Century Britain* (2022), *Uniformità, frammentazione e conflitto* (2022) and *Capitalismo e regime fascista* (2024).

José Luís Cardoso is Research Professor at the Institute of Social Sciences of the University of Lisbon, Portugal. He is author and editor of several books on the Portuguese history of economic thought from a comparative perspective, with special emphasis on the study of the processes of diffusion and assimilation of economic ideas.

Routledge Studies in Fascism and the Far Right

Series editors: Nigel Copsey
Teesside University, UK
Graham Macklin
Center for Research on Extremism (C-REX), University of Oslo, Norway

This book series focuses upon national, transnational and global manifestations of fascist, far right and right-wing politics primarily within a historical context but also drawing on insights and approaches from other disciplinary perspectives. Its scope also includes anti-fascism, radical-right populism, extreme-right violence and terrorism, cultural manifestations of the far right, and points of convergence and exchange with the mainstream and traditional right.

The Metaphysics of Race
Science and Faith in the Nazi Worldview
Amit Varshizky

Imagining Alternative Worlds
Far-right Fiction and the Power of Cultural Imaginaries
Christoffer Kølvraa and Bernhard Forchtner

The Transnational Making of Italian Neofascism
Matteo Albanese

Frege and Fascism
Stephen D'Arcy

Giving Credit to Dictatorship
Authoritarian Regimes and Financial Capitalism in Europe during the Twentieth Century
Edited by Valerio Torreggiani and José Luís Cardoso

For more information about this series, please visit: www.routledge.com/Routledge-Studies-in-Fascism-and-the-Far-Right/book-series/FFR

Giving Credit to Dictatorship

Authoritarian Regimes and Financial Capitalism in Europe during the Twentieth Century

Edited by Valerio Torreggiani and José Luís Cardoso

Routledge
Taylor & Francis Group
LONDON AND NEW YORK

First published 2025
by Routledge
4 Park Square, Milton Park, Abingdon, Oxon OX14 4RN

and by Routledge
605 Third Avenue, New York, NY 10158

Routledge is an imprint of the Taylor & Francis Group, an informa business

British Library Cataloguing-in-Publication Data
A catalogue record for this book is available from the British Library

ISBN: 978-1-032-65616-8 (hbk)
ISBN: 978-1-032-65617-5 (pbk)
ISBN: 978-1-032-65619-9 (ebk)

DOI: 10.4324/9781032656199

Typeset in Times New Roman
by Apex CoVantage, LLC

Contents

Foreword

Youssef Cassis

The question of 'giving credit to dictatorship' is an old issue – think for example of Daniel Guérin's (1936) classic book, *Fascisme et grand capital*, first published in 1936 – but it is also a topical one and this book is an important step in the renewal of a debate in which historians should play a key role. The chapters that follow discuss fascinating case studies, the relationships between finance and authoritarian regimes in twentieth-century Europe, from Spain and Portugal to Greece and Turkey through Italy and Germany, from the 1920s to the 1970s.

In this preface, I would like to offer a few reflections on the relationships between international finance and authoritarian regimes from the late nineteenth to the early twenty-first century. Two questions are at the heart of these reflections, which pertain to the book's central issue and are implicitly or explicitly present in the following chapters. First, are financial markets, and for that matter financial actors, concerned about the nature of the regime of the country to which they lend or in which they invest? Second, is there any correlation between the degree of openness of the world economy – globalisation or deglobalisation – and the amount of credit given to dictators?

For the purpose of these remarks, I have defined international finance as private capital, in terms of activities, especially foreign investment, financial centres, and financial actors. I have only considered dictatorships as authoritarian regimes, with the exclusion of the so-called 'hybrid regimes', but with the inclusion of colonial regimes, which were clearly authoritarian. And I have distinguished between what could be called 'capitalist' and 'communist' dictatorships, which tend to be grouped together in the literature if the former are dominant-party dictatorships. In both cases, the conditions faced by international investors are well worth exploring, in terms of volume of capital inflows and relationships between debtors and creditors.

International finance and authoritarianism

Financial markets and financial actors are primarily concerned with business and profit opportunities and with the safety of their investment, which can be secured or endangered by the advent or the collapse of an authoritarian regime. Some investors are prepared to take higher risks, in an economically or politically unstable environment, but they expect higher returns.

Foreign investors have never hesitated to invest in authoritarian regimes. This can be considered as the default option: there must be a specific reason for *not* investing in an authoritarian regime. On the eve of the First World War, the second largest recipient of foreign investment, Imperial Russia, was an autocracy, as was another major recipient of foreign investment, the Ottoman Empire. Several other capital importing countries were authoritarian or borderline cases. In the interwar years, at any rate in the 1920s, fascist Italy was fully integrated in international finance and was the third largest debtor country, after Germany and Austria. The involvement of international finance in Latin American military dictatorships in the 1960s and 1970s has been well documented. By the late twentieth century, international capital flows had taken a new direction: from rich countries to rich countries or even from poor to rich countries. Nevertheless, in 2000, China was one of the main recipients of foreign investment and the largest amongst emerging economies (Schularick, 2016).

Colonial empires are a clear example of investors' search for safety, often combined with high returns, with complete disregard for the sheer violence inherent to colonial rule, as shown by Caroline Elkins in her recent book on the British Empire (Elkins, 2022). Indeed, the loss of independence of many a country can be attributed, at least in part, to the protection of foreign investors, though the fallen regime was usually autocratic – think, for example, of Egypt in 1882. The authoritarian character of colonial rule guaranteed the safety of investments. As Niall Ferguson and Moritz Schularick argued, less developed British colonies were able to borrow at much lower rates than comparable independent countries (Ferguson and Schularick, 2006).

The world of international finance did not disapprove of authoritarianism and looked favourably at regimes that were not hostile to their interests, even if they did not always condone their excesses. Before the First World War, bankers' value systems were deeply marked by the imperialist culture of the day. For Edgar Vincent, later Viscount D'Abernon, a Governor of the Imperial Ottoman Bank, Arabs, and more particularly Egyptians, suffered from 'an absence of our ideas of honesty, of courage, of disinterestedness'. Fascist Italy had its admirers amongst high financiers, even though they deplored the violence. Thomas Lamont, J.P. Morgan's leading partner, a Republican progressive and champion of the League of Nations, served as banker to Italy during its Fascist period and coached Mussolini on how to appeal to Anglo-American opinion (Chernow, 1990). Half a century later, bankers had a similar view of the military regimes in Latin America and praised them for bringing political stability, eliminating terrorism, and adopting a pro-business attitude (Altamura, 2021). According to a recent article in the *Financial Times*, many Hong Kong expats are glad that the Chinese national security law ended the riots, and few of those who left took a stand against the change (Kinder, 2022).

This raises the related question of why financial actors should shun investing in authoritarian regimes The most obvious reason is the lack of business opportunities. This was mainly the case with poorer countries, including within colonial empires. In 1914, only 9 percent of French foreign assets were invested in its colonies, several of them considered as economically worthless (Marseille, 1984).

A recurrent concern regarding foreign investment has been the risk of default. Analyses of sovereign debt, which have proliferated in recent years, only incidentally distinguish between democratic and autocratic defaulters; and when they do it, they are concerned with specific issues, such as whether a democratic government should inherit the debt of an overthrown despotic ruler (Mallard, 2021). A glance at available data suggests that most defaults were by authoritarian regimes in emerging economies in Africa, Asia, and Latin America (Reinhart and Rogoff, 2009). However, it is not clear whether emerging economies or authoritarian regimes, or a combination of both, were more likely to default.

Whatever their lack of scruples about lending to dictators, international financiers could simply be prevented from doing so. Business opportunities fell dramatically in the Soviet Union after 1918 though they never disappeared and would increase in later periods. Branches of foreign banks were closed or nationalised, including Citibank's Moscow branch, opened on 27 November 1917! Ironically, the international financial community had welcomed the end of the autocratic tsarist regime in February 1917 (Malik, 2018). Foreign banks were also eliminated from China after 1949 though some banks, such as the Hong Kong and Shanghai Banking Corporation, could continue to operate a branch in Shanghai during the 1950s and 1960s. The rise of nationalism in a number of authoritarian regimes, especially in newly independent countries, led to the nationalisation of foreign banks, for example, in the Middle East in the late 1950s and early 1960s – Egypt in 1957, Syria in 1961, and Iraq in 1964. Discriminatory measures could also force them to reduce their activities or to entirely withdraw (Jones, 1993).

Conversely, bankers could be constrained to withdraw from an authoritarian regime because of the political stand of their own government. This happens in times of rising geopolitical tensions and, obviously, wars between their home country and the dictatorship in which they have been involved.

Could public opinion force international finance away from authoritarian regimes? The evidence is patchy but rather negative, even when criticism came from within its own ranks.

Before 1914, the Rothschilds and other prominent Jewish bankers in Europe and America campaigned against antisemitism and threatened to withdraw their support to foreign loans to Tsarist Russia. However, despite their huge influence, Russia continued to borrow on the international financial markets, with the participation of the Rothschilds (Ferguson, 1998). In 1928, the Women's International League for Peace was unable to prevent JP Morgan to issue a loan to Japan for the construction of the South Manchurian Railway. Japan was increasingly moving towards a military dictatorship and imperialist expansion in Northeast China. The Women's League campaign struck a chord with public opinion and its leaders were related through friendship and family links to Thomas Lamont, whom we encountered earlier. And yet JP Morgan was only forced to withdraw its financial support to Japan from 1931, when it clearly went against the American foreign policy (Pak, 2013).

Public criticism of the military dictatorships had no impact on European banks' increasing involvement in Latin America in the 1970s and 1980s, whether through granting loans or opening branches (Altamura, 2021). On the other hand, anti-apartheid campaigns convinced Barclays Bank of the importance of public opinion and political judgement in corporate behaviour. The bank sold its subsidiary in South Africa in 1986 at a heavily discounted price which, it has been argued, benefited White South Africans far more than Black South Africans (Ackrill and Hannah, 2001).

Globalisation and deglobalisation

According to Maurice Obstfeld and Alan Taylor, the ratio of foreign assets to world GDP was 22 percent in 1900 – almost certainly an underestimation because of the lack of data and probably nearer 50 per cent. It had fallen to 8 percent in 1930 and to 6 percent in 1960, before rising to 92 percent in 2000 (Obstfeld and Taylor, 2004). How far have globalisation and deglobalisation affected the involvement of international finance with authoritarian regimes? Not surprisingly, these links were more intense during the period of globalisation – before 1914, and even 1931, and after 1980 – than during the fifty years in between. After all, the collapse of foreign investment affected both autocracies and democracies. But were other factors at play?

The first globalisation was the period when international finance was most involved with authoritarian regimes. On the eve of the First World War, between 35 and 40 percent of the world's foreign assets were invested in authoritarian regimes – about 30 percent of British foreign investment and 55 percent of French foreign investment. Colonial empires, not including Britain's Dominions, represented about half the investments in authoritarian regimes, in other words, less than 20 percent went to independent dictatorships (Woodruff, 1966). Interestingly, while the bulk of British investment in authoritarian regimes were in its colonial empire (78 percent, not including the Dominions), exactly the opposite was true for France (16 percent). Latin American countries and the Austro-Hungarian Empire, all big capital importers, have not been considered as authoritarian regimes.

These investments were mostly portfolio investment. Funds were raised in the leading international financial centres: London, Paris, and Berlin, with New York a latecomer and Brussels playing an ancillary role. Financial centres emerged in authoritarian regimes, but were of different types depending on their role in the global economy and the geopolitical power of the host country. St Petersburg was the political and financial capital of a great power, though it remained a financial centre of regional significance whose main banks were dominated by French capital. Constantinople was the capital of a much weaker power and mainly an outpost for the economic penetration of the Ottoman Empire. In the British colonies, centres like Hong Kong, Bombay, Calcutta, Cairo, or Alexandria played the same role as Shanghai and Peking in a 'semi colony' or Rio de Janeiro and Buenos Aires in countries with 'hybrid' regimes: they were trade centres where a number of British and European multinational banks had opened a branch to finance foreign trade (Cassis, 2010).

International finance was less involved with authoritarian regimes during the phase of deglobalisation lasting from the Great Depression to the end of Bretton Woods. In terms of capital stocks, Russia reneged on its debts in 1918 and virtually ceased to borrow from the West. On the other hand, investment in the colonies increased – from 11 percent of Britain's foreign investments in 1913 to 20 percent in 1938, without taking into account the Dominions. The share of the French colonial empire rose even more dramatically, from 9 percent to 30 percent (Etemad, 2005).

Otherwise, international capital flows virtually came to a standstill in the wake of the Wall Street crash of 1929 – they peaked in 1928. As far as European debtors are concerned, annual capital inflows dropped from about $1.7 billion in 1928 to about $0.5 billion in 1930 (Feinstein and Watson, 1995). The withdrawal of foreign capital, in the first place American, from Germany, the largest capital importer, aggravated the depression and contributed to the advent of the Nazi regime. As a result, international finance was little involved with authoritarian regimes in the 1930s, except for colonial empires – of course in terms of capital flows, not of capital stocks.

Private international capital flows did not resume on a large scale after the Second World War. Between 1955 and 1962, foreign issues floated in New York, by then the world's leading financial centre, barely reached $4.2 billion – a feeble sum compared with the $126.5 billion for domestic issues and the $98 billion in economic and military aid granted by the United States to foreign countries (Nadler, Heller, and Shipman, 1955). So, at an aggregate level, international finance was no more involved with authoritarian regimes in the 1950s than in the 1930s.

The situation started to change with the reopening of the world economy in the 1960s, and especially the 1970s. International finance became involved with both communist and capitalist dictatorships. European commercial banks had been granting credit to the Soviet Union since the 1950s, but most of them opened branches or representative offices in Moscow in the early 1970s, mainly in connection with the financial side of large industrial contracts. With the recycling of the petrodollars from the mid-1970s, international capital flows became dominated by commercial banks' credit to emerging economies, most if not all of them authoritarian regimes, whether Eastern European communist countries, such as Poland, Hungary, or Rumania; Latin American military dictatorships, such as Argentina and Brazil; or non-military, such as Mexico; or African personalist dictatorships, such as Zaire.

The second globalisation, starting in the 1980s led, on the one hand, to a decrease in investment in authoritarian regimes, not only because the number of such regimes had decreased but also because the bulk of foreign investment, over 85 percent in 2000, went to the advanced economies, associated with democratic regimes, of North America, Western Europe, and Japan. On the other hand, and paradoxically, the links between international finance and the authoritarian regimes in power became much closer.

One example of such links is the emergence of leading international financial centres in authoritarian regimes. The most conspicuous example is that of Singapore. The rise of Singapore as a major international financial centre was the result of the systematic effort made on the part of the authorities soon after the country's independence in 1965. They first enabled the Asian dollar market to establish itself from the outset in Singapore and then encouraged the emergence of a bond market. Singapore's financial markets really took on an international dimension from the 1980s reflected, among other indicators, by the number of foreign banks, which reached 185 in 1995.

The rise of Singapore has been widely discussed in the economics and financial literature and seen as an example to be emulated by aspiring financial centres in emerging economies. The authoritarian nature of the regime has only been acknowledged in passing, and if so as a contributing factor to Singapore's success. Since the turn of the twenty-first century Singapore has consistently figured in the top five world's financial centres and considered not as an authoritarian regime, but alongside London, New York, Hong Kong, and Tokyo, as a competitor to Switzerland for wealth management and a rival to Hong Kong for pre-eminence in Asia (Lessard, 1994).

A similar but also a different case is Dubai, which ranked as high as eighth in the *Global Financial Centres Index* in 2019 and has consistently ranked in the top twenty in the last fifteen years. Dubai might be considered as less free than Singapore, but all the leading banks, including HSBC, BNP Paribas, JP Morgan, Citibank, Goldman Sachs, and Morgan Stanley, are present in the Emirates.

The third case is China, which hosts several of the world's leading financial centres, including Shanghai, Beijing, and Shenzhen in addition to Hong Kong, where all the leading transnational banks are represented. As indicated earlier, in 2000, China was the largest recipient of foreign investment amongst emerging economies, and the tenth largest overall while it started accumulating vast amounts of American government bonds.

The contrast with the first globalisation is striking. No autocratic regime, including Russia, had risen to a position of financial pre-eminence, and no financial centre of international significance had emerged in an authoritarian regime. St. Petersburg was far less important at the international level than Shanghai today. And Constantinople in 1913 was in no way comparable to Dubai in 2013.

Concluding remarks

For international finance, giving credit to dictatorships was the norm, not the exception, from Tsarist Russia to fascist Italy, Latin American military dictatorships, and communist China. Considering colonialism as another type of dictatorship has also widened the field of authoritarian regimes, especially from a financial perspective in the first half of the twentieth century. On the other hand, highlighting the normality for international finance to deal with dictatorships can explain the continuity between the first and second globalisation waves, and the intimacy between international finance and authoritarian regimes at the turn of the twenty-first century. From that perspective, the looser links between international finance and authoritarian regimes, mainly observable from the 1930s to the 1980s – the period covered in this volume –could be explained by depression and wars rather than political or ideological factors.

However, such links were more complex at the national level, especially in independent 'capitalist' authoritarian regimes in Europe and Latin America. They tended to be stronger and closer at both personal and institutional levels, if only because authoritarian regimes were able to control the country's financial system and obtain credit through domestic financial institutions. These relationships were affected by many factors, as can be seen in this book's chapters, including, among others, the balance of power between state and finance, existing opportunities and constraints, the prevailing economic climate, the degree of integration in the world economy, and the regime's relationships with international finance. But in the end, whether at the international or national level, the political behaviour of the world of finance remained fundamentally the same: they adapted to events rather than shaped them.

References

Ackrill, Margaret and Hannah, Leslie. *Barclays. The Business of Banking 1690–1996*. Cambridge: Cambridge University Press, 2001.

Altamura, Carlo Edoardo. "Global Banks and Latin American Dictators, 1974–1982." *Business History Review*, 95 (2), 2021.

Cassis, Youssef. *Capitals of Capital. The Rise and Fall of International Financial Centres*. Cambridge: Cambridge University Press, 2010.

Chernow, Ron. *The House of Morgan. An American Banking Dynasty and the Rise of Modern Finance*. London: Simon & Schuster, 1990.

Elkins, Caroline. *Legacy of Violence. A History of the British Empire*. London: The Bodley Head, 2022.

Etemad, Bouda. *De l'utilité des empires*. Paris: Armand Colin, 2005.

Feinstein, Charles H. and Watson, Katherine. "Private International Capital Flows in the Inter-War Period." In Charles H. Feinstein (ed.), *Banking, Currency and Finance in Europe Between the Wars*. Oxford: Oxford University Press, 1995.

Ferguson, Niall. *The World's Banker. The History of the House of Rothschild*. London: Weidenfeld & Nicolson, 1998.

Ferguson, Niall and Schularick, Moritz. "The Empire Effect. The Determinants of Country Risk in the First Age of Globalization." *Journal of Economic History*, 66 (2), 2006.

Guérin, Daniel. *Fascisme et grand capital. Italie – Allemagne*. Paris: Gallimard, 1936 (English translation, *Fascism and Big Business*, 1938).

Jones, Geoffrey. *British Multinational Banking, 1830–1990*. Oxford: Oxford University Press, 1993.

Kinder, Tabby. "Hong Kong Expat Party Continues – But for How Long?" *Financial Times*, September 30, 2022.

Lessard, Donald R. "Singapore as an International Financial Centre". In Richard Roberts (ed.), *Offshore Financial Centres*. Aldershot: Elgar, 1994.

Malik, Hassan. *Bankers and Bolsheviks. International Finance and the Russian Revolution*. Princeton, NJ and Oxford: Princeton University Press, 2018.

Mallard, Grégoire. "We Owe You Nothing: Decolonization and Sovereign Debt Obligations in International Public Law." In Pierre Pénet and Juan Flores Zendejas (eds.), *Sovereign Debt Diplomacies: Rethinking sovereign debt from colonial empires to hegemony*. Oxford: Oxford University Press, 2021.

Marseille, Jacques. *Empire colonial et capitalisme français. Histoire d'un divorce*. Paris: Albin Michel, 1984.
Nadler, Marcus, Heller, Sipa and Shipman, Samuel S. "New York as an International Financial Center." In *The Money Market and Its Institutions*. New York, 1955.
Obstfeld, Maurice and Taylor, Alan M. *Global Capital Markets. Integration, Crisis, and Growth*. Cambridge: Cambridge University Press, 2004.
Pak, Susie J. *Gentlemen Bankers. The World of J.P. Morgan*. Cambridge, MA and London: Harvard University Press, 2013.
Reinhart, Carmen M. and Rogoff, Kenneth S. *This Time Is Different. Eight Centuries of Financial Folly*. Princeton, NJ and Oxford: Princeton University Press, 2009.
Schularick, Moritz. "International Capital Flows." In Youssef Cassis, Richard S. Grosman and Catherine R. Schenk (eds.), *The Oxford Handbook of Banking and Financial History*. Oxford: Oxford University Press, 2016.
The Global Financial Centres Index, published by Z/Yen since 2007.
Woodruff, William. *Impact of Western Man: A Study of Europe's Role in the World Economy, 1750–1960*. New York: St. Martin's Press, 1966.

Contributors

Marianna Astore
Universita dell'Insubria and University of Oxford

Enrico Berbenni
Universita Cattolica del Sacro Cuore
Milano

José Luís Cardoso
Instituto de Ciencias Sociais
Universidade de Lisboa

Federico Castelli
European University Institute
and
Universita di Milano and LEREPS
Sciences Po Toulouse

Joaquim Cuevas
Universitat de Valencia

Žarko Lazarević
Inštitut za novejšo zgodovino
Ljubljana

Tayfun Mertan
Koc University
Istanbul

Mario Perugini
Universita di Catania

Anna Veronica Pobbe
Universita Ca' Foscari
Venezia

Maria A. Pons
Universitat de Valencia

Michalis Psalidopoulos
The American College of Greece and University of Athens

Elena Martínez-Ruiz
Universidad de Alcala
Madrid

Enrique Jorge-Sotelo
Universitat de Barcelona

Ana Tomás
Instituto Superior de Economia e Gestao
Universidade de Lisboa

Valerio Torreggiani
Instituto de Ciencias Sociais
Universidade de Lisboa

Nuno Valério
Instituto Superior de Economia e Gestao
Universidade de Lisboa

Andrea Viola
Universita Cattolica del Sacro Cuore
Milano

Authoritarianism and financial capitalism in twentieth-century Europe

An introduction

Valerio Torreggiani and José Luís Cardoso

Capitalism, democracy and authoritarianism

Over the centuries, the relationship between capitalism and democracy has often faced tensions and challenges. Recent global financial crisis during 2007–2008 and the economic downturn caused by the COVID-19 epidemic have led scholars to re-examine the characteristics and history of the current economic model, which relies on self-regulating markets and a deregulated financial system, as well as its social and political consequences. This re-evaluation encompasses broader issues such as global inequality, environmental challenges, economic regulation, financial rules, progressive taxation and fiscal policies. Moreover, in recent decades, scholars from various disciplines have also focused on the accelerated pace of globalization and observed how financial capitalism can flourish in a variety of social and political contexts, spanning democratic and authoritarian regimes alike (Milanovic, 2019). At the same time, there have been notable increases in various forms of authoritarian governance worldwide – in Russia, China, Hungary, Turkey, North Korea and several Gulf states, just to name a few – a trend that António Costa Pinto has aptly called the "return of dictatorships" (Pinto, 2021). This authoritarian shift marks a significant departure from the transitions witnessed in the second half of the twentieth century, which saw several national movements towards democratization, often referred to as the "third wave of democratization" (Huntington, 1991). Overall, despite their democratic window-dressing (Gandhi, 2008) and their hybrid authoritarianism (Levitsky and Way, 2010), the core undemocratic approach of twentieth-first century authoritarian regimes towards society and economy remains deep-rooted. Besides, the prevalence of authoritarian regimes in major potentially hegemonic nations like Russia and China is a primary cause of concern, especially in terms of global power dynamics.

As Mark Twain had written – the attribution is uncertain – history doesn't repeat itself, but it rhymes. Recent political and economic developments, discarding Francis Fukuyama's speculation on the democratic "end of history" (Fukuyama, 1992), were crucial in reopening an old debate on the relationships among capitalism, freedom and democracy (Kocka, 2015). In this regard, the economist Mordecai Kurtz has recently traced the evolution of capitalism from a promise of freedom and progress to a system marked by the concentration of wealth and influence in the hands of a

DOI: 10.4324/9781032656199-1

few giants, perpetuating social polarization and economic disparity, and ultimately eroding the fabric of democracy (Kurz, 2024). The discourse surrounding the nexus between capitalism and democracy conceals another debate that constitutes the opposite (darker) side of the former, pertaining to the varieties of capitalism that exist in authoritarian regimes.[1] Dictatorial regimes, in fact, are not solely an expression of reactionary or anti-modern forces but are often fostered by the dynamics of capitalism, and their institutions and policies are frequently upheld by the ruling classes in specific historical settings. In these contexts, forms of violent repression are established in parallel to a process of rationalization and modernization of the capitalist structures of the society (Togliatti, 2010; Gramsci, 1971; Fano Damascelli, 1971). Given the current recession of liberal democracy and the increasing prominence of authoritarianism (Wolf, 2023), along with the rise of radical forms of capitalism without democracy (Slobodian, 2023), historical explorations into the nexus between dictatorships and capitalism appear especially relevant. In fact, history, as stated by Youssef Cassis ten years ago, although unable to predict the future, can and must inform debates about the future (Cassis, 2011: 1).

This volume delves into less explored aspects of the debate on capitalism, focusing on the interplay between finance and authoritarian regimes in twentieth-century Europe. In doing so, it aims at promoting the "natural alliance" that Barry Eichengreen (2019: 21) has identified between economic historians trained in economic departments and historians of capitalism from the humanities and social sciences – who must "stop the bickering and join forces", as Marc Flandreau has already stressed (2019: 4). Since the 1980s, the "cultural turn" in the study of fascism has significantly altered the analysis of authoritarian regimes, enhancing our comprehension of their politics, ideology and culture. However, according to Adam Tooze's observation several years ago (Tooze, 2006), this shift has resulted in a disregard for the material economy of dictatorships, which has been analyzed by quantitative economic historians who frequently neglect the impact of political agency and cultural factors.[2] This book seeks to rekindle historiographical interest in the study of the interconnected histories of European dictatorships and the development of both national and international financial systems, emphasizing the importance of time, place and context, while also exploring the connections between ideological, political, economic and financial elements. Overall, the authors of the chapters address the role that some European regimes played in shaping and transforming the financial system, examining various themes and applying diverse methodologies, tools and analytical perspectives. In doing so, by bridging the disciplinary divide between political and economic history, the objective of this book is to explore the intricate network of political and economic relations that existed between authoritarian regimes and financial systems, both domestically and internationally.

The twentieth century brought significant transformations to Europe, influenced by political ideologies, economic systems and global dynamics. The evolution of financial and banking systems towards modernity unfolded not only within the development of Western democracy but also within the intricate web of authoritarian regimes that dotted the continent. From the rise of fascist regimes in Italy and

Germany to the authoritarian dictatorships in Spain, Portugal, Greece and Eastern Europe, both before and after the Second World War, the political context, characterized by centralized power structures and often repressive policies, wielded significant influence over domestic financial systems. Government control and intervention in financial matters were common features, as regimes sought to harness economic resources to consolidate power and pursue their political agendas. In contrast, financial institutions also exerted their sway over economic policies, navigating a delicate balance of power between state control and market forces. While authoritarian regimes sought to shape financial systems to serve their political objectives, financial elites often had their own interests and agendas, leading to complex dynamics of negotiation and compromise. Moreover, the interaction between authoritarian regimes and economic theories and models propagated by intellectuals allied with these regimes played a significant role. In fact, intellectuals and thinkers who were supportive of authoritarian regimes formulated economic theories and models that frequently reflected and reinforced authoritarian ideologies, providing intellectual legitimacy for the regimes' economic policies.

The connection between authoritarian governments and financial systems transcended national boundaries and extended to the global arena, where European regimes engaged with world markets and institutions. In fact, this relationship pertains to the study of the interdependence between the overarching structure of capitalism within a specific historical period, which can be described as a "singular structure" (Wallerstein, 1974), and the various subtypes that evolve within it. The relationship between European regimes and the global stage was characterized by a high degree of dynamism and complexity, as these entities sought to assert their influence through the use of economic power while simultaneously grappling with the pressures and constraints imposed by international economic forces. Therefore, the role of authoritarian regimes in the broader context of global capitalism's transformation was multifaceted. These regimes acted as both agents and products of this transformation, navigating its complexities to consolidate power and advance their agendas. While some regimes embraced state interventionism and protectionism to promote economic development and social stability, others pursued neoliberal economic policies to integrate into the global capitalist system. The diversity of approaches reflected the unique historical, political and economic contexts of each regime. Analysing the specific histories of these regimes reveals fascinating connections as their trajectories intersect with the tumultuous interwar and post-Second World War periods, marked by hegemonic transitions and geopolitical upheaval. The chaotic hegemonic transition of the interwar period significantly influenced the political and economic dynamics of Europe, setting the stage for the rise of authoritarian regimes and the outbreak of the Second World War. This historical backdrop, in turn, influenced the post-1945 establishment of United States world hegemony, shaping the geopolitical landscape of the second half of the twentieth century. In essence, exploring these research questions illuminates the intricate interaction between authoritarian regimes, financial systems, and global dynamics, shedding light on the complex interplay of politics, economics and power that shaped twentieth-century Europe and beyond.

In the historiography of dictatorships in the interwar period, the terms fascism and authoritarianism are often referred to as if they were synonyms. The term fascism usually serves to designate a type of political regime that suspends the practice of democracy, represses individual freedom and promotes the glorification of nationalist and racist ideals. Mussolini's Italy and Hitler's Germany function as a mirror in which similar images are unified by an ideology with common traits that it seems convenient to describe as if it were a single matrix of thought and action. The historiographical contributions on the subject are immense, and it does not seem acceptable to label all totalitarian national regimes – in Europe, South America or East Asia – under just one single and simplified designation.[3] However, the ease with which the word fascism (or the era of fascism) has entered into the definition of so many totalitarian regimes seems to legitimize its application in broad terms, notwithstanding the historical rigor that should be considered for the classification of political regimes. Therefore, fascism has become a general category of analysis that sometimes eludes the specificities of the different varieties of dictatorships. Many authoritarian political regimes, in Europe and elsewhere, may not have fully replicated Italian fascism, nor German nazism, which may have served as their central model of reference. Given the ambiguity in the use of the term fascism, for the sake of historical rigor we shall instead use as guidance the terms dictatorships and authoritarian regimes when referring to the political experiences under analysis in this book.

One of the main features of such authoritarian regimes is that they have an undisputed leader – such as Mussolini, Hitler, Franco and Salazar – who imposes his power and authority and who creates around him an impregnable stronghold of complicity, networks of interests and influences that make it impossible or improbable to overcome them by the vote alone. Furthermore, such a vote cannot be freely exercised, or else its exercise is limited and controlled by an elite with specially reserved access to the administration of power. The undeniable success of these anti-democratic solutions was to some extent due to the crisis of liberal political regimes coupled with an economic depression that definitively called into question the possibility for Western economies to restore social and economic equilibria without strong government intervention.

Thus, the concept of authoritarianism or dictatorship is multifaceted and can vary depending on the historical background and interpretation. In the context of this volume, we have chosen to define authoritarian regimes as those in which the political and economic elites hold power without the presence of free and fair elections. The notion of free elections, as emphasized by Schumpeter (1976), is fundamental to democracy, serving as the cornerstone of the democratic regime. In democratic systems, individuals can participate in the political process by freely choosing their representatives and their economic proposals, through competitive electoral contests. However, in authoritarian regimes, this fundamental aspect of democracy is denied or restricted, leading to a concentration of power in the hands of a select few. Authoritarianism can manifest in various forms, ranging from overt dictatorships characterized by outright repression and suppression of political opposition to more subtle forms where democratic institutions may exist nominally but lack genuine competition and accountability.

This definition aims to capture the essence of authoritarianism by focusing on the absence of democratic processes that allow for the free expression of political will through competitive electoral mechanisms. Nonetheless, the absence of political and civil freedoms does not mean that the dictator ruled alone or enjoyed exclusive decision-making power, especially regarding economic issues. As the authors of the chapters illustrate, an authoritarian regime, while suppressing opposition and eliminating dissent on one hand, secures and maintains its power by promoting a mechanism of mediation and compromise among the most powerful social and economic forces in society. Another relevant issue is that these regimes have almost always been able to find the financial resources to implement political action in the many aspects of government intervention, especially in the economic sphere. This is, after all, the theme explored in this book, through historical examples that prove the inseparable relationship between political agency and economic and financial power. In the twentieth century, as Thomas Piketty wrote, politics is everywhere (Piketty, 2014).

Money, markets and institutions

Over the past twenty years, there has been a substantial increase in the interest of capitalism as a socio-political economic system. Scholars from multiple social science disciplines, including law, sociology, economics, political science and history, have increasingly acknowledged the usefulness of (re)placing capitalism at the centre of their studies, examining its characteristics in contemporary societies, legal frameworks, varieties and historical development[4] and prompting fresh examinations of what is often referred to as "capitalism in action" (Beckert and Desan, 2018). As a result, an increasing number of analyses have focused on the social, political and economic actors of capitalist development, such as social classes, economic interest organizations, businesses, banks, trade unions, political parties and so on. Overall, these analyses investigate the relationships that these actors establish with one another and with the state to set up the rules of the game, as well as the complex set of effects of these interactions on the functioning of the entire system in terms of growth, technological development, systemic crises, expropriation, violence and inequalities. In this regard, it is imperative to acknowledge that the notion of capitalism gives rise to difficulties in definition, as Louis Hyman pointed out (2013). This may be attributed to its dualistic nature as both a social analytical tool and a political category, or it may be ascribed to its flexibility, which can sometimes verge on vagueness.[5] Although the emergence of a new history of capitalism has generated debates and uncertainties among historians (Hilt, 2017; Wilkins et al., 2010; Edwards et al., 2020), the concept appears to have the advantage of bringing the dialectical relationship between social, economic and political groups back to the forefront of reflection, emphasizing the conflictual nature associated with it and its tensions, contradictions, instability and transformation.

The analytical framework provided by the concept of capitalism offers very promising perspectives for rethinking the history of authoritarian regimes. One of the most significant consequences of this approach has been to reestablish political economy as a central category of analysis. Indeed, while economic life is crucial to understanding the history of capitalism, it must be studied as a politically constructed phenomenon. This allows us to highlight the interplay between market dynamics and political structures, as well as to consider the impact of institutions, political movements and legal frameworks, such as debt, contracts and property rights, on both material conditions and ideological beliefs (Beckert and Desan, 2018). In this context, the history of finance can also be better understood as a system constructed by law and politics (Piketty, 2014), while the concept of capitalism can offer new research opportunities in the field (Cassis, 2016). A fundamental characteristic of a capitalist economy, in fact, is related to investing savings and returns in the present with the expectation of higher gains in the future, prioritizing profit as a primary measure of success and accumulating wealth with the aim of fostering innovation and growth. Therefore, the fluctuations of the economic cycle, as Keynes emphasized in the thirties, are driven by the financial sector, which constitutes the primary driving force of capitalism. Nonetheless, Keynes argued that investments are inherently unreliable, as they are influenced by our views and expectations of the future, about which we know so little (Keynes, 1937: 221). Consequently, as Minsky's interpretation of Keynesianism reminds us, the core functioning of a capitalist economy is directly influenced by uncertainty, which profoundly affects the financial structure, namely the relationships between various economic units (Minsky, 1975).

Given the fundamental role of financial interactions in driving economic processes and the inherently political nature of financial systems, it becomes crucial to examine money and the monetary framework as key aspects of historical analysis. Within monetary theories, two primary frameworks emerge. Firstly, the commodity theory posits that specific commodities, particularly gold and silver, serve as the foundation of monetary structures. Conversely, the credit or claim theory of money underscores the significance of debt and credit, acknowledging credit as the essential underpinning of monetary systems (Schumpeter, 1917). In this volume, money is mostly analysed as a social institution, thus as a community-based process of social positioning. Community-wide acceptance, in fact, is crucial because money is characterized *per se* by contractual incompleteness (Giannini, 2011). The primary function of money, namely its capacity to create future obligations and discharge past ones (Lawson, 2016), naturally intertwines with the semantic realm of our future-oriented relationships – encompassing our hopes, fears, expectations, promises and deferred realities. However, because of the uncertainty inherent in the future, monetary contracts cannot provide absolute certainty regarding the future value of money. As a result, social and political interactions, such as conflict, negotiation and compromise, have led to the emergence of political institutions that enforce and implement rules to maintain user confidence in a specific monetary and financial system. This, in turn, shapes its structure and oversees its operations. Consequently, institutions are necessary to safeguard investors who have tied their investments to a particular payment mechanism (Giannini, 2011). Therefore, the overall framework of money, along with its associated elements of monetary and fiscal policies, banking regulations and financial system structures, can be understood as political actions articulated in response to recurring social and economic needs advocated by specific socio-economic groups engaging with policymakers.

This viewpoint regarding the issue of money is essential for understanding the fundamental attributes of any political system and, within our context, of the authoritarian regimes under examination and their interactions with the socio-economic environment in which they emerge. Understanding money, debt and credit as social institutions, whose roles are upheld and regulated by politically constructed norms enforced by governmental authorities, entails interpreting the evolution of financial systems as an ongoing progression shaped by the intricate interplay between divergent socio-economic groups and the political, legal and institutional contexts, both domestic and international. As Woody Holton has noted, in fact, market-making is always a constituent part of nation-building processes (Holton, 2018).

Through the role of money in creating and discharging obligations, complex markets can exist and function. Traditionally, markets have been studied as the result of innate human behaviour. However, this tendency to frame markets as the product of natural human activities and egoistic interests often leads to analytical misunderstandings. This way of thinking about markets is misleading for three reasons. Firstly, it tends to conceal the legal and political foundations of markets, as well as the variety of market relations and different forms of capitalism that arise from these foundations. Secondly, it produces a false separation between private activities and public structures, suggesting that they are completely independent of each other. Finally, it focuses on isolated individuals as the unit of analysis, concentrating on their decentralized activities as buyers and sellers, while neglecting the significance of collective action and socio-economic groups. In contrast to prevailing analysis trends, a more productive approach lies in recognizing markets as political entities, that is, understanding the political underpinnings of specific market types. Additionally, it is essential to abandon methodological individualism and adopt a perspective that considers social classes and socio-economic groups as the primary units of inquiry, specifically in their relationships with the political sphere and decision-making processes. Essentially, understanding economic and financial history in authoritarian contexts as a complex network of interactions, conflicts and compromises between divergent economic interests and priorities involves focusing on collective action and interest group behaviours.

In this sense, to fully understand the concept of financial transactions, it is essential to consider three key dimensions: legal, competitive and political. According to Robert Coase, a transaction is a voluntary action that involves the transfer of goods or services through legal means, such as property rights, money and contracts (Coase, 1987). This legal dimension plays a crucial role in each financial transaction, as the type and effectiveness of the transaction depend on the legal context in which it takes place (Commons, 1950). However, the legal background of the market is not a natural given fact. This is because it arises from a specific geographical and historical context and from the relationships between different political and socio-economic groups. Therefore, in addition to the legal dimension, it is necessary to consider the competitive dimension, which refers to the relationship between the transactor and their competitors. In fact, each transactor's choice is affected by and affects the choices of other transactors (Williamson, 2010). Additionally, the political dimension must be considered, as each economic agent is a political actor who influences and is influenced by the evolution of legal structures that shape the market. Finally, it is important to recognize that these three dimensions are interdependent and affect one another (Vatiero, 2020).

These theoretical perspectives emphasize the paramount significance of social positioning and political economy. In this context, the term political economy refers to the investigation of economic decisions in relation to the influence of political forces. Its primary objective is to comprehend the power dynamics that influence economic outcomes and how socio-economic groups utilize political and ideological resources to promote contentious economic policies (Maier, 1988). Political economy, therefore, in both democratic and authoritarian regimes, is always the result of socio-economic group divisions, preferences, power, influence and actions. Moreover, the intricate interactions between the political economies of different nation-states, which are rooted in non-homogeneous and conflictual dynamics, shape the structure of both domestic and international markets and financial systems.

The most significant implication of these theoretical assumptions for historical research is that understanding the structure and scope of any financial system requires an analysis of its political, legal and cultural bases. In this regard, institutional economists assist economic historians in approaching such complex issues by emphasizing the importance of both formal and informal institutions. Douglas North defines institutions as "the rules governing a society or, more formally, . . . the human-made constraints shaping human interactions" (North, 1990: 3). Throughout history, North maintains that "institutions have been created to bring about order and reduce uncertainty" (North, 1991: 97). Since it is impossible to predict the future, communities establish institutions to mitigate this inherent uncertainty. Consequently, the diverse approaches taken by social groups and political-national communities in addressing this uncertainty shape the types of institutions they create. However, as regulations impact the interests of individuals and groups, they seek to shape the institutional framework and legal rules in line with their economic goals. For this reason, rather than focusing on efficiency, it is more appropriate to describe the institutional process in terms of its effectiveness for specific groups. In this sense, North argues that "institutions are not necessarily or even usually created to be socially efficient; rather, they are created to serve the interests of those with the bargaining power" (North, 1990: 16). Thus, political economy becomes a battleground where choices regarding taxes, tariffs and commercial or banking regulations significantly affect different social groups. Interest groups engage in politics to influence legislators and obtain favourable laws as "products". Ultimately, transformations in institutions follow political channels.

Therefore, understanding how financial institutions and markets are established requires examining various actors including decision-makers, business organizers, consumers, merchants, workers, financers, bankers and speculators.

Accordingly, it is essential to challenge the traditional boundaries between politics and economics and states and markets when analysing financial capitalism in authoritarian contexts. This involves exploring the relationships among money, business and dictatorial political power, as well as the influence of interest groups on decision-making processes and political regulation. In fact, the destruction of democratic processes does not eliminate politics or the need to make compromises but rather leads to the development of new, opaque mechanisms of political bargaining that exclude certain social forces while allowing different sections of the dominant classes to participate (Maier, 1975). In these contexts, the study of finance must be approached as a product of both authoritarian law and politics, while authoritarian law and politics must be viewed as products of socio-economic group negotiation. Ultimately, the interaction between dictatorial governments and economic systems is part of a narrative that revolves around "the connection between money and force" (Tilly, 1990: 16), and it contributes to understanding what Charles Tilly defined as "the two interdependent master processes of the [modern] era: the creation of a system of national states and formation of a worldwide capitalist system" (Tilly, 1984: 14).

Giving credit to dictatorship in twentieth-century Europe

In his historical view, Commons distinguished the three economic stages of scarcity, abundance and stabilization. The stage of scarcity, which preceded the industrial revolution, was one of little individual liberty along with a great deal of governmental control at a time when national welfare was subordinated to the demands of a war economy. The following stage of abundance covered the first hundred years of the industrial revolution. This was the era of employer capitalism when the manufacturer found himself at the helm of the economic system. In this age of abundance, there was a maximum of individual liberty of action and a minimum of governmental interference. After 1850, a notable shift occurred as the world transitioned into the stabilization era, which characterized the twentieth century. The earlier stage of employer capitalism became the era of banker capitalism, an era of widespread stabilization movements in which each vested interest seeks to protect its own position as against all other competing interests (Commons, 1934: 773).

Within this era of banker capitalism, vested interests and stabilization, twentieth-century European history was clearly marked by the rise of authoritarian regimes, in different epochs and countries. Through historical examples, this book explains how that rise intertwines with domestic and international financial systems and provides a European answer to the problem in the form of a complex set of different responses and interchanges. While there is no ideal model of how to give credit to dictatorship, or how authoritarian regimes exert their influence on the domestic financial system or how they interact with the international context, the response to the question of how authoritarian regimes deal with financial matters is the sum of different national outcomes. Besides, if on the political level fascist Italy could have been a model that other authoritarian regimes tried to adopt and reshape, in relation to financial issues there was no authoritarian national model that proved ideal or dominant.

The first case study provides a rationale for a better understanding of the emergence, evolution and collapse of the new Catalan banking elite during the interwar period, particularly on the role of the Banco de Cataluña (1920–1931) and its connections with Primo de Rivera's Dictatorship (1923–1930). Drawing on new archival evidence, Enrique Jorge-Sotelo discusses the idiosyncrasies of this alliance, in terms of both its historical political origins and its implications for banking management at the dawn of the Great Depression. Overall, the chapter stresses the importance of understanding the role played by political factors and political regimes in financial and banking crises throughout history, namely the consequences of political actions regarding the shaping of institutions dealing with situations of financial fragility.

In 1927–1928, Portugal asked for the support of the League of Nations to issue a foreign loan, but its negotiations failed. More or less at the same time, Greece succeeded in a similar process. This is the historical background of Chapter 2, which tries to explain the reasons for the different outcomes of negotiations and to identify the consequences of this difference. According to Ana Tomás and Nuno Valério, there were political reasons – not structural characteristics, nor the short-term situation – explaining the different outcomes of negotiations. The main consequence was a delayed consolidation of Portuguese monetary stabilization as against Greek immediate adoption of gold-exchange standard. However, this did not ensure a better financial and political Greek performance in the medium term. Approaching the topic through the lens of comparative historical analysis and exploring the interactions between nation-states and international institutions suggest that investors do not discriminate between democratic regimes and dictatorships, under similar profitability and credibility conditions, although democratic regimes seem able to provide higher confidence.

The relationship between politics and the functioning of the banking sector is the main topic of Chapter 3, by Zarko Lazarevic, which deals with the Yugoslavia experience. The royal dictatorship and the subsequent authoritarian regime in the 1930s have shaped Yugoslav society and economic life. The dictatorship itself did not represent a turning point in the concepts of economic or banking regulation. The continuity of the basic principles of regulation is beyond any doubt. In the 1930s, there was major state intervention in the structure and business policy of banks. The reason was the great economic crisis that coincided with the emergence of the authoritarian regime. Economic stabilization, including the restructuring of the banking sector, became a precondition for political and social stability. This chapter also explains how the state banking sector has played a decisive role in economic policy during and after crisis. Government intervention preserved the functioning of the private banking sector. By prescribing business policy, the government diverted part of the private banking sector's resources to finance government spending at the expense of the real sector and the population.

The authors of Chapter 4, Marianna Astore, Mario Perugini and Valerio Torreggiani, address the practice and theory of wartime financing in fascist Italy between 1935 and 1943, mainly in relation to the role of the central bank. Therefore, this essay focuses on the role of the Bank of Italy in giving credit to the war effort, looking at the case of 'Consorzio Sovvenzioni sui Valori Industriali', created in December 1914. In addition to the medium-term financing, starting from the mid-thirties, the Consorzio undertook a series of operations defined as "special". The special operations constituted almost all the total amount of the Consorzio's activities during the Second World War and were essentially financed through monetary circulation, that is, by the Bank of Italy. Additionally, the chapter delves into the financing of fascist warfare through the lens of the history of economic thought. In this regard, particular emphasis is placed on the development of the theory known as the "circuit of capital", which was formulated within the Institute of National Corporatist Finance, established in 1939 by the Bank of Italy.

Countries faced many challenges in restoring their external accounts during the Great Depression due to increased protectionism. Italy provides a perfect case study to demonstrate the various provisions that were put in place to safeguard the country's gold reserves, as explained by Enrico Berbenni and Andrea Viola on Chapter 5. The devaluation of the currency was an intervention aimed at rebalancing a structural deficit in the trade balance, which was an important part of the problem. This chapter examines how the 1936 devaluation affected Italy's trade balance and the potential impact it had on foreign counterparts and the overall dynamics of Italian trade. It reveals that the structural impact on imports, exports, or the overall trade balance is not significant. Conversely, the international sanctions imposed on Italy following the war in Ethiopia, in addition to escalating political tensions, appear to have a great influence on Italian trade dynamics.

In Chapter 6, still dealing with the Italian experience, Federico Castelli offers new insights into the financing of the fascist dictatorship following the economic sanctions imposed by the League of Nations between 1935 and 1936. Firstly, attention is given to the role of Banca Commerciale Italiana (Comit), particularly its London branch, in the normalization of Anglo-Italian financial relations after the sanctions. The director, Carlo Lovioz, focused his efforts at the primary London clearing banks to reopen acceptance credits, which were crucial for short-term trade financing. During the sanctions and after their removal, Italy faced a substantial deficit in raw materials, primarily those imported by sea. Consequently, starting in 1936, there was a heightened need to acquire tankers and steamships to transport goods to Italy and its colonies. This shift occurred after many years, during which the ministerial budget had continued to support the reinforcement of the fascist war industry. Therefore, this contribution aims to examine Comit's proactive role in extending credits to Italian shipping companies for the acquisition of merchant ships.

Chapter 7, by Anna Veronica Pobbe, explains the economic strategy used in Gemany by the nazis, which should be defined as a robbery, rather than a planned economy of war. This essay examines how German banks supported nazi projects, using a specific case study: the Polish-occupied territories. The first part of the chapter is devoted to the support provided by some banks to the invasion of Poland. Not only did they provide credit for the operations, but they also established a series of branch offices in the territories directly annexed to the Third Reich (such as the Warthegau) as early as October 1939. Secondly, the essay discusses how specific tools, such as Sonderkontos ("special bank accounts"), were used to draw resources from activities such as deportations, killing operations, and the liquidation of ghettos and camps. Finally, this chapter addresses the active role played by German banks in the complex relationship between productivity and profitability. Overall, the picture that emerges from this analysis is a dark one, highlighting how the Nazis were able to draw resources from their criminal activities with the support of the German banking system.

The financial repression of the Franco regime in Spain between 1940 and 1975 is the main topic analyzed by M. Angeles Pons, Elena Martínez-Ruiz and Joaquim Cuevas in Chapter 8, with a particular focus on regulatory mechanisms such as banking regulation, stock market regulation and exchange rate controls, along with their impact. The main effects on the banking system included the lack of competition, inefficiencies within the banking sector, distortions arising from privileged credit circuits, the Bank of Spain's limited authority to regulate the entire credit system, and the absence of genuine banking supervision. From a monetary policy perspective, the use of financial repression had significant implication for inflation. While the Spanish level of financial repression was relatively high, it closely aligned with the average of most European countries. However, the distinctive characteristic of this case lies in the political regime, given Spain's status as dictatorship. Consequently, financial repression likely served not only as a mechanism to guarantee government revenues but also as a means to reallocate financial resources to benefit the economic and political groups that supported the Franco regime.

Michalis Psalidopoulos is the author of Chapter 9, which is devoted to the analysis of macroeconomic management and development policy of the Greek dictatorship (1967–1974), with an emphasis on the evolution of economic thought in Greece. During this period, an old generation of Greek economists, mostly exposed to interwar German Historical Economics, went into retirement, and a new generation with an Anglo-Saxon graduate education assumed the conduct of economic policy. Views and policies pursued by these economists and the different expansionary roles played by the central bank and by specialized development banks during that period are discussed in this chapter. Monetary expansion, planning and *ad hoc* intervention were pronounced as keys for growth in the place of monetary stability. Fiscal policy was used through incentives and exemptions rather than to monitor effective demand. Changing international economic conditions after the breakdown of the Bretton Woods system in 1971 were also considered, and they revealed that the dictatorial regime lacked alternatives and a long-term strategy for the Greek economy. Economic growth met an impasse and led, next to foreign policy blunders, to high inflation and the breakdown of the dictatorship.

The last chapter, Chapter 10, is authored by Tayfun Mertan, who examines the process of transformation in Turkey between 1980 and 1983, as a consequence of a neoliberal hegemony. Framed as a solution to socio-economic instability that emerged towards the end of the 1970s, the January 24, 1980, decisions marked the start of the neoliberal transformation of the relations of production and the form of state in Turkey, aiming at transitioning its economic system into an open market economy. However, internal ideological conflicts prevented the minority government from implementing neoliberal policies. The Junta rule that took power on September 12, 1980, ended the crisis of hegemony in the country and adopted the pre-coup neoliberal agenda. Until the general elections in November 1983, the Junta rule realized a legal and institutional transformation and received both ideological and material support from the United States as well as from international organizations such as the International Monetary Fund, the World Bank, the European Union, and NATO. This final case study illustrates in a clear way one of the underlying topics of this book, dealing with the relationship among political regimes, financial systems, international dynamics and economic changes.

Taken together, the historical examples gathered in this book offer a broad and diverse perspective on how authoritarian political regimes obtain financial support for the development of their policies, as well as on the political backing that financial institutions receive from the governments they support. The lessons of these historical examples are relevant to understanding similar situations in the present day. History does not serve to legitimize or condemn today's political decisions or financial strategies. But it certainly offers a pretext for reflection on similar issues that continue to worry us. We hope that readers will share this conviction about the importance of enriching learning through historical case studies.

***

This volume is an outcome of a conference convened at the Institute of Social Sciences of the University of Lisbon in November 2022 under the theme "Giving Credit to Dictatorship: Authoritarian Regimes and Financial Capitalism in the Twentieth Century". We wish to express our appreciation to the Institute of Social Sciences of the University of Lisbon and the scientific committee of the conference for their support. We also extend our gratitude to Youssef Cassis, who delivered the keynote lecture at the conference, enriching our discussions with his expertise. Additionally, we acknowledge the anonymous referees for their rigorous feedback, which has contributed to the scholarly rigor of this work. Our thanks are also extended to the editorial team at Routledge for their professionalism and support throughout the publication process. Lastly, we are thankful to all the authors who have contributed their expertise and dedication to this collaborative effort.

Notes

1 For some recent analysis, see Mattei (2022) and Astore and Torreggiani (2024).
2 For details on the limits of the cliometric school, see Fenoaltea (2019, 2020).

3 Among the numerous studies on fascism viewed from a comparative perspective, due to their systematic and comprehensive nature, see, above all, Payne (1995), Paxton (2004), Pinto (2011) and Griffin (2018).
4 Just to give a few examples, see Hall and Soskice (2001), Mueller (2012), Neal and Williamson (2014), Kocka and Van der Linden (2016), Slobodian (2018), Milanovic (2019), Pintor (2019) and Martin (2022).
5 For details on the advantages and disadvantages of not precisely defining capitalism, see the various positions expressed in Beckert et al. (2014).

Bibliography

Astore, Marianna and Torreggiani, Valerio (eds.). "Capitalismo e regime. Classi sociali e gruppi d'interesse nell'Italia fascista", *Studi storici*, vol. 65, no. 1, 2024.

Beckert, Sven, Burgin, Angus, et al. "Interchange: The History of Capitalism", *Journal of American History*, vol. 101, no. 2, 2014: 503–536.

Beckert, Sven and Desan, Christine (eds.). *American Capitalism. New Histories*. New York: Columbia University Press, 2018.

Cassis, Youssef. *Crisis and Opportunities. The Shaping of Modern Finance*. Oxford: Oxford University Press, 2011.

Cassis, Youssef. "Economic and Financial Crises", *Capitalism. The Reemergence of a Historical Concept*, edited by Jürgen Kocka and Marcel Van der Linden. London and New York: Bloomsbury, 2016: 13–31.

Coase, Robert. *The Firm, the Market and the Law*. Chicago, IL: University of Chicago Press, 1987.

Commons, John Robert. *Institutional Economics*. New York: Macmillan, 1934.

Commons, John Robert. *The Economics of Collective Action*. New York: Macmillan, 1950.

Edwards, Andrew David, Hill, Peter and Neves-Sarriegui, Juan. "Capitalism in Global History", *Past and Present*, vol. 249, no. 1, 2020. https://academic.oup.com/past/article/249/1/e1/6007772.

Eich, Stefan. *Currency of Politics. The Political Theory of Money From Aristotle to Keynes*. Cambridge, MA: Princeton University Press, 2022.

Eichengreen, Barry. "Financial History, Historical Analysis, and the New History of Finance Capital", *Capitalism: A Journal of History and Economics*, vol. 1, no. 1, 2019: 20–51.

Evans, Peter B., Rueschemeyer, Dietrich, and Skocpol, Theda. *Bringing the State Back In*. Cambridge: Cambridge University Press, 1985.

Fano Damascelli, Ester. "La 'restaurazione antifascista liberista'. Ristagno e sviluppo economico durante il fascismo", *Il movimento di liberazione in Italia*, vol. 23, no. 104, 1971: 47–99.

Fenoaltea, Stefano. "Spleen: The Failure of the Cliometric School", *Annals of the Fondazione Luigi Einaudi*, vol. LIII, no. 2, 2019: 5–24.

Fenoaltea, Stefano. "Choler: The Failure of the Cliometric School", *Annals of the Fondazione Luigi Einaudi*, vol. LIV, no. 1, 2020: 231–242.

Flandreau, Marc. "Border Crossing", *Capitalism: A Journal of History and Economics*, vol. 1, no. 1, 2019: 1–9.

Fukuyama, Francis. *The End of History and the Last Man*. New York: Free Press, 1992.

Gandhi, Jennifer. *Political Institutions Under Dictatorship*. Cambridge: Cambridge University Press, 2008.

Giannini, Curzio. *The Age of Central Banks*. Aldershot: Edward Elgar, 2011.

Gramsci, Antonio. *La costruzione del Partito Comunista (1923–1926)*. Torino: Einaudi, 1971.

Griffin, Roger. *Fascism. An Introduction to Comparative Fascist Studies*. Cambridge: Polity Press, 2018.

Hall, Peter A. and Soskice, David (eds.). *Varieties of Capitalism. The Institutional Foundations of Comparative Advantage*. Oxford: Oxford University Press, 2001.

Hilt, Eric. "Economic History, Historical Analysis, and the 'New History of Capitalism'", *Journal of Economic History*, vol. 77, no. 2, 2017: 511–536.

Holton, Woody. "The Capitalist Constitution", in *American Capitalism. New Histories*, edited by Sven Beckert and Christine Desan. New York: Columbia University Press, 2018: 35–62.
Huntington, Samuel P. *The Third Wave. Democratization in the Late Twentieth Century*. Norman, OK: University of Oklahoma Press, 1991.
Hyman, Louis. "Why Write the History of Capitalism?", *Symposiuam Magazine*, 2013. http://www.symposium-magazine.com/why-write-the-history-of-capitalism-louis-hyman
Keynes, John Maynard. "The General Theory of Employment", *The Quarterly Journal of Economics*, vol. 51, no. 2, 1937: 209–223.
Kocka, Jürgen. *Capitalism: A Short History*. Cambridge, MA: Princeton University Press, 2015.
Kocka, Jürgen. "Introduction", in *Capitalism. The Reemergence of a Historical Concept*, edited by Jürgen Kocka and Marcel Van der Linden. London and New York: Bloomsbury, 2016: 1–10.
Kocka, Jürgen and Van der Linden, Marcel (eds.). *Capitalism. The Reemergence of a Historical Concept*. London and New York: Bloomsbury, 2016.
Kurz, Mordecai. "How Capitalism Became a Threat to Democracy", *Project Syndicate*, March 15, 2024. https://www.project-syndicate.org/onpoint/how-capitalism-became-a-threat-to-democracy-by-mordecai-kurz-2024-03
Lawson, Tony. "Social Positioning and the Nature of Money", *Cambridge Journal of Economics*, vol. 40, no. 4, 2016: 961–996.
Levitsky, Steven and Way, Lucan A. *Competitive Authoritarianism. Hybrid Regimes After the Cold War*. Cambridge: Cambridge University Press, 2010.
Maier, Charles S. *Recasting Bourgeois Europe. Stabilization in France, Germany and Italy in the Decade After World War I*. Princeton, NJ: Princeton University Press, 1975.
Maier, Charles S. *In Search of Stability*. Cambridge: Cambridge University Press, 1988.
Martin, Jaimie. *The Meddlers. Sovereignty, Empire, and the Birth of Global Economic Governance*. Cambridge, MA: Harvard University Press, 2022.
Mattei, Clara. *The Capital Order*. Chicago, IL: Chicago University Press, 2022.
Milanovic, Branko. *Capitalism Alone. The Future of a System That Rules the World*. Cambridge, MA: Harvard University Press, 2019.
Minsky, Hyman P. *John Maynard Keynes*. New York: Columbia University Press, 1975.
Mueller, Dennis C. (ed.). *The Oxford Handbook of Capitalism*. Oxford: Oxford University Press, 2012.
Neal, Larry and Williamson, Jeffrey G. *The Cambridge History of Capitalism*. Cambridge: Cambridge University Press, 2014.
North, Douglas. *Institutions, Institutional Change, and Economic Performance*. Cambridge: Cambridge University Press, 1990.
North, Douglas. "Institutions", *Journal of Economic Perspectives*, vol. 5, no. 1, 1991: 97–112.
Paxton, Robert. *The Anatomy of Fascism*. New York: Vintage Books, 2004.
Payne, Stanley. *A History of Fascism, 1914–1945*. London and Madison, WI: The University of Wisconsin Press, 1995.
Pinto, António Costa (ed.). *Rethinking the Nature of Fascism: Comparative Perspectives*. London: Palgrave Macmillan, 2011.
Pinto, António Costa. *O Regresso das ditaduras*. Lisbon: Fundação Francisco Manuel dos Santos, 2021.
Pintor, Katharina. *The Code of Capital. How the Law Creates Wealth and Inequality*. Princeton, NJ: Princeton University Press, 2019.
Piketty, Thomas. *Capital in the Twenty-First Century*. Cambridge, MA: Harvard University Press, 2014.
Pitteloud, Sabine, Ballor, Grace, Clavin, Patricia, Perrone, Nicolás M., Rollings, Neil and Slobodian Quinn. "Capitalism and Global Governance in Business History: A Roundtable Discussion", *Harvard Business School Working Paper*, no. 22–081, 2022.

Ricardo, David. "Letter to Thomas Malthus, October 9, 1820", in *The Works and Correspondence of David Ricardo*, vol. 8 (1819–1821), edited by Piero Sraffa. Cambridge: Cambridge University Press, 1951: 278.
Schumpeter, Joseph A. "Money and the Social Product", *International Economic Papers*, vol. 6, 1956, ed. or. 1917: 148–211.
Schumpeter, Joseph A. *Capitalism, Socialism and Democracy*. London: Routledge, 1976.
Slobodian, Quinn. *Globalists: The End of Empire and the Birth of Neoliberalism*. Cambridge, MA: Harvard University Press, 2018.
Slobodian, Quinn. *Crack-Up Capitalism: Market Radicals and the Dream of a World Without Democracy*. New York: Metropolitan Books, 2023.
Smith, Adam. *An Inquiry into the Nature and Causes of the Wealth of Nations*, edited by Edwin Cannan. London: Methuen, 1904, ed. or. 1776.
Tilly, Charles. *Big Structures, Large Processes, Huge Comparisons*. London: Russell Sage Foundation, 1984.
Tilly, Charles. *Coercion, Capital, and European States, AD 990–1990*. London: Basil Blackwell, 1990.
Togliatti, Palmiro. *Corso sugli avversari. Le lezioni sul fascismo*, edited by Francesco M. Biscione. Torino: Einaudi, 2010.
Tooze, Adam. *The Wages of Destruction. The Making and Breaking of the Nazi Economy*. London: Allen Lane, 2006.
Vatiero, Massimiliano. *The Theory of Transaction in Institutional Economics. A History*. London: Routledge, 2020.
Wallerstein, Immanuel. *The Modern World-System I. Capitalism Agriculture and the Origins of the European World-Economy in the Sixteenth Century*. New York: Academic Press, 1974.
Wilkins, Mira, Thelen, Kathleen, Whitley, Richard, Miller, Rory M., Martin, Cathie Jo, Berghahn, V. R., Iversen, Martin Jes, Herrigel, Gary and Zeitlin, Jonathan. "Varieties of Capitalism Roundtable", *Business History Review*, vol. 84, no. 4, 2010: 637–674.
Williamson, Oliver E. "The Economics of Governance", *American Economic Review*, vol. 95, no. 2, 2005: 1–18.
Williamson, Oliver E. "Transaction Cost Economics: An Overview", in *The Elgar Companion to Transaction Cost Economics*, edited by Michael E. Sykuta and Peter G. Klein. Aldershot: Edward Elgar, 2010: 8–26.
Wolf, Martin. *The Crisis of Democratic Capitalism*. London: Penguin Books, 2023.

1 Convergence in decay

Primo de Rivera and the new Catalan banking elite, 1925–1931

Enrique Jorge-Sotelo

> "We should have faith in the final result of our campaign; its fruit, early or late, will come; but wait; it will take time, because this is about evolution; don't aim at picking today the fruit from the tree you planted yesterday; nor believe in the efficacy of partnership born out of circumstance or as the product of artificially created states of opinion."
>
> (Joan Nualart, *Societat d'Estudis Econòmics*, Barcelona, 1907, 34)

1.1 Introduction

By September 1923, when General Miguel Primo de Rivera led a coup d'état that imposed a nearly seven-year period of authoritarian rule in Spain, the country's first industrial engine and home to its largest city, Catalonia, had no important local banks. Starting in the late nineteenth century, banking business in Barcelona had succumbed to the superior means of foreign banks; the expansion of Madrilean and Basque banks' branches in Catalonia at the turn of the twentieth century had only added to the increasingly marginal role of Catalan financial capital. From 1925, however, a new emerging financial elite saw an opportunity to regain the ground lost by establishing personal and professional links with Primo de Rivera and his Minister of Finance José Calvo Sotelo through two newly created institutions: Banco de Cataluña (1920) and Banco Exterior de España (1929). The narrow cooperation between the Dictatorship and the emerging Catalan financial elite of the 1920s – new financial institutions, their managers and key figures within different strands of political Catalanism – was not an obvious one. Given the two sides' a priori remarkable ideological disparities, the traditional explanation is that entrepreneurs, whatever their underlying liberal political views, had no other chance of progressing and contributing to economic development than playing by the existing rules, and these were written by Primo de Rivera – a dynamic that did not apply only to Catalan financial elites but to Spanish businessmen in general during the Dictatorship of 1923–1930 (Cabana 1965, 1972, 2003; Cabrera and del Rey 2007).

Historians have documented how Catalan conservative political elites not only welcomed but also supported Primo's military coup, mostly in exchange for

DOI: 10.4324/9781032656199-2

protection against anarchist organizations that had been gaining ground among Barcelona's working classes, and after a promise of state decentralization and devolution (Molas 1972; Riquer 1977; Balfour 1995; Quiroga 2008, 2013, 2022). However, it did not take long before these very same elites became disenchanted with Primo de Rivera's actual plans for Catalonia. Once Primo seized power, the prosecution and repression of Catalan political, cultural and social institutions unfolded as part of the Dictatorship's plans to force the Spanish masses under a single national identity (Quiroga 2008). Economic historians have also discussed how the corporatist nature of the Dictatorship raised the value of certain political connections, thus explaining liberal elites' connivance with authoritarianism (Velarde 1972; Fraile 1991; Cabrera and del Rey 2007). Much less has been written about how and why Catalan financial elites continued to support and partner with Primo de Rivera until he resigned in January 1930.[1] To a large extent, the views summarized earlier do not address the question of why the links between the Dictatorship and a new, emerging financial elite became so strong when they did, that is, during the late 1920s, when Primo had already been in power for more than five years, when the threat of social unrest had waned and when the Dictatorship had made clear its repressive stance towards Catalonia's political institutions and culture.

In this chapter, I argue that the rationale for the emergence of such narrow ties and their timing can be explained by the similarity in the diagnostics reached by both groups – the Dictatorship and the new Catalan financial elite – about the illness affecting their respective patients. For Primo de Rivera, the ailing body was, naturally, Spain and its national identity, trapped by the institutional, political and economic decay epitomized by the colonial Disaster of 1898. Primo built his political discourse around the shadow that colonial defeat projected over the country's self-perception. In his view, a diagnosis of more than twenty years of continued decay called for a single-handed, even if openly undemocratic, leader until a definitive cure was found. Reestablishing order by any means necessary was required to free the country from "a series of miseries and immoralities that started in 1898 and that threatened Spain with a tragical and painful outcome" (Casassas 1983, 81–87). For the new Catalan financial elite, in turn, it was Catalan banks that lay in hospital bed. The loss of relevance of Catalan banking capital in the whole of Spain but more importantly in Catalonia called for a new institution that, given the incapacity and passivity of the existing ones, would finally address these long-standing disorder and disadvantages to bring decay to a halt. Tellingly, when Banco de Cataluña was founded in 1920, it was presented as the institution that would "put financial development in Catalonia in order, who would be the bank of Catalan banks, which would lead, with its strength, common sense, and patriotic commitment, the renovation of banking that, firstly in Catalonia and later in Spain, should bring the reaffirmation of economic independence" (Recasens 1918, 25).

A simultaneous perception of decay favored the convergence of both sides' rhetoric, while colonial defeat also activated an authoritarian drive, not only among the military but also among certain factions of some Catalan political elites returning from Cuba (Casals Meseguer and Ucelay-Da Cal, 2023). As it is apparent from these selected quotes, both discourses embraced the regenerationist narrative that emerged after the colonial Disaster of 1898. Both alluded directly to the rhetorical figures of *disease, decay, order* and *renaissance*. But what did align the pecuniary interests of these two groups? Why was the new Catalan banking elite, and not the Basque or the Madrilean elite, the one that established such strong and idiosyncratic partnerships with Primo de Rivera? I argue that it was the acceleration of the global economy over the second half of the 1920s, which opened a simultaneous window of opportunity. The recovery of international trade and international capital flows from 1925 allowed the initiation of a *reaction of salvation*, of what ought to be the cornerstone of Spain's "return" to have a say in the Americas – this time through non-colonial trade – and a new opportunity for the renaissance of Catalan banking to compete with foreign banks in the financing of international trade in Barcelona. In turn, this backdrop of a fast-growing domestic and international economy provided Primo de Rivera with the possibility of partially delivering the promised devolution towards the Catalan financial and industrial elite for supporting his coup in 1923.

Thus, the convergence and ad-hoc agreements between an autocrat responsible for selective killings of dissidents and who incessantly persecuted Catalan social and political institutions, its language and culture and an a priori modernizing, reformist and Catalanist financial elite committed to the promotion of precisely what the Dictatorship was aiming at eradicating can be explained by the mutual need of delivering *salvation* to their respective patients – their constituencies – and by the belief in the cure that the roaring 1920s promised to bring about. Primo de Rivera built his charisma and reputation as a Dictator on the basis of presenting himself as the only credible option to *save* the country from its own maladies.[2] The new Catalan financial elite surrounding Banco de Cataluña presented the bank as the only institution that would care to take the responsibility of *saving* Catalan banking from a seemingly unstoppable decay.

1.2 The disaster and the *iron surgeon*

The shadow of end-of-century colonial defeat loomed large and well into the twentieth century. The imprint of national decay that the loss of Cuba, Puerto Rico and the Philippines in 1898 – the so-called Disaster – left on Spanish politicians, intellectuals and the public in general shaped their discourse in the following decades and was one of the cornerstones of Primo de Rivera's ascent to power in 1923. The significance of Spain's loss of its last colonial domains can perhaps fit a less dramatic interpretation if framed into the inevitable fate of a small colonial power within the tectonic dynamics of nineteenth-century imperialism. However, it had important contemporaneous effects on domestic politics and an asymmetric impact on economic and financial elites, triggering a series of reactions that embraced different forms of a narrative of regeneration. In the political arena, during the 25 years that separated the Disaster and Primo de Rivera's military coup, a new authoritarian right emerged, turning Spanish nationalism into a fundamental piece of its political discourse. The interpretation of the Disaster allowed for this new authoritarian right to not only enhance its traditional catholic, imperial, corporatist and antidemocratic elements but also add new ones, such as radical militarism and a strong stance against peripheral nationalisms, and an aim to mobilize the masses in these directions (Balfour 1995, 421; Quiroga 2008, 60).

Shortly after the Disaster, as the credibility of the political regime of the Restoration continued to erode, the regenerationist discourse gained track, particularly against the ongoing two-party system. Elections were openly fraudulent, with local caciques acting as a clientelist network for ruling parties. An initial attempt at unifying regenerationist opposition to the Restoration regime took place under the leadership of intellectual and politician Joaquín Costa, who called for a reconsideration of the state of the nation in 1901. Besides all-important reform of a dysfunctional political system, an economic agenda was also considered. Having lost the main overseas market, economic development had to be fostered from within. Calls for educational reform emerged, as well as the need for a large effort in building and modernizing basic public infrastructures such as irrigation, housing, roads and railways. At first, Costa managed to unify different strands of regenerationism. However, attempts at reform did not materialize. Disenchanted with the idea of a feasible alternative to the corrupt two-party system, Costa abandoned his hitherto gradualist approach and ended up advocating radical revolution. Reforming Spain required reaching the root of all Spanish maladies, and for this, Costa argued, an *iron surgeon* had to take over and heal the injured body of a nation in decay: "this surgical policy, I insist, should be the responsibility of an iron surgeon, who is well versed in the anatomy of the Spanish people and feels an infinite compassion for them" (Costa 1901, 86).[3]

Political instability complicated agreement over needed economic reforms. The first mass general strikes in Spain took place in 1901 and inaugurated a period of confrontation between a discredited political regime and a growingly organized working class.[4] This conflict was particularly acute in Catalonia, as a consequence of the collapse of colonial demand. The Catalan textile industry received a strong blow; textile exports collapsed and labor conflict ensued, with a growing presence of anarchist factions. In turn, textile workers were put under growing pressure by industrialists to raise their productivity in order to regain competitiveness after demand for Catalan textiles from the protected colonial market disappeared (Sudrià 1982, 1983). The double threat suffered by the Catalan industrial bourgeoisie – increasing social conflict and the pecuniary losses caused by the Disaster – shaped an initial agreement between the latter and Spanish regenerationists. The Catalan industrial bourgeoisie embodied by the newly founded party *Lliga Regionalista* – led by Enric Prat de la Riba first and Francesc Cambó later – would embrace conservative Spanish plan for regeneration 'from above' in exchange for protection of Catalan industry and a certain degree of administrative devolution (Riquer 1977, 140).

The unfolding macroeconomic consequences of the Disaster limited regeneration efforts and in doing so, they quickly weakened Catalan industrial and financial elites' initial support. Colonial defeat was accompanied by a sharp increase in short-term government debt and base money and a subsequent depreciation of the peseta – by then already inconvertible to gold – after the monetization of government bonds by Banco de España to finance the war (Comín 2012). During the war, Spain had issued large amounts of colonial debt; as per the Treaty of Paris, military defeat brought the acknowledgment of these debts, which so far had not been adding to domestic debt. Spanish public finances became unsustainable, with debt service exploding to 43% of fiscal expenditure (Comín 2012). As a consequence, the first years after the Disaster witnessed a strong rethinking of Spanish fiscal and monetary affairs.

In 1899, Raimundo Fernandez-Villaverde was appointed Minister of Finance and took over the post-colonial fiscal and monetary reckoning (Comín 2000). Fiscal reforms involved the consolidation of the Treasury's debt in redeemable debt, the exchange of redeemable debt into non-redeemable debt and a 20% tax on all government debt interest earnings – this last reform aimed directly at reducing the debt service burden. Part of the debt conversion took the form of an *affidavit* to which holders of Spanish foreign debt could adhere and by which foreign debt was converted to domestic debt, thus no longer payable in gold but in pesetas (Comín 2012, 380). Reforms also took place in the tax system. Existing taxes such as the unpopular *consumos,* an indirect tax on food, fuel and drink, were raised. New taxes were also introduced, such as a tax on capital gains (*Contribución sobre las utilidades de la riqueza mobiliaria*), which set the stage for the income tax in 1920 and the rationalization of other existing taxes (Comín 2002, 192–193).

Fernandez-Villaverde's agenda also included monetary orthodoxy after war finance (Comín 2001). Since the establishment of Banco de España as the sole issuer of bank notes in Spain in 1874, the government had the option of resorting to the direct monetization of public deficits, something that was not in direct conflict with the promise of redeeming notes in gold, as Spain had abandoned gold convertibility of the peseta in 1883 (Martín-Aceña et al. 2011). Even if monetization of public debt did not become a systematic recourse, it surged during the war years (Comín 2012, 382). After this episode, several measures were introduced between 1899 and 1902 to curb monetary financing of fiscal deficits. First, limits on maximum fiduciary issuing were reduced, and then there was a 50% reduction in interest payments on the Banco's holdings of Overseas Debt (*Deuda de Ultramar*). Second, Banco de España cut the interest rate in the early 1900s in order to make Fernandez-Villaverde's debt conversion easier. Finally, in 1902, a law and an agreement between Banco de España and the government were passed, and they limited direct debt monetization and increased the backing of its monetary liabilities with short-term assets (Tortella 1970, 295–299). The main result of the law was a gradual contraction in the monetary base, followed by a timid increase from 1909. Overall, by 1913, the monetary liabilities of Banco de España remained where they were right after the post-colonial reforms; from a purely monetary standpoint, the period 1902–1913 mirrored the overall symptoms of relative decay after the Disaster, with not much happening to the monetary base of the country (Martín-Aceña 1985).

In comparative terms, the Spanish post-colonial fiscal and monetary reforms resulted in the third largest government debt consolidation recorded in Europe during the nineteenth and twentieth centuries and the one in which the contribution of primary budget surpluses was larger.[5] Such drastic adjustment succeeded in restoring macroeconomic stability but came at a price. The unavoidable distributional conflict that emerged with Fernandez-Villaverde's plan hit the incipient, timid agreements on a nationwide regenerationist movement. In particular, it caused the reaction of the Catalan industrial elite, a fundamental element in the eventual materialization of a reformist agenda. In 1899, the increase in taxation to an already ailing bourgeoisie was confronted with the so-called *Tancament de Caixes* (shutting of coffers), a movement through which Barcelona's merchants united around the *Lliga de Defensa Industrial i Comercial* and announced that they would not pay their *Contribución Industrial*, a tax on trade and industry already characterized by fraud among large industrialists (Riquer 1977, 142–154; Moreno Lázaro 2017). This first reaction worked as a catalyst for a new political agenda for Catalanism which run parallel to the specific interests of the Catalan bourgeoisie. In addition, the local incidence of the colonial shock contributed to this elite split between Catalan support for long-standing Spanish political parties and the new regional elite, culminating in the creation of *Lliga Regionalista* (1901), the leader of political Catalanism in the following two decades (Vall-Prat 2023). Later on, *Unió Federal Nacionalista Republicana* (1910) was founded as the main opposition to *Lliga* within political Catalanism (Riquer 1977, 161, 2022).

The growth of political Catalanism was soon interpreted by Spanish regenerationism as a façade for separatism, resulting in increasing opposition to the original plans of regional devolution. In parallel, growing social conflict in Barcelona, mostly stemming from the reaction of the working class to worsening conditions in industry continued to threaten social order. The economic benefits of colonial protection for Catalan textile exports had managed to align divergent views within Catalanism in the late nineteenth century. Both rural, catholic conservative on one side and the middle-class internationalist factions on the other saw progress in protection from the state. However, the collapse of colonial demand and the response of Spanish fiscal authorities changed this view and deepened the perception of a divided Spain: a modernizing outward-oriented periphery that was bearing most of the post-colonial shock, and a stagnated center that held the reins of the state.

Economic and social conflict within Catalonia and political elite conflict within Spain meant that the Catalan bourgeoisie was trapped, as Sebastian Balfour put it, in the classic dilemma of the lesser bourgeoisie: "threatened as a class by economic change and the rise of working-class protest, they remained ideologically tied to the old regime, despite their intense desire for change" (Balfour 1995, 414). This implied that the Catalanist institutional, economic and political modernization plan, which depended on the massive support among the working classes, ended up coexisting, already in the early 1900s, with the violent repression of the very same working classes in Barcelona by the state's armed forces, a connivance that would deepen during Primo de Rivera's Dictatorship between 1923 and 1930 (Casals Meseguer and Ucelay-Da Cal 2023).

1.3 The decay of the Catalan banking elite

In parallel to the disenchantment that the Disaster projected in the whole of Spain and in Catalonia in particular, another narrative of decay gained ground within Catalan financial and political circles. As an outward-oriented region, Catalonia had experienced substantial financial and banking instability during the late nineteenth century, both in the 1880s, during the Paris Bourse crash and the so-called *Febre d'Or* (gold fever), and following the Baring's crisis of 1890. Despite "Catalan banks suffered from a tradition of discredit" due to recurrent instability, up to the Disaster of 1898, they had still managed to retain the lion's share of the Spanish non-issuing banking business (Cambó 1915, 320).[6] The blow to Catalan banks and the subsequent decline in the importance of Catalan financial capital is presented in Figure 1.1, which shows how right after the loss of the protected colonial market in 1898, banks in Catalonia entered into a phase of continued decay vis-à-vis those of Madrid and Bilbao.

As explained earlier, the sudden collapse of protected colonial demand for textile products and a new scenario of international competition meant that Barcelona did not enjoy the impulse to local capital that the cities of Madrid and Bilbao experienced

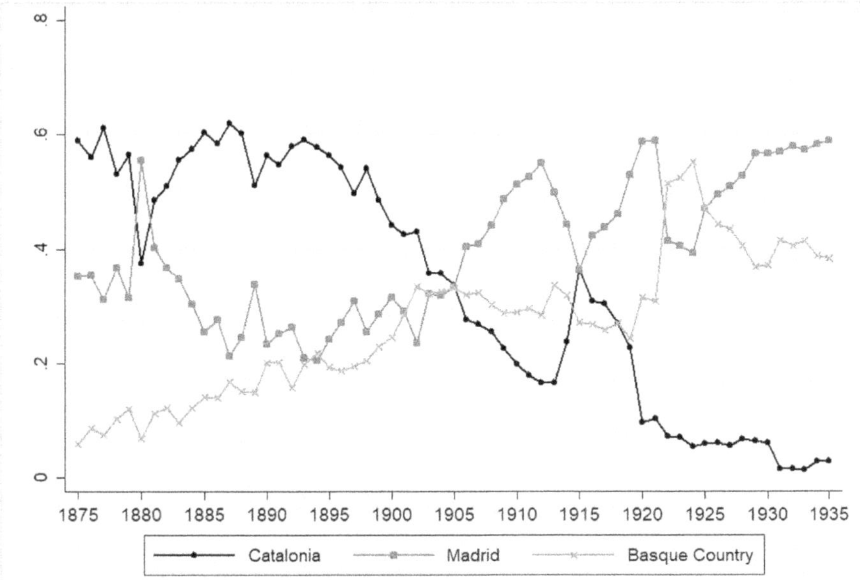

Figure 1.1 The decay of Catalan banking (1875–1935).

Source: Own calculations based on Tedde (1974), *Anuario Financiero de Sociedades Anónimas* (1916), *Anuario Financiero del Banco de Vizcaya* (1919, 1920, 1921), *Anuario Garciceballos* (1918) and *Boletines del Consejo Superior Bancario* (1922–1935).

Note: Percentage values represent the share of checking accounts (*cuentas corrientes acreedoras*) in each region as a percentage of the sum of the three. Selection of banks follows Tedde (1974). Inclusion or exclusion of individual banks does not alter the trend and the magnitude of the changes in crisis times during the first years of the twentieth century (Riquer 1977, 64). The most illustrative case is perhaps Banco Hispano Colonial (1876), a bank born under the auspices of trade globalization and colonial trade; right after the defeat, between 1899 and 1901, the bank underwent a capital reduction of 50% and did never regain preeminence in Barcelona (Rodrigo 2001). Moreover, capital repatriation from ex-colonies resulted in the creation of three new banks: Banco Hispano Americano (1900), Banco Español de Crédito (1902) and Banco de Vizcaya (1901). The first two, headquartered in Madrid, became the largest and most widely branched banks in Spain during the interwar years, while the latter joined Banco de Bilbao (1857) in underpinning the support to heavy industry in the Basque Country.[7] The three of them quickly understood that an important part of their business ought to be done in Barcelona, particularly given the blow to Catalan financial capital caused by the 1898 defeat, and so they were quick to open branches in the city.

Importantly, foreign banks expanded their role in the city, deepening the decline of local banks. This growing presence of foreign banking interests in Barcelona was quickly flagged by local industrial and financial elites as a fundamental weakness. In 1907, for example, a series of conferences was held in Barcelona's *Societat d'Estudis Econòmics* in order to discuss the "problems of Catalan banking" and the "promotion of the banking industry" (see heading quote). The conclusion reached by economists, politicians and financiers attending the meetings was that after the Disaster, Catalan industrial firms were at a disadvantage over other countries' industrial exporters because they lacked a stable and cheap source of short-term commercial and international trade finance. Relying on foreign banks had proved disastrous in the past:

> [a bank] not being able to find business in international trade in a city [Barcelona] in which the latter amounts to 2.600 million pesetas is to be incapable to find any business at all. Some find it, though: foreign banks. But, foreign banks! They are the police! The most important banking house, during the [Cuban] war, asked for the liquidation of all loans at a moment in which the exchange rate was above 100. Now, it is already thinking about cutting back on credit to the factories that are affected by the recent floodings. All this means that a large share, almost all, of our imports and exports are in the hands of foreigners.
>
> (Graell 1908, 4)

It was in 1915 when Francesc Cambó, head of *Lliga Regionalista* and the leading figure of political Catalanism, framed the situation in terms of long-standing decay:

> During these years in which Catalan banks have suffered a considerable decay, we have witnessed a tenfold increase in Banco de España's operations in Barcelona; we have witnessed the establishment of branches of the Banco Alemán Transatlántico [Deutsche Überseeische Bank], Banco del Río de la Plata and of Banco di Roma, each of them outgrowing Barcelona's most important local bank [Banco de Barcelona]. What is more, we have seen a Madrilean bank, Banco Hispano Americano, establish a branch here that operates more than any other local bank.
>
> (Cambó 1915, 315)

The narrative of decay matched the interests of the Catalan financial elite in order to recover the ground lost by local capital after the Disaster, but it did not necessarily imply that neither Catalonia had experienced a period of financial leadership in the previous decades to which it aimed at returning nor the region was underbanked (Sudrià 2007). Arguments about foreign "invasion" and the "non-Catalan" origins of banks' expanding business in Barcelona emerged, but the new Catalan financial elite's understanding of fundamental weaknesses went well beyond that rhetorical device. Just as in the narratives emerging among Spanish regenerationists following the Disaster of 1898 alluded to a dysfunctional status quo, there was a common perception among the main leaders of political Catalanism – Francesc Cambó or Pere Coromines, leader of *Unió Federal Nacionalista Republicana* – as well as among emerging financial leaders – Eduard Recasens, Director of Banco de Cataluña – that the incumbent, old banking elite in Barcelona had been refusing to take the role as the financial engine of the Catalan economy. This was thwarting potential economic development and, in turn, Catalonia's ability to exert growing influence in Spanish political and economic affairs (Jorge-Sotelo 2023). Consolidated banking elites profited from their incumbent privilege and limited their actions to passive banking that ensured a continued, stable and conservative stream of dividends, while foreign and non-Catalan banks received the rewards from innovation and risk. Banco Hispano Colonial had been de facto wiped out of the scene by the aftermath of the war. In the view of these new emerging elites, it was Banco de Barcelona (1844), the oldest bank and largest non-issuing bank in Spain, that had repeatedly declined to take the responsibility of bearing the risks of long-term lending and international trade finance alongside outward-oriented industrial enterprises, allowing foreign banks to take over Barcelona (Blasco and Sudrià 2010, 2016). Decay continued and the incumbents looked the other way.

Just as with Joaquin Costa's *iron surgeon,* which contemplated the need for a radical intervention to attack the origins of the Spanish' nation's maladies and ignite the regeneration of the nation, financial circles surrounding and underpinning political Catalanism reached a similar conclusion. Incumbent Catalan financial elites were sitting too comfortably in their conservative, risk-less business models. Trying to get the board of Banco de Barcelona involved into a renaissance of Catalan banking implied the herculean task of dealing with the interests of an established, accommodated and alienated elite, who enjoyed the large benefits brought by incumbency in banking. The renaissance of Catalan banking required a "reaction of salvation", as Francesc Cambó put it in 1915 (Cambó 1915, 316). Cambó's diagnosis and his suggested cure were shared in the debates among Catalan financial and political elites, particularly among a group of emerging politicians and financiers close to political Catalanism. Among them stood out Eduard Recasens, by then a relatively unknown figure in the Catalan and Spanish banking circles, who summarized the need for an elite replacement:

> Some argue that the Catalan bank that will conduct our financial affairs could be one of the already established, perhaps widening its range of operations, but we disagree with this view, because we understand that the governing functions of Catalonia's trade, industrial and banking development can only

> be undertaken with decisive influence by Banco de Cataluña, which should, precisely, be named like that.
>
> (Recasens 1918, 23)

Catalan industrial exports boomed during the First World War, given Spain's non-belligerent stance in the conflict. This pushed Catalan financial and industrial circles to seek the opportunity to ride a new expansion with the eventual resumption of global trade. With opportunity, however, came the threat that foreign banks would seek precisely the same by expanding their business in Barcelona. Eduard Recasens expressed this view eloquently, when already in 1918, he warned:

> "It is necessary that banks, particularly Catalan banks – because they will be more affected by the international nature of our trade – are well prepared to adapt to . . . the post-war days. Business will see a formidable reaction, international trade . . . will acquire an extraordinary level of development . . . and industrialists and merchants from some parts of the world will try to come and absorb and dominate us, and so a strong effort of anticipation is convenient in order to not be defeated in this battle for trade.
>
> (Recasens 1918, 17)

The export-boom during the First World War was thus seen as the right moment to give birth to the new institution in charge of the renaissance of Catalan banking. Banco de Cataluña was founded on 23 June 1920 in order to "facilitate the quick commercial and industrial development of Catalonia" and, in accordance with the concerns described earlier, to "build a wall to prevent the invasion of foreign banks that are taking over Catalonia, particularly Barcelona".[8] Crucially, mere six months after Banco de Cataluña was born, the old incumbent banking elite suffered a fatal blow – once again – from the sudden collapse of external demand for Catalan industrial produce. The end of hostilities and the resumption of industrial activity in Europe caused the collapse of textile exports, from 12.230 tons in 1915 to 1.124 in 1020 (Sudrià 1983). Asset and commodity prices plummeted. The crisis hit Banco de Barcelona particularly hard, as it had finally seen the War boom as an opportunity to modernize its banking practices and tried to effectively compete with foreign banks in Barcelona. Perhaps evidencing the inherent shortcomings of long-standing pleasant incumbency, the departure of the main exponent of the old banking elite from its conservative business model resulted in excessive risk-taking, speculation in foreign exchange markets and the collateralization of its loans with commodities valued at war-time prices (Cabana 1978; Muñoz 1988; Blasco and Sudrià 2010, 2016; Jorge-Sotelo 2019). Banco de Barcelona – the oldest financial institution in Spain – failed on Christmas Day 1920. Naturally, a similar shock hit newborn Banco de Cataluña, which was very close to following the same fate; during 1921, it went through several episodes of stress and underwent large losses but, a relatively liquid and very small bank at the time, with a narrow depositor base, it managed to stay afloat due to the provision of emergency liquidity by Banco de España on eligible collateral (Jorge-Sotelo

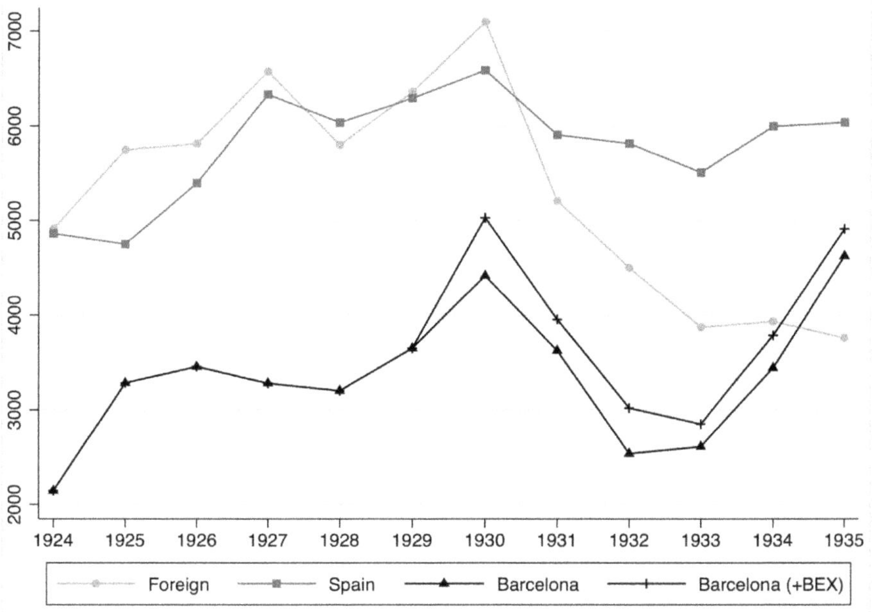

Figure 1.2 Annual settlement volume at the Barcelona Clearinghouse (1924–1935).
Source: Memorias de la Cámara de Compensación de Barcelona (various years)

2022, 2023). Therefore, after the short-lived boom of the First World War, Catalan banking continued to lose ground during the first half of the 1920s, with Banco de Cataluña slowly recovering from the 1921 shock (Figure 1.1). The dominance of Madrilean, Basque and foreign banks did not cease, as it is depicted in Figure 1.2, which shows the balances settled by each group of banks in the Barcelona clearinghouse. The failure of the old banking elite and the difficulties experienced by the new one provided undeniable grounds to the narrative of decay. The only chance for reverting the decay of Catalan banking was in the hands of Banco de Cataluña and its Director Eduard Recasens. The importance of the personification of this expected revival in the figure of Eduard Recasens is perhaps captured by the fact that Banco de Cataluña was soon called by the name of "Banco de Recasens" among the public (Cabana 2003, 85).

1.4 Giving credit to dictatorship: Banco de Cataluña and Banco Exterior de España

The interwar years saw the birth of state-backed banks and credit agencies, particularly of those involved in international trade finance. Expectations of recovering global trade and the need to generate foreign exchange revenues to return to exchange rate stability during the first half of the 1920s resulted in the creation of such institutions in Britain, Germany and the United States, among others.[9] Developments in the leading economies did not go unnoticed to Primo de Rivera and the banking community in Spain. In 1925, the Dictatorship called for proposals for the creation of such an institution in Spain – initially called *Banco de Crédito al Comercio Exterior*. Representatives of Catalan industry and banking took a leading role in the debate.[10] Banco de Cataluña had already partnered with the Dictatorship in 1924, when Primo de Rivera issued a Municipal Statute as part of his plan to incentivize infrastructural investment by local municipalities; Eduard Recasens wrote to Primo suggesting the creation of *Banco Municipal de España*, a state-backed bank that would lend to local corporations to underpin urban expansion (Matés-Barco and González-Ruiz 2019). Shortly after, Recasens's proposal won the public bid and the bank was chartered under the name of *Banco Local de Crédito de España,* BCLE.[11] Primo de Rivera's Minister of Finance José Calvo Sotelo was appointed President, Eduard Recasens Vice-President, and Eduard's brother Francesc was appointed Director.[12] From the onset, and under Banco de Cataluña directors' effective management, BCLE loans promoted local development across Spain, becoming an important engine for urban development in the 1920s (Matés-Barco and González-Ruiz 2019, 108–113).

While the creation of BCLE initiated narrow cooperation between Banco de Cataluña and the Dictatorship, it did not address their respective narratives of decay. The global economy was recovering fast. Unlike Spain, France and Italy had finally managed to stabilize their currencies, even if at the cost of devaluation. Capital was flowing at unprecedented rates from the United States to Central Europe, after the German stabilization. The growing import capacity of the United States had taken over as the main destination for Latin American exports. Both Primo de Rivera and Eduard Recasens saw this process as an opportunity to recover the lost ground. To Primo de Rivera, this could mean Spain's return to the Americas through the establishment of global trade links with the ex-colonies; Cuba or Chile's renewed export potential could be fostered with the presence of Spanish financial capital. This would also raise foreign exchange reserves for the government and help stabilize the peseta for an eventual return to the gold standard, after the Dictatorship had deemed the external value of the peseta as the thermometer of the regime's international reputation (Eguidazu 1979; González Calleja 2005; Jorge-Sotelo 2020). To Eduard Recasens – now the undeniable leading figure in Catalan banking – this was the long-awaited chance to regain the ground lost after the 1898 and 1920 shocks.

By mid-1928, Eduard Recasens approached his personal friend and Minister of Finance José Calvo Sotelo to readdress the idea of creating a new export-fostering state-backed bank. Shortly after, Primo de Rivera opened a public tender for the charter of state-backed Banco Exterior de España (BEX). Two groups entered the bid: a group led by Banco Urquijo de Madrid and more than ninety banks, including all the largest banks in Spain and a group led by Banco de Cataluña, two of its subsidiaries (Banco de Reus de Descuentos y Préstamos and Banco de Tortosa) and another six banks, most of them headquartered in Barcelona.

Given the nature and the potential rents stemming from the management of such an institution in the roaring 1920s, stakes were high. As Barcelona's financial newspaper *Economia i Finances* put it, "*whoever wins the bid will have, with the backing of the state, the key to virtually all trade and Spain's trade expansion*".[13] Minister of Finance José Calvo Sotelo's decision to grant the charter of BEX to Banco de Cataluña was highly controversial. The Council of State recommended a joint agreement in which the two bidding groups were merged, something that the international financial press had also assumed as the most likely solution. Banco de España and the Supreme Banking Council also expressed their disagreement, but Calvo Sotelo alluded to potential collective action problems of a joint management and the decision to grant BEX to Banco de Cataluña won by one vote. The controversial granting of BEX to such a narrow and geographically concentrated group of bankers can be interpreted, to a large extent, as part of the administrative devolution from Primo de Rivera to the Catalan financial and industrial elite, something the dictator had promised in exchange for supporting his coup in 1923.

BEX opened its doors on 3 June 1929, and through the rediscount of foreign bills and the provision of credit to international trade-oriented Spanish firms, it was expected to become "the first serious attempt at structuring our country's trade policy over concrete realities".[14] Eduard Recasens was appointed the first Director of BEX and his brother Francesc took the role of the second Director. The state was also represented in the BEX board: the Ministry of Finance, the Ministry of National Economy, the Council of National Economy, the Supreme Banking Council, the Trade Chambers, the National Board of Spanish Overseas Trade and Banco de España. However, if something characterized the management of BEX during its first years of existence it was discretion enjoyed by its Directors, who could ". . . use the bank's signature in . . . all types of receipts, payments, giros, deposits, current accounts and credit accounts, acceptances, endorsements and all similar operations".[15] This reduced the board's ability to control the bank and allowed Recasens to run the bank with a large degree of discretion. For instance, it allowed to take unilateral decisions such as a highly controversial credit policy, consisting in charging cheaper rates to short-term credit operations at the BEX discount window to the group of banks managing BEX – that is, to Recasens' own Banco de Cataluña – and therefore charging higher rates to the banks that had lost the bid for BEX charter (Jorge-Sotelo 2022).

Both the Dictatorship's decision to grant such a large enterprise to a narrow group of bankers and Recasens' management of the institution put BEX on the spotlight as yet another corporatist and crony institution created by Primo de Rivera and Calvo Sotelo.[16] Beyond that, discretion, privileged access to credit and the implicit backstop of the regime – which had bailed out affine insolvent banks before – had effects on how both BEX and Banco de Cataluña were managed (Jorge-Sotelo 2023). Moral hazard materialized in credit misallocation through politically motivated insider lending, creating solvency problems for both banks, and led to the accumulation of exceptionally high levels of foreign exposure and liquidity risk at the dawn of the Great Depression.

1.5 Poor governance, the great depression and democracy

As soon as Eduard Recasens was granted the management of BEX, Banco de Cataluña embarked into an unprecedentedly rapid and risky expansion (Figure 1.3). Relying on continued liquidity provision by BEX and on the expectation that solvency risk would be ultimately bore by the Dictatorship, Recasens brought about a radical change to the balance sheet and the business model of Banco de Cataluña. As Table 1.1 shows, Banco de Cataluña developed a uniquely risky and illiquid portfolio right after being granted the BEX charter. While all banks relied on holding public debt as the main liquid money market security, Banco de Cataluña now had a unique source of liquidity for commercial paper stemming from international trade transactions with remarkably lax credit controls (Jorge-Sotelo 2023). Importantly, BEX was the only state-backed institution that could rediscount these types of securities, as Banco de España was only obliged – by law – to provide liquidity to banks through short-term loans collateralized by domestic public debt. Having privileged (Recasens managed both Banco de Cataluña and BEX) and cheaper access to the rediscount of commercial paper originated in foreign trade meant that Banco de Cataluña could not only grow in size but also get rid of its public debt portfolio, as it now relied on BEX as its self-managed lender of last resort, and

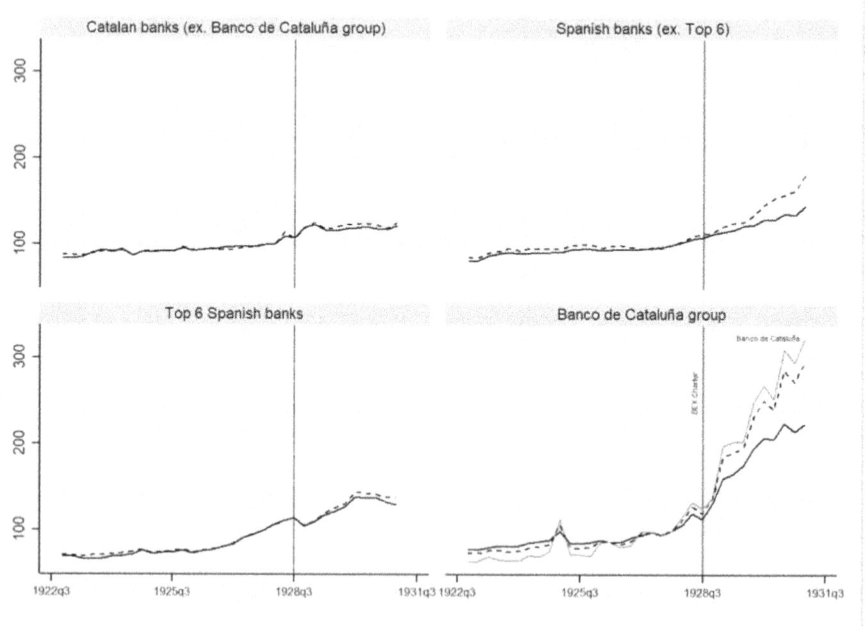

Figure 1.3 Banco de Cataluña's growth compared, 1922–1931.

Source: Jorge-Sotelo (2022)

Note: The solid line indicates non-weighted average and the dashed line indicates asset-weighted average.

Table 1.1 Portfolio composition of Spanish banks, 1927–1931

	Public debt as % securities			*Public debt as % of call deposits*			*Call deposits as % of total deposits*		
	1927q4	*1929q1*	*1931q1*	*1927q4*	*1929q1*	*1931q1*	*1927q4*	*1929q1*	*1931q1*
B. Español de Crédito	26	29	37	41	39	65	50	56	44
B. Hispano Americano	41	42	46	33	39	43	93	79	72
B. de Bilbao	43	47	49	55	63	69	52	51	48
B. de Vizcaya	48	50	42	73	100	75	44	41	40
B. Urquijo de Madrid	23	35	35	25	65	65	68	50	47
B. Central	20	26	32	37	49	83	44	35	31
B. Guipuzcoano	41	36	38	57	52	57	52	47	38
B. de Cataluña	**23**	**42**	**16**	**18**	**52**	**12**	**70**	**62**	**70**
B. Pastor	47	53	41	81	136	107	36	28	25
B. Herrero	63	62	60	87	48	48	53	87	90
B. Mercantil	62	67	61	113	171	153	38	29	29
B. de Aragón	55	51	47	105	89	104	48	41	31
B. de Valencia	59	55	54	54	61	96	71	57	29
Average	**42**	**46**	**43**	**60**	**74**	**75**	**55**	**51**	**46**

Source: Jorge-Sotelo (2022).

Note: Call deposits is the sum of "Sight Deposits" and "Deposits in foreign exchange".

in case solvency concerns arose, it could count on Primo de Rivera (Jorge-Sotelo 2022, 2023). Relying on the backstop of the Dictatorship, Banco de Cataluña jumped off the cliff into the international economy from 1929, just as the world was approaching real and financial collapse.

The implicit bailout clause provided by the Dictatorship did not only generate liquidity risks. The political influence of Catalan conservative political elites did also affect decisions made by Recasens, both in BEX and in Banco de Cataluña. Getting closer to Primo de Rivera had caused growing internal division within the board of Banco de Cataluña between the monarchic conservatives – *Lliga Regionalista* – who had seen less ideological conflict with siding with Primo, and the republicans – *Unió Federal Nacionalista Republicana* – who found it less compatible with their political convictions. The result was that the bank got increasingly under the influence of *Lliga* members, in both strategic and financial matters (Coromines 1972, 56, 1975, 40–43; Recasens 1985, 51–52; Cabana 2003, 85). Within these internal power dynamics, the most striking episode was the creation, one week after the Black Thursday of October 1929, of a gigantic international trust of firms in the cork industry. On November 1929, Francesc Cambó (*Lliga Regionalista)* and Eduard Recasens (Director of Banco de Cataluña and BEX) created *Compañía General del Corcho SAE (Cogeco)*, a holding of 17 industrial cork producers across 9 countries, most of them in Europe but also in the North of Africa. The official aim of the company was to compete in the international cork market with US trust Armstrong Cork Company, which was increasingly dominating the European cork market. Cork was Spain's first industrial export at the time, and the cork industry was particularly important in Catalonia, where it had centuries-long tradition, and where Armstrong had just purchased the largest industrial cork exporter, *Manufacturas del Corcho SA* (Vilar 1934; Parejo-Montuno 2010). Against this backdrop, the operation was soon given personal authorization by Primo de Rivera, as it was an easy-to-sell opportunity in his discourse of nationalizing industry; it would allow to "control the lion's share of cork industry in Europe and the North of Africa and thus take advantage of one of Spain's most important commodities" and "prevent this commodity from falling into foreign hands . . . a danger that has pushed the Government to approve the operation" (Jorge-Sotelo 2022).

Preventing foreign capital dominance was undoubtedly a crucial motivation for the creation of *Cogeco*, but there was more to it. The operation masked something else, namely yet another bailout of an insolvent bank close to the Dictatorship. In this case, this was organized by Francesc Cambó as a personal favor to Banco Central's manager José Luis de Ussía y Cubas, Count of Gaitanes, with whom he was close friends. Cambó used his influence on BEX and Banco de Cataluña through Eduard Recasens to purchase insolvent Belgian cork producer *Compagnie Commerciale et Industrielle du Liège* (CIL) from the hands of Banco Central. Removing these assets from Banco Central avoided its insolvency and failure. Although CIL's insolvency was well known, it was incorporated as *Cogeco*'s largest firm in the trust. Tellingly, the largest Spanish banks were offered to participate in *Cogeco*, but they all refused. Unsurprisingly, dissenting and warning views were raised at the board of BEX. The most important one was Banco de España's, who, right at the inception of *Cogeco,* warned that the operation was too risky, enough information was missing and had been decided unilaterally by Eduard Recasens without informing the board. These views were written down in the minutes of BEX but mostly ignored. Francesc Cambó was appointed President of *Cogeco* and Eduard Recasens sat at the Board of Directors, while the company was presented as yet another salvation reaction against the dominance of foreigners that suited both sides' narratives. Once again, foreign dominance caused a simultaneous threat to both Primo de Rivera's regime and the Catalan banking elite and this time in the all-important cork industry.

The project was appealing to both sides, particularly if the 1929 stock market shock was just a temporary correction, meaning that these companies were being purchased at a bargain. The downside was intentionally obscured, however large and anticipated it was, for these operations resulted in state-backed BEX becoming the main shareholder and provider of liquidity to an eminently insolvent gigantic international trust – *Cogeco* – at the same time that Banco de Cataluña depended on BEX for its own liquidity needs and both banks were discretionally managed by the same individual. Mutual aims at fighting foreign dominance, the rhetoric that accompanied them and the crony dynamics and individual interests underlying these operations pushed the Catalan financial elite to bank on the Primo de Rivera, implicitly accepting BEX as part of the devolution that the Dictator had promised.

The promise of a bailout vanished soon after the *Cogeco* operation had materialized, leaving the new Catalan banking elite without a safety net. After years of mounting discredit – of which the *Cogeco* operation constitutes is a prime example – Primo de Rivera and Calvo Sotelo resigned in January 1930, as the Great Depression was beginning to unfold. As the collapse of global trade ensued and the rise of protectionism deepened the crisis in all exporting industries, solvency problems mounted for *Cogeco* and also for BEX. Banco de Cataluña's fate, and with it the fate of the revival of Catalan banking, hinged on the evolution of an insolvent cork trust and a state-backed bank chartered by a discredited Dictator now gone. During the year and half between the resignation of Primo de Rivera and the failure of Banco de Cataluña in July 1931, Eduard Recasens did not only ignore warnings from his bank's main and most qualified financial advisors but also double down on the expansion of the bank by purchasing yet another ailing Barcelonian bank that was in French hands – Banca Arnús – thus reaching inexplicable levels of liquidity risk, given the nature of Spanish money markets described earlier (Jorge-Sotelo 2022, 2023).

The sudden proclamation of the Second Spanish Republic in April 1931 was accompanied by financial crisis. There was a widespread bank run, capital flight ensued, asset prices collapsed and pressure mounted on the exchange rate, threatening the collapse of the currency. By early June 1931, however, liquidity problems for most banks had been addressed, even if the shock had caused a sharp contraction in credit to the real economy (Jorge-Sotelo 2020). Right after Primo had left in the early 1930s, members of the BEX board had started to ask more questions about the solvency of *Cogeco* and the concentrated exposure of the state-backed bank to Banco de Cataluña, flagging that the collapse of the international economy was now hitting the bank due to its unilateral, politically motivated but financially unsound decisions. Distrust and heated discussions ensued within the BEX board, with accusations of mismanagement, loose credit policy to dubious signatures, discretion in large loan operations, credit misallocation through insider lending and the use of a public bank for politically motivated interests. Pressure mounted as news about the deterioration of *Cogeco*'s assets reached the board of BEX, resulting in the resignation of Eduard and Francesc Recasens. News of the state of BEX and Banco de Cataluña quickly reached Republican fiscal authorities and in mid-June 1931, the provisional Republican Minister of Finance Indalecio Prieto claimed in a newspaper interview that the Republic saw banks that had used connections with the Dictatorship as members of "a cacique domain" and a private instrument for the enrichment of "half a dozen gentlemen", thus compromising the likelihood of a state-backed bailout.[17]

A bailout was eventually required. On 24 June 1931, as financial panic began to unfold in Central Europe, *Cogeco* announced that it would miss its 1 July bond coupon payment. Panic ensued within the board of BEX, as all expectations quickly materialized. Foreign banks cut liquidity to BEX, and its board – now without Banco de Cataluña's representation – turned to protect its balance sheet and to generate liquidity. BEX drastically cut lending in order to grow its cash reserves and this left Banco de Cataluña – which depended on continued BEX credit – without its main source of liquidity. Before, during and after *Cogeco*'s default on the bond payment and until Banco de Cataluña failed on 7 July 1931, the latter borrowed heavily from Banco de España against all its remaining eligible assets, but to no avail. Banco de España proposed that the rest of banks headquartered in Barcelona provide a joint guarantee to back an additional emergency loan for Banco de Cataluña, but local banks refused. When the bank ran out of eligible assets to borrow from Banco de España and without the support of the rest of the Barcelona banking community, Banco de Cataluña's directors turned to the Ministry of Finance. Several emergency meetings took place, but Republican fiscal authorities (including the President of the Republic), who had already expressed their skepticism, were not persuaded to extend a public guarantee on the bank's assets as Primo de Rivera had done in the past with affine bankers.[18] Banco de Cataluña failed on 7 July 1931.

The benefits of being connected to Primo de Rivera had paid off until the Dictator resigned in the early 1930s, the Great Depression unfolded, and the arrival of the Second Spanish Republic in 1931 eliminated the certainty of a bailout clause. Against the backdrop of collapsing trade, international financial crisis and political uncertainty, cronyism and fundamentally unsound banking quickly revealed its shortcomings: balance sheet mismanagement, credit misallocation through politically motivated insider lending and poor credit control put the final nail in the coffin of Catalan financial capital.

1.6 Conclusion

A new Catalan financial elite emerged in the early 1920s to fight incumbency and foreign financial dominance and to restore Catalan capital's share in the Spanish banking system. Despite its fundamental disagreement over Primo de Rivera's idea of Spain – particularly of Catalonia and its political, social and cultural institutions – this new elite gambled its survival and the renaissance of Catalan banking on its connections with the Dictatorship. These materialized in support for his coup in 1923 and the corresponding devolution in 1929, through the controversial granting of the discretionary management of a state-backed bank. Both Primo de Rivera and the new Catalan financial elite's agenda converged in a discourse of regeneration and resurgence. These connections paid off to all parts involved during the roaring 1920s, which set the timing of these agreements, while the resignation of Primo de Rivera and the international economic collapse of the 1930s caused their fragility to surface. The case of Banco de Cataluña and Banco Exterior during the late 1920s highlights the importance of different political regimes not only in shaping the way monetary and fiscal institutions have dealt with financial shocks in the past, but perhaps, more importantly, the role they have played in designing the institutional framework in which banks grow unstable.

Notes

1 This chapter draws from Jorge-Sotelo (2019, 2020, 2022, 2023).
2 For a detailed discussion on Primo's rhetoric and "charismatization", see Quiroga (2008).
3 There is a historiographical debate about the actual content of Costa's idea and vague allusions to such a figure, both regarding its intellectual origins and the self-proclamation of Primo de Rivera first and Francisco Franco later as *iron surgeons*. See Fernandez

Clemente (1984), Balfour (1995), Lorente (1997), Quiroga (2008, 2013, 2022), Ben Ami (2012) and Alcusón (2013).

4 Membership of the Socialist Union increased from around 6,000 members in 1896 to 57,000 in 1904 (Tuñón de Lara 1972, 331).

5 Only after the UK in 1947–1956 and Ireland in 1996–2005. See Eichengreen and Esteves (2022, 10).

6 For the history of Banco de Barcelona, see Blasco and Sudrià (2010, 2016).

7 For a recent compendium of histories of Spanish banks and bankers, see Tortella and Quiroga (2023).

8 *"De les terres catalanes", La Veu de Catalunya,* N. 7614, 6/08/1920, Ed. Vespre, 9.

9 See Myles (2021) for a recent detailed analysis of the role and nature of such institutions.

10 *Informe sobre el proyecto de creación de un Banco de Crédito al Comercio Exterior,* Publicaciones de Fomento del Trabajo Nacional, Barcelona: Imprenta Hijo de Domingo Casanovas, 1925.

11 *Real Decreto Ley de 24/05/1925, Artcíulo 3, sección b.*

12 Primo de Rivera vetoed the participation of Pere Coromines, who had drafted the statutes of the bank and who was a key figure at Banco de Cataluña up to that point. In short, Coromines seems to have been less inclined to link Banco de Cataluña with the Dictatorship, both on ideological grounds, but also regarding the financial implications that siding with Primo de Rivera ended up implying for the management of the bank. This meant that as Banco de Cataluña approached the Dictatorship in successive agreements, Coromines was progressively relegated to irrelevance within the bank. For details on the implications of this internal division within the bank, see Jorge-Sotelo (2023).

13 "El Projecte del Banc de Crèdit Exterior i el problema de l'exportació", *Economia i Finances,* 25/08/1928, 4.

14 Memorias, Banco Exterior de España, 1929.

15 Acta 1, Consejo de Administración del Banco Exterior de España, 03/06/1929, 4 *et passim.*

16 For a recent study on economic corruption and cronysm under Primo de Rivera, see Muñoz (2016).

17 "*Don Indalecio Prieto nos habla de la situación financera de España, del problema monetario, del presupuesto, del mercurio y del monopolio de Petróleos*", Entrevistas de Crisol, Crisol, 16/06/1931, 8.

18 For a discussion on the diverging views on Republican authorities' motivations to deny a bailout to Banco de Cataluña, see Jorge-Sotelo (2022, 2023).

References

Alcusón, Antonio, "Ecos del Cirujano de Hierro: la utilización política de Joaquín Costa por parte de la dictadura de Primo de Rivera en Aragón (1923–1930)", *Anales de la Fundación Joaquin Costa*, 27, 2013, pp. 89–98.

Balfour, Sebastian, "Riot, regeneration and reaction: Spain in the aftermath of the 1898 Disaster", *The Historical Journal,* 38, 2, 1995, pp. 405–423.

Ben Ami, Shlomo, *El cirujano de Hierro. La dictadura de Primo de Rivera (1923–1930)*, Barcelona, RBA Libros, 2012.

Blasco, Yolanda and Sudrià, Carles, *El Banco de Barcelona, 1844–1874: Historia de un Banco de Emisión*, Madrid, LID, 2010.

Blasco, Yolanda and Sudrià, Carles, *El Banco de Barcelona 1874–1920: decadencia y quiebra*, Madrid, Marcial Pons, 2016.

Cabana, Francesc, *La banca a Catalunya*, Barcelona, Edicions 62, 1965.

Cabana, Francesc, *Bancs i banquers a Catalunya*, Barcelona, Edicions 62, 1972.

Cabana, Francesc, *Història del Banc de Barcelona (1844–1920)*, Barcelona, Edicions 62, 1978.

Cabana, Francesc, *Eduard i Francesc Recasens: dos empresaris de Reus*, Reus, Cambra de Comerç de Reus, 2003.
Cabrera, Mercedes and del Rey, Fernando, *The power of entrepreneurs. Politics and economy in contemporary Spain*, Oxford, Berghan Books, 2007.
Cambó, Francesc, "La banca catalana", en Lliga Regionalista (ed.), *El pensamiento catalán ante el conflicto europeo: conferencias de los parlamentarios regionalistas, Marzo, Abril y Mayo de 1915*, Barcelona, Imprenta Hijos de Domingo Casanovas, 1915, pp.278–306.
Casals Meseguer, Xavier and Ucelay-Da Cal, Enric, *El Fascio de Las Ramblas: los orígenes catalanes del fascismo español*, Barcelona, Ediciones de Pasado y Presente, 2023.
Casassas, Jordi, *La Dictadura de Primo de Rivera (1923–1930)*, Barcelona, Anthropos, 1983.
Comín, Francisco, "La obra de Raimundo Fernández Villaverde en Hacienda", en Universidad de Zaragoza (ed.), *La Hacienda desde sus ministros: del 98 a la Guerra Civil*, Zaragoza, Prensas Universitarias de Zaragoza, 2000, pp.23–60.
Comín, Francisco, "Raimundo Fernández Villaverde: la personificación de la ortodoxia financiera clásica en España", in Enrique Fuentes Quintana (dir.), *Economía y economsitas espanyoles,* Vol. 5, Galaxia Gutenberg, 2001, pp.273–284.
Comín, Francisco, "El plan de estabilización de Raimundo Fernández Villaverde", *Cuadernos de Información Económica,* 168, 2002, pp.189–196.
Comín, Francisco, "Default, rescheduling and inflation: public debt crises in Spain during the 19th and 20th centúries", *Revista de Historia Económica, Journal of Iberian and Latin American Economic History,* 30, 3, 2012, pp.353–390.
Coromines, Pere, *Obres completes*, Barcelona, Editorial Selecta, 1972.
Coromines, Pere, *Diaris i records de Pere Coromines III: La República i la Guerra Civil*, Barcelona, Curial, 1975.
Costa, Joaquín, *Oligarquia y caciquismo como la farma actual de gobierno en España: urgencia y modo de cambiarla*, Madrid, Imprenta de los Hijos M. G. y Fernández, 1901.cl.
Eguidazu, Fernando, "La crisis de la peseta y la caída de la Dictadura", *Cuadernos Económicos del ICE*, 10, 1979, pp.299–352.
Eichengreen, Barry and Esteves, Rui P., "Up and away? Inflation and debt consolidation in historical perspective", *Oxford Open Economics*, 1, 2022.
Fernández Clemente, Eloy, "Retórica regeneracionista y pseudocostismo en la Dictadura de Primo de Rivera", in *Legado de Costa*, Ministerio de Cultura/Diputación General de Aragón, 1984, pp.139–173.
Fraile, Pedro, *Industrialización y grupos de presión. La economía política de la protección en España, 1900–1950*, Madrid, Alianza Editorial, 1991.
González Calleja, Eduardo, *La España de Primo de Rivera (1923–1930): La modernización autoritaria*, Madrid, Alianza, 2005.
Graell, Guillem, "Informe de clausura", en Societat d'Estudis Econòmics (ed.), *Información pública sobre la necesidad de crear banca catalana*, Barcelona, Societat d'Estudis Econòmics, 1908.
Jorge-Sotelo, Enrique, *'Escaping' the Great Depression: monetary policy, banking and financial crises in Spain, 1921–1935*, PhD Dissertation, London School of Economics and Political Science, 2019.
Jorge-Sotelo, Enrique, "The limits to lender of last resort interventions in emerging economies: evidence from the Gold Standard and the Great Depression in Spain", *European Review of Economic History,* 24, 1, 2020, pp.98–133.
Jorge-Sotelo, Enrique, "Politicians, bankers and the Great Depression: the Spanish banking crisis of 1931", *EABH Working Papers,* 2022.
Jorge-Sotelo, Enrique, "El Banco de Cataluña (1920) y Eduard Recasens (1884–1939)", in Gabriel Tortella and Gloria Quiroga (eds.), *Bancos y banqueros. Dos siglos de crédito privado en España y sus protagonistas*, Madrid, Comares, 2023.
Lorente, José Domingo Dueñas, "Notas sobre la interpretación mesiánica de la figura y obra de Joaquín Costa", *Anales de la Fundación Joaquín Costa*, 14, 1997, pp.97–122.
Martín-Aceña, Pablo, *La cantidad de dinero en España, 1900–1935,* Madrid, Servicio de Estudios del Banco de España, 1985.

Martín-Aceña, Pablo, Martínez-Ruiz, Elena and Nogues-Marco, Pilar, "Floating against the Tide: Spanish Monetary Policy, 1870–1931", in A. Ögren y L. F. Øksendal (eds.), *The Gold Standard Peripheries: Monetary Policy, Adjustment and Flexibility in a Global Setting*, Basingstoke, Palgrave Macmillan, 2011.
Matés-Barco, Juan Manuel and González-Ruiz, Luis "La actividad inversora del Banco de Crédito Local de España en su primera época (1925–1936)", *Investigaciones de Historia Económica – Economic History Research,* 15, 2, 2019, pp.102–118.
Molas, Isidre, *Lliga catalana: un estudi d'estasiologia,* Barcelona, Edicions 62, 1972.
Moreno Lázaro, J., "El fraude en el pago de la Contribución Industrial y de Comercio en España: el caso de los harineros, 1845–1907", *Investigaciones De Historia Económica,* 15, 3, 2017, pp.165–176.
Muñoz, Juan, *El fracaso de la burguesía financiera catalana. La crisis del Banco de Barcelona,* Madrid, Endymion, 1988.
Muñoz, Jaume, *La España corrupta. Breve historia de la corrupción (de la Restauración a nuestros días, 1854–2016),* Madrid, Comares, 2016.
Myles, J., *Steering the wheels of commerce: state and enterprise in international trade finance, 1914–1929,* Thesis doctoral, Université de Genève, 2021.
Nualart, Joan, *La banca catalana: informe dirigit a la Societat d'Estudis Econòmics,* Barcelona, L'Avenç, 1907.
Parejo-Montuno, Francisco, *El negocio del corcho en España durante el Siglo XX,* Estudios de Historia Económica, N. 57, Madrid, Banco de España, 2010.
Quiroga, Alejandro, *Haciendo españoles. La nacionalización de las masas en la Dictadura de Primo de Rivera (1923–1930),* Madrid, Centro de Estudios Políticos y Constitucionales, 2008.
Quiroga, Alejandro, "Cirujano de Hierro. La construcción carismática del general Primo de Rivera", *Ayer. Revista De Historia Contemporánea,* 91, 3, 2013, pp.147–168.
Quiroga, Alejandro, *Miguel Primo de Rivera: dictadura, populismo y nación,* Barcelona, Crítica, 2022.
Recasens, Eduard, "Petites notes sobre la banca en el present i en l'avenir", en *Conferència de D. Eduard Recasens i Mercadé, donada en el Centre Autonomista de Dependents del Comerç i de la Industria el dia 16 de Maig de 1918, per encàrrec de la Secció Permanent d'Educació i Instrucció,* 1918.
Recasens, Josep, *Vida inquieta: combat per un socialisme català,* Barcelona, Empúries, 1985.
Riquer, Borja de, *La lliga regionalista, 1898–1904,* Barcelona, Edicions 62, 1977.
Riquer, Borja de, *Cambó. El último retrato,* Barcelona, Crítica, 2022.
Rodrigo, Martín, "El Banco Hispano Colonial y Cuba, 1876–1898", *Illes i imperis: estudios de historia de las sociedades en el mundo colonial y post-colonial,* 4, 2001, pp.49–70.
Sudrià, Carles, "Desarrollo industrial y subdesarrollo bancario en Cataluña, 1844–1950", *Investigaciones Económicas,* 18, 1982, pp.137–176.
Sudrià, Carles, "La exportación en el desarrollo de la industria algodonera española 1875–1920", *Revista de Historia Económica,* 2, 1983, pp.369–386.
Sudrià, Carles, "La banca catalana en los años de entreguerras y el debate sobre la decadencia: una revisión", *Revista de la historia de la economia y de la empresa,* 1, 2007, pp.269–287.
Tedde, Pedro, *La Banca Española en la Restauración, Tomo II, Datos para una historia económica,* Madrid, Servicio de Estudios del Banco de España, 1974.
Tortella, Gabriel, "El Banco de España entre 1829 y 1929. La formacion de un Banco Central", in *El Banco de España. Una Historia Económica,* Madrid, Banco de España, 1970.
Tortella, Gabriel and Quiroga, Gloria (eds.), *Bancos y banqueros: dos siglos de Crédito privado en España y sus protagonistas,* Madrid, Comares, 2023.
Tuñón de Lara, Manuel, *El movimiento obrero en la Historia de España,* Madrid, Taurus, 1972.
Vall-Prat, Pau, "Economic shocks, mobilization, and regional elite splits", *Comparative Political Studies,* 56, 2, 2023, pp.193–227.
Velarde, Juan, *Política económica de la Dictadura,* Madrid, Guadiana de Publicaciones, 1972.
Vilar, Pierre, "L'Espagne et le commerce mondial du liège", *Annales de Géographie,* XLIII, 1934, pp.282–298.

2 Portugal in a Greek mirror

The failed attempt of a foreign loan supported by the League of Nations, 1927–1928

Ana Tomás and Nuno Valério

2.1 Introduction

On November 24, 1927, the Portuguese Minister of Finance addressed a letter to the League of Nations asking for the support of the League for the issuing of a foreign loan with the purpose of promoting the financial restoration, the monetary stabilization and the economic development of the country.

On December 5, 1927, the Council of the League of Nations authorized the Financial Committee and the Secretariat to study the financial situation of Portugal and to report to the Council in its next session.

The negotiations on the support of the League of Nations to the Portuguese loan came to a failure on March 10, 1928, as recorded in the minutes of a new meeting of the Council. This meant that the planned foreign loan was not issued and the consolidation of the Portuguese monetary and financial stabilization had to be postponed.

More or less at the same time, Greece asked for a similar support and succeeded. This text tries to explain the reasons for the different outcomes of negotiations (Section 2.2) and to identify the consequences of the different outcomes of negotiations (Section 2.3), drawing some conclusions on the interaction of financial and political matters in the process. It is based on the archives of the League of Nations and on previous studies of Portuguese and Greek monetary and financial situation at the epoch.

2.2 Reasons for the different outcomes of Portuguese and Greek negotiations

The different outcomes of Portuguese and Greek negotiations might be explained by the structural characteristics of the Portuguese and Greek national economies, by the short-term situation of both economies or by the political situation of both countries. This section will explain why the first two possibilities are not likely and the last one is a potential explanation for the difference.

The structural characteristics of the two economies that must be considered are the size and degree of development, the links to the international economy and the monetary systems.

DOI: 10.4324/9781032656199-3

The economic activity of the 6.1 million inhabitants of Greece produced in 1927 a value added that may be estimated at 43 billion drachmas (around 115 million pounds at current prices, 11.5 billion euros at prices of the beginning of the third decade of the 21st century). This implies that per capita income was around 7 thousand drachmas (roughly 18.5 pounds at current prices, 1850 euros at prices of the beginning of the third decade of the 21st century).[1]

The economic activity of the 6.5 million inhabitants of Portugal produced in 1927 a value added that may be estimated at 9 billion escudos (around 90 million pounds at current prices, 9 billion euros at prices of the beginning of the third decade of the 21st century). This implies that per capita income was around 1.45 thousand escudos (roughly 14.5 pounds at current prices, 1445 euros at prices of the beginning of the third decade of the 21st century).[2]

Thus, the national economies of Greece and Portugal had not very different sizes, although Greece was slightly larger; and both had medium degree of development: Greece slightly above the world average of the epoch and slightly above 40% of the level of Great Britain, the leading European economy, and Portugal somewhat below the world average of the epoch and slightly above 30% of the level of Great Britain.[3]

Links to the international economy were, however, quite different. Portugal had Great Britain as its main trade and financial partner and had a large colonial empire (eight territories scattered in Western Africa, Eastern Africa, India, China and Indonesia, with around 8 million inhabitants), which did not play a significant role as an outlet market, but afforded some advantages as a supply market of tropical and mineral products for consumption and re-exportation. Greece had its main trade and even financial partners in the Mediterranean world and had no colonial empire.

Thus, the Portuguese national economy seemed to have some potential advantage from the point of view of its links to the international economy, which might compensate its smaller size and lower per capita gross domestic product.

Concerning the monetary systems, Portugal was the first country to follow Great Britain into the gold standard in 1854 (Reis, 1996) and one of those that had to leave the system while it remained the standard monetary system of the contemporary world economy – in July 1891 in the wake of a financial crisis (Mata and Valério, 1996).[4] The depreciation of the Portuguese currency until the First World War was relatively moderate – in July 1914, £1 = 5.3 escudos as against the par £1 = 4.5 escudos.[5]

Greece attempted to abide by the rules of the classical gold standard as a member of the Latin Union. Although it was not able to sustain convertibility in the late 19th and early 20th centuries, it was able to keep the exchange rate not far from the par (£1 = 25.22 drachmas) until the beginning of the Balkan wars.[6]

Concerning the short-term situation, it is necessary to consider the involvement in wars and the monetary upheavals experienced by both countries.

Greece was involved in the Balkan wars against Turkey between 1912 and 1913, with significant territorial gains (Greece's area increased from around 80 thousand square kilometres to nearly 120 square kilometres, mainly in Epirus, Thessaly and

South Macedonia at the cost of Turkey), participated in the First World War as a member of the winning alliance, with further territorial gains (Greece's area increased to around 130 square kilometres, mainly in Western Thrace at the cost of Bulgaria) and engaged in further war against Turkey over Eastern Thrace and Western Anatolia until 1922 without success. Besides a significant war debt and a slice of war reparations from defeated powers, the main consequence of these conflicts were refugee movements of Greeks from Eastern Thrace and Anatolia to Greece and of Turks from Greece to Turkey, especially in the wake of the last war.

Portugal was actively involved in the First World War, in colonial theatres (Angola and Mozambique), Atlantic submarine war and sending an expeditionary force to the European Western Front. The result was a significant war debt, almost negligible territorial gains in Mozambique and a slice of war reparations from defeated powers.

War triggered significant inflation and depreciation in both countries. By the mid-1920s, exchange rates stabilized at levels very far from the old par (respectively £1 = 94.75 escudos in Portugal and £1 = 375 drachmas in Greece) and prices also stabilized at roughly corresponding purchasing power levels (slightly above 20 times the pre-war level in Portugal and slightly less than 15 times the pre-war level in Greece).

Thus, both countries had been deeply affected by war in the second and early third decades of the 20th century, although somewhat differently and were staging some economic recovery and financial and monetary stabilization in the mid-1920s. Once more, the differences of the short-term situation do not seem to allow the explanation of the different outcomes of Portuguese and Greek negotiations.

Anyway, monetary and financial stabilization seemed precarious in both countries until the new gold-exchange international monetary system recommended by the Genoa Conference of 1922 was adopted. By 1927, the possibility of such a move seemed to depend on significant foreign loans.

The technical reason for such need may be perceived by the analysis of the balance sheet of the Bank of Portugal at the time of the negotiations with the League of Nations (Table 2.1).

The result of the monetization of public deficits, both during and immediately after the world war, was what was perceived as an excessive weight of government

Table 2.1 Balance sheet of the Bank of Portugal

Total assets 2514	*Total liabilities 2483*
Gold and exchange reserves 44	Banknotes issued 1857
Government debt 1614	Other short-term liabilities 200
Other assets 856	Other liabilities 426
	Net capital 31

Source: Banco de Portugal, Relatório do Conselho de Administração, 1927.

Date: December 31, 1927.

Unit: million escudos, £ 1 = 94.75 escudos.

debt in total assets (almost two-thirds). The bulk of the other assets were the result of the current commercial activity of the Bank, as both first-order (to non-financial firms) and second-order (to financial intermediaries) lender. Gold and exchange reserves seemed tinny, covering only slightly more than 2% of the banknote issue and all short-term liabilities.

This situation implied that the key point of the stabilization process should be a significant increase of the reserves to provide the confidence needed to avoid any run on them. The way to ensure such increase seemed to be the repayment of a significant part of the government debt. Thus, the main goal of the foreign loan to be issued by the government should be the repayment of a significant part of the government debt towards the Bank and the simultaneous reinforcement of the Bank's reserves.

The result of such a process may be illustrated by the balance sheet of the Bank of Greece when it opened business after stabilization (Table 2.2).

Gold and exchange reserves exceeded government debt in the Bank's assets (commercial paper was almost irrelevant as a new central bank – Bank of Greece – was created, and most previous loans, especially first-order loans, were retained by the old issuing bank – National Bank of Greece). Banknote coverage reached 84% and coverage of all short-term liabilities reached 55%.

The Portuguese government contacted London bankers on the possible issue of a foreign loan, and received the advice to get support from the League of Nations as a device to obtain more favorable terms. This is the background to the request of November 24, 1927, and the opening of negotiations on December 5, 1927.

The international conference convened by the League of Nations to Genoa in 1922 issued a set of recommendations that became the package of financial orthodoxy recommended afterwards by the League of Nations.[7] These recommendations involved three main items: the existence (or creation) of an independent central bank; reaching a balanced budget; and ensuring gold convertibility of the currency (usually indirectly, as direct convertibility was only achievable by anchor currencies, namely the American dollar, the British pound sterling and the French franc).

The League of Nations stimulated the adoption of these measures by supporting loans in the main international capital markets for countries attempting to adopt the gold-exchange system. Several countries benefited from these procedures, namely: Austria in 1923, Hungary in 1924, Estonia in 1927, Greece in 1927 (after a first

Table 2.2 Balance sheet of the Bank of Greece after stabilization

Total assets 7930	*Total liabilities 7529*
Gold and exchange reserves 4067	Banknotes issued 4863
Government debt 3760	Other short-term liabilities 2636
Other assets 103	Other liabilities 30
	Net capital 401

Source: Archives of the League of Nations R2936/10E/911/911.

Date: May 14, 1928.

Unit: million drachmas, £ 1 = 375 drachmas.

loan in 1924 linked to the need to settle refugees from Anatolia in the wake of the war with Turkey) and Bulgaria in 1928 (after a first loan in 1926 also linked to the need to settle refugees from Anatolia).

As might be expected, the League of Nations recommendations and demands presented to the Portuguese government were not significantly different from those presented to the countries just mentioned. Once more, it is not possible to find here a reason for the different outcomes of the negotiations.

Turning now to the political situation, it is important to stress that neither Greece nor Portugal had achieved stability in the mid-1920s. Greece witnessed the replacement of the constitutional monarchy by a republican regime (1923) but managed to keep a formal constitutional democracy in the process. Portugal, whose constitutional monarchy had been overthrown earlier (1910), was unable to keep a formal constitutional democracy in the 1920s, the constitutional regime being replaced by a military dictatorship in 1926.

Thus, while there was no question on the legitimacy of the Greek government to commit the Greek state to the foreign loan and the demands of the League of Nations, the question of the legitimacy of the Portuguese government was raised by the representatives of the former government, led by the President of the Republic deposed by the military coup, Bernardino Machado, who was exiled in France.[8] However, this did not prevent the League from presenting a proposal of agreement to the military government. The legitimacy issue cannot also be presented as the explanation for the different outcomes of negotiations.

As a matter of fact, it was the Portuguese government that rejected the conditions proposed by the League of Nations. The reason presented was the fact that they were offensive to national honor. However, they were similar to those presented to other potential borrowers and accepted by them. It is difficult to accept the idea of a special sensitivity of the Portuguese to such demands. It is more likely to suggest that the military government feared that the acceptance of the conditions proposed might provide a propaganda weapon to the opposition forces, especially among some parts of the armed forces, which were crucial to the survival of the new political order.

2.3 Consequences of the different outcomes of negotiations

It is now time to discuss the consequences of the different outcomes of negotiations. Immediate consequences and medium-term consequences must be distinguished.

The main short-term consequence of the different outcomes of negotiations for Greece and Portugal was that Greece was able to immediately adopt gold-exchange standard, while Portugal had to postpone such a move.

The failure of the attempt to issue the foreign loan that seemed a necessary condition for monetary and financial stabilization triggered a fresh depreciation of the Portuguese currency, which slipped from £ 1 = 94.75 escudos to £ 1 = 108.25 escudos in the following months. However, the fiscal year 1928–1929 witnessed the balancing of the Portuguese public accounts, and such a situation was maintained in the following years in spite of the stress brought to foreign payments by the Great Depression.

Thus, in 1931, the Portuguese government believed it was possible to peg the escudo to the pound although at a slightly depreciated exchange rate (£ 1 = 110 escudos), reaching, at last, the long wished formal monetary stabilization. On July 1, 1931, the Portuguese currency was at last declared convertible into the pound sterling.[9]

How was it possible for the Bank of Portugal to ensure credibility of its commitment to convertibility? An analysis of its balance sheet after the monetary stabilization (Table 2.3) provides the answer and, at the same time, a picture of the differences between such stabilization and the standard stabilization as achieved by Greece three years earlier.

Government debt was reduced by roughly one third, not by any genuine repayment but through an accounting operation. Gold and exchange reserves changed their legal value because of the nominal devaluation of the monetary unit. As the old par was £ 1 = 4.5 escudos and the new par was £ 1 = 110 escudos, the monetary reform multiplied the escudo value of the reserves by a factor of 24.(4). As a consequence, it was possible not only to reduce government debt (from more than 1.5 million escudos to around 1 million escudos) but also (i) to increase the escudo value of the gold and exchange reserves (from around 50 thousand escudos to around 1 million escudos), banknote coverage to 48% and total short-term liabilities coverage to 42%; and (ii) to increase the capital of the Bank by a factor of around 6 (from around 30 thousand to around 180 thousand escudos).

Was such a purely nominal operation enough to ensure credibility? The answer of practice was Yes. However, it may be stressed that the real key point was not gold and exchange reserve revaluation, but balancing public accounts and convincing economic agents that there would be no more monetization of public deficits. It is true that consolidation of public accounts had started in 1922 and had been gradually brought forward by constitutional republican and military dictatorship governments, but it was in 1928 that it was concluded. As a consequence, the man in charge of the Ministry of Finance at the time, Oliveira Salazar, was able to reap the political fruits of the process and become the often challenged, but never toppled, leader of the country until his physical incapacity in 1968 (Valério, 1994).

However, Portuguese participation in the gold-exchange standard system did not last long, because the anchor chosen, the pound sterling, left the system less than three months later (September 21, 1931). Thus, apparently, Portuguese participation in the gold-exchange standard system came too late to have any long-lasting effect.

Table 2.3 Balance sheet of the Bank of Portugal after the 1931 reform

Total assets 3101	*Total liabilities 2921*
Gold and exchange reserves 982	Banknotes issued 2062
Government debt 1069	Other short-term liabilities 279
Other assets 1050	Other liabilities 580
	Net capital 180

Source: Banco de Portugal, Relatório do Conselho de Administração, 1931.

Date: December 31, 1931.

Unit: million escudos, £ 1 = 110 escudos.

Anyway, stabilization was not entirely lost. Pegging the Portuguese currency to the pound sterling lasted until the Second World War without significant disturbances (Valério, 1984).[10] And this even allowed some political stabilization: in 1933, military dictatorship was replaced by a new constitutional regime, although one of strict right-wing authoritarian character, which lasted until the 1970s.

Meanwhile, Greek financial and political situation deteriorated during the 1930s. On the one hand, it proved impossible to sustain the drachma/pound exchange rate, which depreciated until £ 1 = 545 drachmas. On the other hand, the constitutional republican regime was replaced in 1935 by monarchy again, and it was not a democratic monarchy, as it witnessed a military dictatorship until, in 1941, Italy invaded the country.[11]

2.4 Conclusion

Consideration of the Portuguese and Greek negotiations with the League of Nations in 1927–1928 and their financial and political consequences may suggest some interesting points about the relations between financial and political processes. These points may be summarized into two questions: (i) do investors discriminate between democratic regimes and dictatorships? and (ii) do financial and political stability (and instability) go hand in hand with each other?

The Portuguese and Greek experience during the 1920s and 1930s suggests a negative answer to the first and a positive answer to the second of these concluding questions.

In fact, neither investors in general nor the League of Nations seemed to discriminate between the Greek democratic regime and the Portuguese dictatorship under similar profitability and credibility conditions. Anyway, the Greek democratic regime proved more able to avoid internal stress on acceptance of the League conditionality than the Portuguese military dictatorship. This may lead to a different question: are democratic regimes able to provide higher confidence because they promote larger domestic involvement of different political and social forces in financial decisions, especially borrowing decisions? And now, the answer suggested by our example is positive.

Similarly, the performance of the two countries during the 1930s shows that the better Portuguese financial performance coincided with higher political stability (although not a democratic one), while the less successful Greek financial performance led to a situation of political instability (and to the end of the democratic regime).

Of course, looking at the Portuguese and Greek experience during the 1920s and 1930s is insufficient to substantiate any generalization of the answers suggested. Comparison with cases in other times and places, such as those presented in this volume, is needed to confirm such suggestions.

Sources

Archives of the League of Nations

- dossier R2926/10E/2436/203 – Restauration financière du Portugal – Réorganisation de la Banque du Portugal

- dossier R2927/10E/2098/203 – Restauration financière du Portugal – Organisation de la Banque du Portugal
- dossier R2927/10E/2565/203 – Restauration financière du Portugal – Rapport du Comité Financier au Conseil mars 1927
- dossier R2936/10E/911/911 – Finances de la Grèce – Réorganisation de la Banque de Grèce

Notes

1 According to Bolt and van Zanden (2020), in 1927, the per capita gross domestic product was 3,539 international dollars and the population was 6,127 thousand in Greece. Hence, the gross domestic product amounted to 21.7 million international dollars. The PPP equivalent of 1 international dollar was roughly 2 current drachmas.

2 According to Bolt and van Zanden (2020), in 1927, the per capita gross domestic product was 2,627 international dollars and the population was 6,538 thousand in Portugal. Hence, the gross domestic product amounted to 17.2 million international dollars. The PPP equivalent of 1 international dollar was roughly 0.55 current escudos. We believe that the 9 billion escudos estimate of 1927 gross domestic product for Portugal is a bit underestimated but have retained it to ensure source similarity with the Greek figures.

3 According to Bolt and van Zanden (2020), in 1927, the per capita gross domestic product was 8462 international dollars in Great Britain. There is no estimate of the world average, but it seems likely that the relative situation presented in Maddison (2001) for the pre-First World War year – Greece 1592 international dollars, Portugal 1244 international dollars, world average 1510 international dollars – remained valid in the mid-1920s. It must be borne in mind that these figures were not computed at the time and, thus, were not available to decision-makers, although some intuition of their amount and meaning might exist.

4 Notice that, at the same time, banknote issue was concentrated at the Bank of Portugal.

5 The depreciation of the Portuguese currency until the First World War was studied by Salazar (1915).

6 Greece had two issuing banks – the Ionian Bank (created in 1839 in the then British colony of the Ionian Islands, ceded to Greece in 1864) and the National Bank of Greece (created in 1841) – but in 1903 an agreement was reached for the gradual withdrawal of the former's issue until 1920, which was accomplished. For more details on this topic, see Lazaretou (2015) and Valério (2012).

7 For more details on this topic, see Bordo, Edelstein and Rockoff (NBER WP 7186).

8 Documents about these initiatives were published in the work of Marques (1976).

9 The post-World War I evolution of the Portuguese currency was studied at the time by Caetano (1931) and more recently by Santos (1996). Mention should also be made of a modern overall analysis of the Portuguese evolution from leaving the gold standard until establishing a gold-exchange standard (Mata, 1987).

10 In a certain sense, monetary stabilization was prolonged during the war and under Bretton Woods international monetary system until the 1970s.

11 For details on the Greek evolution from gold-exchange standard in the late 1920s to financial instability in the 1930s, see Christodoulakis (2013).

References

Bolt, Jutta and Jan Luiten van Zanden, "Maddison's Style Estimates of the Evolution of the World Economy. A New 2020 Update", in *Penn World Table* (www.rug.nl), 2020.

Bordo, Michael, Michael Edelstein and Hugh Rockoff, "Was Adherence to the Gold Standard a 'Good Housekeeping Seal of Approval' During the Inter-Was Period?", NBER WP 7186.

Caetano, Marcelo, *A depreciação da moeda depois da Guerra*, Coimbra, Coimbra Editora, 1931.

Christodoulakis, Nicos, "Currency Crisis and Colapse in Interwar Greece: Predicament or Policy Failure?", in *European Review of Economic History*, 17 (3), pp. 272–293, 2013.
Lazaretou, Sophia, "The Evolution of Banking and Central Banking in Modern Greece: A Historical Retrospect", in *History of Economic Thought and Policy*, 2015 (1), pp. 59–82, 2015.
Maddison, Angus, *The World Economy. A Millennial Perspective*, Paris, OECD, 2001.
Marques, A. H. de Oliveira (editor), *A Liga de Paris e a ditadura militar 1927–1928*, Mem Martins, Publicações Europa-América, 1976.
Mata, Maria Eugénia, *Câmbios e política cambial na economia portuguesa 1891–1931*, Lisboa, Sá da Costa, 1987.
Mata, Maria Eugénia and Nuno Valério, "Monetary Stability, Fiscal Discipline and Economic Performance – The Experience of Portugal Since 1854", in Jorge Braga de Macedo, Barry Eichengreen and Jaime Reis (editors), *Currency Convertibility – The Gold Standard and Beyond*, London and New York, Routledge, 1996.
Reis, Jaime, "First to Join the Gold Standard, 1854", in Jorge Braga de Macedo, Barry Eichengreen and Jaime Reis (editors), *Currency Convertibility – The Gold Standard and Beyond*, London and New York, Routledge, 1996.
Salazar, António de Oliveira, *O ágio do ouro, sua natureza e suas causas*, Coimbra, Imprensa da Universidade, 1915.
Santos, Fernando Teixeira dos, "Last to Join the Gold Standard, 1931", in Jorge Braga de Macedo, Barry Eichengreen and Jaime Reis (editors), *Currency Convertibility – The Gold Standard and Beyond*, London and New York, Routledge 1996.
Valério, Nuno, *A moeda em Portugal 1913–1947*, Lisboa, Livraria Sá da Costa Editora, 1984.
Valério, Nuno, *As finanças públicas portuguesas entre as duas guerras mundiais*, Lisboa, Cosmos, 1994.
Valério, Nuno, "National States and Central Banks in the Mediterranean World in the Interwar Period", in John A. Consiglio, Juan Carlos Martinez Oliva and Gabriel Tortella (editors), *Banking and Finance in the Mediterranean*, Farnham and Burlington, Ashgate, pp. 197–212, 2012.

3 Dictatorship, authoritarian regime, and the banking sector in Yugoslavia during the 1930s

Žarko Lazarević

3.1 Introduction

In the 1930s, the Yugoslav state was shaped by two decisive events with far-reaching consequences. The establishment of the dictatorship on January 6, 1929, fundamentally changed the political life of the country, while the economy was affected by the Great Depression. Yugoslavia belonged to the group of Central and Eastern European countries that abandoned the liberal-democratic model and slipped into dictatorship. At the same time, it was also an example of a dysfunctional political system that could not find the necessary consensus on the country's development model within the framework of parliamentary life. The "pretext" for the introduction of dictatorship was political instability, which reached its peak only after ten years of the state's existence and threatened its survival. Then, the Great Depression shook the country's economic system to the core. This chapter looks at efforts to resolve these dilemmas using the example of banking regulation – within the framework of the dictatorship and authoritarian regime of the 1930s, of course. The first argument is that the introduction of dictatorship for banking or financial policy was not a critical development in terms of the banking regulatory system. The continuity of concepts and practices was maintained. However, the real turning point came with the arrival of the Great Depression, which hit Yugoslavia with a little delay. It set in when the dictatorship was already on its way to becoming an authoritarian regime and was seeking the broader social (political) support it needed to consolidate its legitimacy. Under these exceptional circumstances, the government policy was redesigned. Economic recovery became a precondition for political stabilization. Thus, the "justification" for the dictatorship shifted from the political to the economic sphere. The crisis management of society and the economy gradually came to the fore.

Since the present discussion focuses on the banking sector, we should first outline its basic characteristics. As Yugoslavia was underdeveloped in economic terms, this was also true for the banking sector. It had all the characteristics of an underdeveloped banking system, which can be summarized in a few points. Due to the historical, economic, cultural, and political heterogeneity of the state, the banking system was also heterogeneous. This applies to the types of banks, their size, their business operations, and the type of management. Although there were

DOI: 10.4324/9781032656199-4

a high number of banking institutions, they had only modest capital and operated locally. In each Yugoslav province, there were only a limited number of regionally relevant banks and only a few banks were of national importance. The reasons for the fragmentation of the banking sector varied, ranging from purely economic to political, ethnic, and religious. The banks had modest capital and were mostly organized according to the universal banking model. To maintain or increase their revenues and profits under conditions of such limited opportunities, they had to pursue a wide range of activities. They were involved in all types of banking operations as well as direct investments in the real sector. The Yugoslav banking system was characterized by an imbalance between capital supply and demand. This led to disproportionately high interest rates on loans and caused an excessive transfer of funds from debtors to creditors, which further hampered the already moderate economic development. Finally, foreign capital played a crucial role in the banking sector (Tomašević 1938, 227–229; Dimitrijević 1958, 17–27).

The banking system was made up of public and private financial institutions. At its head was the central bank, the Narodna banka Jugoslavije (National Bank of Yugoslavia), which was founded in 1920 after the transformation of the Narodna banka Kraljevine Srbije (National Bank of the Kingdom of Serbia). The central bank took over the branches of the former Austro-Hungarian bank and founded several new ones, thus expanding its scope of activity to the entire state. Two banks were directly owned by the state: Državna hipotekarna banka (State Mortgage Bank), which collected long-term assets and granted mortgage loans or municipal loans, and Poštanska štedionica (Postal Savings Bank). In addition, the state held significant stakes in two other banks: Priviligovana agrarna banka (Privileged Agricultural Bank), which granted loans for agriculture, and Zanatska banka (Craftsmen's Bank), which financed economic activities in urban areas. The number of private banks was considerable at around 700, while around 14% of total capital was still owned by foreign banks. There were also sixty-one local savings banks. Credit unions – 466 in urban areas and 4146 in rural areas – were the most widespread banking institutions, which is why they played an important role in collecting people's savings.[1]

3.2 The dictatorship and the authoritarian regime

In the 1920s, the Kingdom of Serbs, Croats, and Slovenes, which was later renamed Yugoslavia, was an unstable country in political terms. The reason for this instability was the structure of the state. When it was founded in 1918, it comprised very different territories with different histories, belonging to different states, traditions, and political cultures. This was also accompanied by considerable differences in the level of economic and social development. Yugoslavia was indeed a country of contrasts and contradictions. Its integration took place in a contradictory political atmosphere, far away from the official rhetoric of idealized unification. The process of integration and legislative unification lasted until the Second World War but was never fully completed. Due to divergent interests, political fragmentation, and political instability, the adoption of legislative proposals through parliamentary procedures was mostly impossible. In the twenty-two years before the Second

World War, Yugoslavia had no fewer than forty-one governments. The average term of office of a government was therefore only half a year (Perovšek 2009, 237). The new state simply took over the old laws and extended their application indefinitely. Most of the legal unification of the state took place in the 1930s, during the dictatorship and under the authoritarian regime.

The individual regions were at such different levels of socio-economic development that the differences were barely measurable. The Serbian political elites had a decisive say in controlling the political decision-making mechanisms. There were political and economic inequalities in the state. Political, administrative, and military power was concentrated in Belgrade, while economic power was concentrated in Slovenia and Croatia. The holders of political supremacy were therefore not able to exercise economic supremacy. On the one hand, the Kingdom of Serbs, Croats, and Slovenes was a new state, while on the other it maintained legal and political continuity with the Kingdom of Serbia Kršev (2012, 115). The same applied to the economic sphere, where the legislation and state institutions of the Kingdom of Serbia formed the core of the economic system (Gnjatović 2007, 92). Both facts contributed to the fact that the state was conceived, organized, and administered as an extended Serbia, that is, in the way the Serbian administrative and political elites were used to. Based on this model, Yugoslavia was designed as a relatively closed, protectionist market.

The fundamental conflict in Yugoslavia before the Second World War took place at the level of Serbian–Croatian relations. It was about two different perceptions of state order and political space. It was a question of regional autonomy or the country's unitary system and of decentralization or centralization of state power. The dominant Croatian political elites believed only decentralization could create the conditions for overcoming regional differences and guarantee the long-term stability of the state. However, the prevailing position of the Serbian political elites was a firm insistence on centralism as the only model for achieving stability and overcoming regional differences, even at the cost of dictatorship in the 1930s.

In the 1920s, during the period of parliamentarism, this dilemma was not resolved. The policy of marginalizing political opponents could not bring stability to the country. Matters escalated to uncontrollable proportions in 1928, when a shoot-out took place in the Yugoslav parliament. The leader of the largest Croatian party was shot dead along with several other MPs. Croatian political representatives began a boycott of parliamentary life. The legitimacy of the parliament and the state itself was called into question. In this tense atmosphere, it was decided to abolish parliamentarianism and introduce a royal dictatorship on January 6, 1929, after securing international support. The dictatorship was intended to achieve several goals. The most important was to reduce political tensions in the state, which is why political parties and all other ethnic-based organizations were banned. Only economic and religious organizations were allowed. The fragmentation of the political space along ethnic lines was identified as the main cause of instability. This was also linked to the fact that particularism was given priority over national interests in political action. Thus, the dictatorship was supposed to unite the population and political actors on the basis of the Yugoslav state idea, the "Yugoslav" culture, and possibly the Yugoslav nation. The state was therefore symbolically renamed Yugoslavia. The dictatorship was intended to enable better governance at all levels and not just at the government level. This led to an administrative reorganization of the state. The aim was to involve more professionals in the administration, with technocrats expected to adhere to the principles of meritocracy and be politically neutral.

The dictatorship went through several phases. Until 1931, it took the form of a personal dictatorship of the king, based on military support. In the second phase, in 1931, the king promulgated a new constitution, which did not, however, abolish the principles of the dictatorship. It was merely introduced to give the impression that parliamentary life had been restored. New political parties were now officially allowed, but they had to operate on a national level without regional or ethnic designations. In practice, only one national party was allowed. This allowed members of otherwise banned political parties to operate publicly. Mobilization in the only legal party also meant public support for the fundamental goals of the dictatorship. The attitude towards the dictatorship also determined the political division of the country. At the same time, the new party – the Yugoslav National Party – was also an instrument for strengthening the legitimacy of the dictatorship. The situation gradually changed in the second half of the 1930s after the assassination of the Yugoslav king in 1934. The regime began to calm down somewhat and sought broader political support, even in those circles that did not approve of the dictatorship. However, the foundations of the regime did not change. The government remained authoritarian until the end of the Second World War. In 1935, a new political formation was founded: the Yugoslav Radical Union (JRZ), a "coalition" of the former (banned) parties, the largest Slovenian party, the Bosnian-Muslim party, and some Serbian parties. With this step, the parties that had previously been banned (for ethnic reasons) legalized their political existence in a new guise. This political organization then took power in the country in the second half of the 1930s.

Initially, the dictatorship was greeted with relief, even by the general public. Prominent representatives of various business associations also explicitly supported the dictatorship. Their support was based on the hope that the political situation would stabilize. Disappointment with parliamentarianism for its ineffective management of the state and the economy was omnipresent. The instability of the political arena was attributed to the country's poor governance, which hindered economic development. The supporters of the dictatorship publicly expressed their hope for a more efficient administration of the country and the economy. The representatives of the various business associations also offered their personal involvement (Gašparič 2011, 223–236). The authorities accepted the offer and involved them as experts in political decision-making at the government level. This ensured a continuous dialog between the business associations and the authorities in the 1930s, which was reflected in the banking sector.

3.3 The economic crisis

In the first decade of its existence, the country did not achieve the expected economic stabilization. The path to economic recovery and the development of a new national economic sphere was slow and even extremely sluggish due to political instability. The favorable conditions in 1929, which was considered the most favorable year economically until the Second World War, raised hopes for better times (Marn 1935, 169–172). The Great Depression followed the same pattern as elsewhere (Marcus et al. 2020, 188–215). It first affected agriculture in 1930 and continued a year later as a financial crisis. When it also turned into an industrial crisis, economic activity was paralyzed. The consequences were the same as in other countries and can be summarized in a few points. Firstly, the crisis led to a collapse in the export trade of agricultural products, a fall in prices, and a decline in farmers' purchasing power. It is not difficult to imagine what this meant in a predominantly agrarian society. Agriculture contributed a significant proportion of the national product, followed by the industry and the service sector. It was a time of uneasy expectations for the future. Due to the interrupted flow of money, the banking system came to a standstill, whereupon prices in industry and production and workers' wages fell and unemployment skyrocketed (Mirković 1958, 359–369; Vučković 1976, 197–227).

Agriculture suffered the most during the crisis. Falling prices, which even halved, drove farmers to the brink of ruin. Their purchasing power was decimated and their ability to pay was destroyed. The average earnings per farm in 1933 were less than 40% of what they had been in 1926 (Lazarević 1994a, 44), which was reflected in a sharp decline in the standard of living of the farming population, reportedly by up to 80% (Marn 1935, 170–172). Peasant indebtedness was an expression of the long-standing crisis in agriculture, which was exacerbated during the Great Depression. The consequences of an unfavorable, fragmented land ownership structure dominated by small farms became clear. The latter did not have sufficient strength and economic potential to overcome the crisis. Due to their large numbers, farmers gradually became the country's central economic and socio-political problem. The 1930s brought the painful realization that the agricultural cooperatives, in which great hopes had been placed, could not solve the problems of the agricultural population in times of crisis. The cooperatives were helpless due to their illiquidity. In the struggle for survival, they concentrated mainly on themselves and waited for state support (Lazarević 1994b, 53).

During the Great Depression, price pressure or a disproportionate fall in agricultural and industrial prices also became critical. In 1933 and 1934, when the crisis reached its peak, the gap was almost 40% to the detriment of agriculture.[2] In Yugoslavia, price pressure led to changes in the shares of individual sectors in national income. During the crisis, the contribution of industry grew, rising from 8% to 13% between 1931 and 1935 (Potočnik 1939, 245–246). The textile industry was a notable exception among the industrial sectors: not only was it spared from the crisis, but it was also even able to increase its capacity. Its expansion, even during the crisis, can be explained by the fact that the import of textiles was one of the most important items, while imports were limited due to the shortage of foreign currency during the crisis. At the same time, the textile industry was still in its infancy and was therefore far from its growth thresholds (Kresal 1976).

Due to shrinking production, unemployment has risen enormously. In Slovenia, the most developed region of the country, 27% of all industrial workers lost their jobs during the crisis (Kresal 1970, 91–92). The actual percentage of the active unemployed population was considerable but was not statistically determined. The overpopulation in agriculture was particularly worrying as it revealed the true picture of the unemployed population in the countryside (Tomasevich 1955, 208–227). The shadow economy was booming and included unemployed skilled workers, craftsmen, and merchants who abandoned their professions en masse during these years (Traven 1939a, 257–268). Compared to 1929, the wages of industrial workers fell by 40% (Kresal 1970, 97). The quality of life in the industrial centers deteriorated drastically as the relationship between income and the cost of living became extremely unfavorable. The relevant statistics showed that in Slovenia, the most industrialized region, only 34% of workers had a satisfactory income that was above the subsistence level, 12% were at the subsistence level, while everyone else had to contend with more or less extreme poverty (Kresal 1982, 114). Due to the radical loss of purchasing power and the extreme austerity measures, the crisis also affected the crafts and trade sectors, which were ultimately left without any means of rationalizing business processes, as small family businesses and a modest cottage industry predominated (Traven 1939b, 381–390; Šink 1939, 393–396).

The financial crisis of 1931 was the most pressing problem. The banking sector struggled with severe liquidity problems, while cash shortages became chronic as individuals and banks hoarded while the government pursued deflationary policy. In addition to internal weaknesses, such as the injection of short-term funds into long-term investments, banking institutions were particularly affected by the extensive cash run. As their income fell, people began to draw on their savings. The tight monetary policy associated with the short-term hundred-day gold parity of the national currency (dinar) also contributed to the deterioration of the situation. Instead of encouraging the inflow of foreign capital by lifting restrictions on foreign payments, such a policy facilitated the smooth outflow of foreign capital from the country (Vučković 1976, 206–210, 215–220; Gnjatović 1991, 154–160; Marcus et al. 2020, 198–204). Farmers were the first to stop repaying debts, followed by other business entities. The liquidity crisis spread distrust in everyone and everything. Fearing for their deposits, people turned up en masse at bank counters and demanded their money immediately. To maintain confidence and stem the tide, bankers initially paid out unlimited amounts in savings deposits. However, when the panic did not subside for several months, they were eventually forced to stop paying out due to exhaustion (Gnjatović 1991, 154–160). During the summer of 1931, commercial bank deposits on a national level fell to 17% (Nikolić 2016, 88).

The Great Depression shook the concepts and practices of governance to the core. The dictatorship faced major challenges. When it was introduced, the first item on the agenda was to stabilize the country politically, consolidate it, and ensure the legitimacy of the new government among the population; and also with the idea of creating a "Yugoslav" nation in response to the country's ethnic diversity. It turned out that the dictatorship only had one year at its disposal, as there were already signs of an impending economic crisis in 1930. In the years that followed, the dilemmas of the Great Depression occupied most of the government's attention, both during the open dictatorship and during the authoritarian regime that followed. When the great economic crisis of the 1930s brought entirely different issues onto the agenda, questions about the best way forward became even more pressing. Under the conditions of such a profound crisis, the economic, social, and political issues became acute. Moreover, the crisis tested the long-term viability of all social and economic institutions, not just those that had been established during the dictatorship. The Great Depression called into question the legitimacy of the dictatorship and the authoritarian regime that followed. When the dictatorship began, no radical interventions in the economy were planned. It was assumed that the policies that were already in place or under discussion before the dictatorship would be continued. The economic crisis completely changed social priorities and thus the objectives of economic policy. As a result of the crisis, the focus of the government's actions shifted. Political stability remained the primary goal, but the order of importance changed. To achieve political stability in the 1930s, the economy had to be stabilized first. Political stability was no longer threatened only by ethnic particularisms, but also by the state of the economy and the growing social crisis, especially in the countryside.

3.4 Banking regulation and reconstruction

With the outbreak of the Great Depression, the issue of bank regulation became urgent. In the 1920s, regulation was lenient, faith in the liberal model was strong and bankers had great reservations about state regulations (Tomašević 1938, 225). In the first years of the dictatorship, the projects begun in the 1920s were continued. The dictatorship was not a turning point. It was the Great Depression that was decisive. The 1930s were characterized by extensive state intervention in the economy. The government intervened heavily in banking because the Great Depression had exacerbated the problem of liquidity and solvency in the banking system. There was an urgent need to restructure the banking system so that it could fulfill its economic role and fully support the economic recovery. Intervention was gradual as the situation escalated.

The continuity of regulation can be seen in the draft Banking Act of 1930. The new banking legislation was supposed to standardize the legal basis for banking transactions, reduce fragmentation, and regulate auditing and supervision. The dialog between the authorities and the bankers was not interrupted during dictatorship. It is therefore not surprising that the government commissioned a proposal for a banking law from the president of one of the most influential banking associations. The proposal envisaged the Ministry of Commerce as the supervisory authority. The security of citizens' deposits was the focus. It was therefore proposed that a link be established between the volume of business and the share capital. The maximum ratio was to be 3:1, which would also promote the concentration of banks. The intentions of the proposed legislation were good, but they did not consider the differences in the banking structure in the Yugoslav regions. In the northern parts of the country, it meant that banks had to either raise capital or limit the scope of their operations. Despite the dictatorship, there was no consensus among bankers, so the law could not go through the procedures (Kršev 1998, 77–78, 2007, 275–276). Entry into the banking market was then partly regulated by the Companies Act of 1931, which mainly dealt with the issue of capital. The relatively high capital requirements by Yugoslav standards were introduced to alleviate the pressing problem of the dominance of small banks. An exception to this rule were the savings banks founded by the local authorities, which also guaranteed the liabilities. In addition to permission to conduct business in the areas of deposits, loans, bills of exchange, and foreign exchange, banks also had to obtain a special license to trade in securities (Gaćeša 2001, 268–269).

The decision to introduce the gold standard was decisive for financial policy. In this case, too, it was a continuation of the efforts begun in the second half of the 1920s. The final act took place during the severe economic crisis in the spring of 1931, at an unfortunate time when it was practically impossible to maintain the stability of the national currency through central bank intervention alone. The decision to ensure convertibility resulted from international political conditions. If Yugoslavia wanted to join the Bank for International Settlements (BIS) and thus continue to receive German reparations without interruption, it had to switch to the gold standard. The Yugoslav government accepted this challenge after effectively stabilizing the national currency for several years, convinced that meeting international conditions would bring long-term benefits to the domestic economy. At the same time, however, it was also aware of the considerable short-term risks that the transition to the gold standard entailed in the context of profound economic and political instability.

The successive bankruptcies of the leading German and Austrian banks, the Hoover moratorium, and the abandonment of the gold standard in the UK had an impact on the situation in Yugoslavia. All this threatened the foreign exchange component of the monetary base of the National Bank of Yugoslavia and the balance of payments flows. The daily outflow of foreign currency from the country could only be prevented by the suspension of convertibility, which took place on October 7, 1931. The convertibility of the national currency (dinar), which had been proclaimed on June 28, 1931, thus lasted only 101 days. Convertibility was formally abolished with the rules restricting free trade in foreign exchange, which laid down a list of prohibitions and restrictions on foreign exchange transactions. The National Bank was given the right to purchase half of the country's foreign exchange inflows. However, only a few banks were granted the right to conduct foreign exchange transactions. Borrowing abroad was only possible with the express permission of the Ministry of Finance. As the situation did not improve, on the last day of 1931 the government stipulated that exporters who brought foreign currency into the country had to offer up to 80% of it to the Yugoslav National Bank for repayment. Eventually, the measures implemented began to take effect and the parity of the dinar remained at 9 Swiss francs for 100 dinars until the end of 1931. From May 1932, however, its international value began to fall again and reached its lowest point in October, when 100 dinars were worth only 6.60 Swiss francs in Zurich. To stop the further devaluation of the dinar due to the latent outflow of foreign currency from the country, the government inevitably switched to clearing trade. In 1932, clearing agreements were concluded with nine European countries, which helped to stop the devaluation of the dinar (Gnjatović 2006, 27–40; Nikolić 2016, 84–87; Marcus et al. 2020, 198–204).

The agony of the banking sector began in the summer and especially in the fall of 1931. The collapse of prominent Central European banks, particularly the Creditanstalt debacle, fueled mistrust in the domestic banks. The illiquidity and insolvency of the banking system required rapid and thorough intervention. The central bank continued to pursue its policy of securing liquidity, while the Ministry of Trade and Industry was responsible for regulating and restructuring the banking system. In September 1931, the banks stopped paying out deposits in full and depositors could only receive limited amounts. The bankers undertook to pay out all new deposits they received without restriction. They put pressure on the government to finally set a temporary cap on payouts.[3]

Between 1932 and 1934, the necessary laws were passed to restructure the banking sector. As the government, on the one hand, temporarily exempted the farmers from repaying their debts, similar measures had to be taken on the other. Thus, one of the articles of the Farmer Protection Law (1932) allowed financial institutions to legalize the existing regulations, that is, the non-payment of savings deposits or the payment of deposits in long-term installments. These were only supposed to be temporary measures. However, with further regulations, they remained in force throughout the 1930s. Efforts to mitigate the consequences of the banking crisis intensified in 1935, when the first bank restructuring decisions were issued. The decisions on the rehabilitation of banks were based on the 1934 Decree on the Protection of Financial Institutions, which stated that all financial institutions that were unable to meet the claims of their creditors could apply for protection. Based on an application made in agreement with the owners, the Ministry of Trade and Industry ordered the deferral of payments, reorganization, or non-bankruptcy liquidation.

All these procedures had to be approved by the owners at the general meetings. Special government commissioners monitored the implementation of the protective measures adopted. These commissioners had the right to be present at all meetings of the management committees and they also supervised the work of the management boards of the banking institutions. Financial institutions that applied for legal protection and benefited from the rights based on it (i.e., suspension of payments or restructuring) had to consolidate their balance sheets and write off all losses. These were to be covered from the reserve fund and other funds. If this was not sufficient, which was often the case, the financial institutions had to resort to writing down the share capital by the amount outstanding. Measures to alleviate the situation of protected banks under the 1934 decree included revaluation of real estate holdings and encouragement to merge with banks that were in better shape.

The Ministry of Trade and Industry permitted the deferral of payments for a maximum period of six years. This only applied to old claims, that is, those that had arisen before the moratorium on the payment of deposits came into force in April 1932. Banking was divided into old and new business. For new business, the normal rules applied without any restrictions. The banks had to draw up payment plans for the old deposits based on the six-month inflow of the old claims. A minimum interest rate of 2% and a maximum interest rate of 4% applied to the old claims, depending on the performance of the institution to be protected. Priority was given to small investors, to whom the banks had to pay out proportionally more deposits in a timely manner than to creditors with larger deposits. The conversion of creditors' claims into equity, but only up to 40% of the claims, was one of the most important measures in the restructuring process. The conversion of claims into ordinary and preference shares was only possible with the agreement of the creditors. Otherwise, the creditors' claims became part of special reserve funds. These claims were settled gradually and pro rata, possibly from net profits, after the banks had first endowed the reserve funds (which were to account for half of the share capital) and after the dividends on the preference shares had been paid. The authorization to convert the old claims into shares also implied the authorization to increase the capital proportionally. If necessary, a non-bankruptcy liquidation was carried out by a commissioner on behalf of the government and in agreement with the creditors' committee. Public announcements of non-bankruptcy liquidation had to be made. Savings account holders did not have to register their claims, while all others had to register their claims within three months of the public announcement. The management had to inform known creditors of the start of the bankruptcy-free liquidation.

In the reorganization proceedings, the publicly owned savings banks were placed on a completely equal footing with the joint stock banks. The founders of the savings banks (municipalities, cities, and regional governments) had to guarantee their losses and endow their operating and reserve funds. To this end, they were allowed to issue bonds. The situation of credit cooperatives was also special. The restructuring of credit cooperatives was only possible after the reserve funds had been written off. At the same time, the Ministry required every cooperative in the process of restructuring to make payments due to the reserve funds from its members.[4] Credit cooperatives could only apply for protection (suspension of payments, restructuring, and non-bankruptcy liquidation) through their cooperative associations. The same provisions also applied to cooperative unions.[5]

Restructuring also included the regulation of the banks' business policy. Banks could invest available funds from new business in state or state-guaranteed securities. They could also invest in foreign exchange transactions but only up to a third of their own funds. At the same time, they had to cover one tenth of these investments with cash deposits at Narodna banka (National Bank), Poštanska štedionica (Postal Savings Bank), or Državna hipotekarna banka (State Mortgage Bank). These deposits could be withdrawn at any time without restriction. The maximum amount of a single loan was also prescribed, which could be up to one tenth of the banks' own funds. The list of restrictions was even more extensive. Banks undergoing restructuring were not allowed to grant loans to members of their management and supervisory boards, grant mortgage loans, or purchase real estate or goods for their own account. The banks' participation in other non-bank public limited companies was also restricted.[6] Banks were also instructed to reduce or control their costs. It was explicitly required that the salaries and other benefits of management had to fall in the same proportion as those of other employees. During the restructuring regime, the members of the Executive Board and Supervisory Board and other senior executives were not entitled to bonuses, remuneration, year-end and Christmas bonuses, distributable profits, or other benefits. All such claims and similar claims that had not been recovered by the time of rehabilitation were forfeited and could not be claimed in court. The banks abolished all collective and individual contracts. Employees had eight days to sign new employment contracts or were dismissed with modest severance payments. Pensions from the banks' pension funds were also cut. These provisions, which were tailored to public limited companies, also applied mutatis mutandis to savings banks and credit cooperatives and their unions. Similar provisions also applied to associated companies or subsidiaries.[7]

By initiating the reorganization process, the state tackled a complicated task. In 1936, the government completed the comprehensive restructuring of the banking system with the decree on the liquidation of farmers' debts. With this decree, half of the peasants' debts were written off to neutralize the halving of prices, while the rest had to be repaid to the Privileged Agricultural Bank within twelve years at a significantly reduced interest rate. The farmers' solvency was restored at the same time as the banking system was restructured. The government included the written-off debts and the debts that the agricultural bank had taken over from other banks in the national debt, while the financial institutions received government bonds for their bad debts. They were able to redeem these bonds by pledging them and thus obtain the money they urgently needed. The Ministry of Trade and Industry, which was responsible for the important long-term project of restoring liquidity to the banking system, was inundated with requests. In the second half of the 1930s, almost half of the banking sector was in the process of being restructured (Dugalić 1999).

Regulation of the entire banking sector was also continued. Interest rates were capped. The central bank's discount rate became the benchmark. In 1934, it stood at 7%.[8] The interest rate cap, which depended on the discount rate, was an attempt to standardize the maximum interest rate level in the state. The state also intervened in interest rates in 1935 when it severed the direct link between interest rates and the central bank's discount rate. The interest received was set at a maximum of 10% and the interest paid was not allowed to exceed 4%. The only exception allowed was fixed-term deposits, where savers could be rewarded with a maximum of 5% interest.[9] Banking institutions were also instructed to build up reserve funds amounting to half the nominal value of the share capital. This was to be achieved in some years at the expense of net profit sharing. Each year, 10% of the net profit was to flow into the reserve funds. Once the banks had reached the prescribed level of reserve funds, they had to maintain this ratio permanently. Half of the reserve funds had to be invested in government securities. The banks were also not allowed to sell these securities without the approval of the Ministry of Trade and Industry. The other half of the reserve funds could be invested at the banks' discretion but only in liquid securities or real estate.[10]

In the second half of the 1930s, after stabilization had been achieved, the banking system began to be overhauled. To make it more crisis-proof, the criteria for establishing banks and conducting their business were to be tightened. In 1938, the Savings Banks Decree was the first to be passed. The authorities' desire to ensure the long-term liquidity of savings banks, the security of deposits, and sound business operations was more than obvious. Savings banks were only allowed to operate with the approval of the Ministry of Trade and Industry after the local municipalities, as founders, had declared that they would guarantee all savings banks' liabilities with their entire assets. Savings banks were only allowed to invest in secure businesses: mortgage loans, government securities, Lombard loans, short-term bills of exchange, deposits with other private or state banks and, in exceptional cases, in the real estate sector. They were not allowed to offer long-term loans to their founders and could only grant short-term loans for a maximum period of six months. The investment structure was prescribed: a maximum of 20% of deposits could be invested in long-term loans (mortgages and securities), 15% in short-term deposits with other banks, 10% in short-term loans for the founders, and 50% in government securities, particularly treasury bills. The reserve funds of the savings banks were set at 15% of the total amount of all deposits, which had to be invested according to the principle already mentioned. Therefore, half of the reserve funds had to be invested in government securities. The Ministry could, at its own discretion and at any time, conduct an audit of the business operations or, if necessary, assign a commissioner to the savings bank to ensure the safety and regularity of the savings bank's business operations.[11]

Later, there was an initiative to reorganize the joint stock banks as well. The bill provided that the latter could be established based on a license (concession) granted by the Ministry of Trade and Industry, provided that the conditions for increasing the share capital were met. The amount of share capital required depended on the location where the bank was to be established and on local competition. In the larger centers with several competing banks, the capital requirements were stricter. Foreign bank branches also had to meet appropriate capital requirements. In addition to the provisions on share capital, the proposal also included the requirement to set aside significantly larger reserves than before. Restrictions on business activities were also tightened. The intention was to restrict the banks to pure banking business: the acceptance of savings deposits and the granting of loans to companies and population. The plan was to ban long-term mortgage loans, while the scope of other long-term investments was also to be restricted. Banks were only allowed to invest one third of their share capital in shares in other companies. Compared to the 1930 proposal, the new draft provided for a stricter ratio between the banks' deposits and own funds. In the long term, banks were to maintain a ratio of 2:1 between deposits and own funds. The total amount of all liabilities of the banks was not allowed to exceed five times their own funds. The restrictiveness was also reflected in the definition of liquidity: 20% of sight deposits and term deposits of up to 30 days had to be always liquid. In addition, 15% of all banks' liabilities had to be invested in short-term (three-month) bills of exchange, warrants, some Lombard loans, and foreign currencies. With these specific provisions, the government wanted to prevent possible risks in banking operations in advance. As far as lending policy is concerned, the government wanted to ensure the diversification of the loan portfolio: lending to a single borrower was allowed to account for a maximum of 10% of the banks' own funds. The proposal also aimed to limit the issuance of guarantees so that only licensed (larger and more prominent) banks could issue guarantees to their clients. Due to the conflict of interest, transactions with members of the Executive Board and Supervisory Board were expressly prohibited. In addition, the responsibility of the members of the Executive and Supervisory Boards for profit or loss was tightened.

The state or the Ministry of Trade and Industry assumed control of banking transactions. The state exercised supervision in two ways: regular and extraordinary supervision. Regular supervision included the obligation for banks to submit three-month, six-month, and annual financial statements to a specific auditing body. To ensure the comparability and uniformity of balance sheet items, the Ministry would prescribe a special balance sheet form. Regular control also included an audit of each bank's transactions every two years. Extraordinary control meant that if the state suspected irregularities or a threat to liquidity criteria in a particular bank, it had the right to conduct an extraordinary audit of its operations. If necessary, the ministry had the right to send a commissioner to the bank in question to ensure constant monitoring of business operations (Tasić 1992, 203–205). In 1939, the year the Second World War began, political and economic priorities changed. The initiative for the new legislation, which was intended to radically intervene in the banking system, stalled – not only because of the tense international situation but also because of the bankers who continued to oppose any restrictions on banking before and during the dictatorship and under the authoritarian regime. In fact, the proposed banking legislation also represented a continuity with the concepts of banking regulation from the 1920s. The only difference was that much greater emphasis was placed on the long-term security of business activities and public deposits.

3.5 Conclusion

The Yugoslav banking system operated in an environment of profound political, economic, cultural, social, and ethnic differences. The political situation was also precarious. In the 1930s, during the open dictatorship and subsequent authoritarian regimes, these differences were not overcome but merely suppressed. The diversity and political instability caused by the differences in development also affected the characteristics of the banking system itself. The banking system had the characteristics of an underdeveloped banking system. It was characterized by a high degree of fragmentation and many smaller banks based on the universal banking model. The banks were not efficient enough in financial intermediation and the prices for their services were too high, especially in lending. Yugoslavia was a country where the gap between the available capital and demand was significant. The consequences on the capital market only reflected this situation.

During the global economic crisis, the issue of banking regulation became urgent. The role of the state became indispensable. The public banking sector played a crucial role in the recovery from the economic crisis. Government intervention helped to preserve the private banking sector. The government combined the restructuring of the banking system with the restoration of farmers' solvency. Initially, the creditors' short-term claims on the banks were legally converted into long-term claims. This was the first measure aimed at reorganizing the banking system and at the same time included the regulation of banking transactions. The government prescribed business policies, liquidity ratios, interest rates, cost-cutting measures, wage policies, etc., to the banks undergoing restructuring – half of the country banking sectors in total. All the measures that the government initially tested on the banks during the restructuring process were then implemented at a systemic level. By prescribing business policies, the government diverted some of the private banks' resources into financing state spending for the real sector and the population. The state also strengthened its supervisory role. The fundamental requirement of regulation was to ensure the safety of bank deposits. The measures arose from and were determined by the weaknesses of the banking system. In the turbulent 1930s, society longed for long-term stability and security. At the same time, crisis management brought with it new problems and misunderstandings. State intervention meant greater centralization – not only political and administrative centralization but also the concentration of capital by state banks. This exacerbated the conflicts even further, as was the case before the dictatorship. The centralist state model had been highlighted as the main reason for the economic disadvantage of some regions, either due to insufficient understanding of regional economic needs or due to real and imagined disadvantages in budget transfers and investments (Shoup 1968, 227).

The dictatorship failed to resolve the fundamental contradictions in the organization of the state and the management of the economy, including banking. Instead, it even exacerbated them. The Croatian–Serbian political conflicts were shifted from the public to the political backstage, where they continued unabated. This also perpetuated the contradiction between the centralist and autonomist concepts of state development. This situation continued until 1939, when an agreement was finally reached between the Serbian and Croatian elites. Shortly before the Second World War in Yugoslavia, the Serbian political elites wanted to stabilize the country politically. It was impossible to accomplish this task permanently without coming to terms with the most important Croatian party, the Croatian Peasant Party (HSS). After lengthy secret negotiations, an agreement was finally reached that forced the Serbian elites to abandon the centralist principle. This agreement led to an institutional change in Yugoslavia and the creation of a separate Croatian autonomous entity. With certain territorial extensions, Banat Croatia united most of the Croatian population. The newly created entity had a special confederal status, and its autonomous government had a comprehensive list of powers. In comparison, the central government retained powers in the areas of defense, monetary policy,[12] foreign policy, international economic cooperation, and the state's transport infrastructure. The remaining powers were transferred to the Banat of Croatia, which was also given legal and financial autonomy with its own tax system (Čulinović 1954, 296–303). Although the outbreak of the Second World War prevented the comprehensive functioning of the Croatian Banat, an important precedent was nevertheless set. Even contemporaries compared the Croatian Banat with the special status enjoyed by Hungary within the Habsburg Monarchy during the period of dualism. The status of the Croatian Banat was far higher than Croatia's position within the Hungarian half of the monarchy (Tomasic 1940, 591). Croatia became a kind of Confederate Island in a rigid centralized system that also applied to the other Yugoslav regions (Lampe 1994, 83). The question of whether this would have brought lasting stability to the country was rendered irrelevant by the Second World War.

Notes

1 Statistički godišnjak 1940.
2 Kriza zemljoradnje i njena zaduženost u svetlu privredne statistike. Bilten Priviligovane agrarne banke, 19, 1935.
3 Poročilo o delovanju Društva bančnih zavodov v Dravski banovini za dobo 1930–1935. Izdano ob priliki proslave petnajstletnice društvenega obstoja (28. 12. 1921–29. 12. 1936) na dan 29. decembra 1936. Ljubljana, 1936: 8–11.
4 Uredba o zaščiti denarnih zavodov in njihovih upnikov". In Službeni list kraljevske banske uprave Dravske banovine, No. 100 (1934): 965–974; "Uredba o izpremembi uredbe o zaščiti denarnih zavodov in njihovih upnikov z dne 23. novembra 1934". In Službeni list kraljevske banske uprave Dravske banovine, No. 87 (1935): 819; No. 88 (1936): 806; No. 95 (1937): 921; No. 22 (1938): 205.
5 "Uredba o zaščiti kmetijskih kreditnih zadrug in njihovih zvez". In Službeni list kraljevske banske uprave Dravske banovine, no. 100 (1934): 976–977.
6 "Uredba o zaščiti denarnih zavodov in njihovih upnikov". In Službeni list kraljevske banske uprave Dravske banovine, No. 100 (1934): 968.
7 "Uredba o zmanjšanju režijskih stroškov gospodarskih podjetij". In Službeni list kraljevske banske uprave Dravske banovine, No. 100 (1934): 977–979.
8 Narodna banka, p. 217; "Uredba o maksimiranju obrestne mere". In Službeni list kraljevske banke uprave Dravske banovine, No. 100 (1933): 1153–1154; "Uredba o maksimiranju obresti". In Službeni list kraljevske banke uprave Dravske banovine. No. 68 (1934): 712–713.
9 "Uredba o izpremembi uredbe o maksimiranju obresti". In Službeni list kraljevske banke uprave Dravske banovine, No. 11 (1935): 101.
10 "Uredba o ustanovitvi poslovnih rezerv in rezervnih skladov pri zavarovalnih podjetjih, ustanovah socialnega zavarovanja, denarnih zavodih in zadružnih organizacijah, kakor tudi o delnem nalaganju teh rezerv in rezervnih skladov v državne vrednostne papirje". In Službeni list kraljevske banske uprave dravske banovine, No. 64 (1938): 681–683.
11 "Uredba o občinskih hranilnicah". In Službeni list kraljevske banke uprave dravske banovine, No. 98 (1938): 911–916.
12 According to some sources, an agreement between the Yugoslav Central Bank (National Bank of the Kingdom of Yugoslavia) and the Banate of Croatia on the introduction of a parallel Croatian currency was also reached. Drafts of the Croatian currency were supposedly also designed, which are now kept at the Croatian Central Bank (http://www.hnb.hr/novcan/povijest/h-nastavak-4.htm).

Literature

Čulinović, Ferdo. *Državnopravna historija jugoslovenskih zemalja 19. i 20 vijeka*. Zagreb: Školska knjiga, 1954.
Dimitrijević, Sergej. *Strani kapital u privredi bivše Jugoslavije*. Beograd: Nolit, 1958.
Dugalić, Veroljub. *Narodna banka 1884–1941*. Beograd: Jugoslovenski pregled, 1999.
Gaćeša, Nikola (ed.). *Istorija bankarstva u Vojvodini*. Novi Sad: Matica Srbska, 2001.
Gašparič, Jure. "The country at a standstill: Yugoslavia and Slovene politics in the 1930s". *Nationalities Papers: The Journal of Nationalism and Ethnicity* 39, No. 2 (2011): 223–236.

Gnjatović, Dragana. *Stari državni dugovi: prilog ekonomskoj i političkoj istoriji Srbije i Jugoslavije: 1862–1941*. Beograd: Ekonomski institut, 1991.
Gnjatović, Dragana. "Sto in en dan konvertibilnega dinarja med svetovnima vojnama". *Prispevki za novejšo zgodovino* XLVI, No. 2 (2006): 27–40.
Gnjatović, Dragana. *Ekonomija Srbije – privredni sistem, struktura i rast nacionalne ekonomije*. Beograd: Megatrend univerzitet, 2007.
Kresal, France. "Delavstvo med gospodarsko krizo na Slovenskem", *Prispevki za zgodovino delavskega gibanja* 10, No. 1–2 (1970): 81–99.
Kresal, France. *Tekstilna industrija v Sloveniji*. Ljubljana: Borec, 1976.
Kresal, France. "Nastanek in razvoj socialne politike na Slovenskem do 1941". *Prispevki za zgodovino delavskega gibanja* 22, No. 1–2 (1982), 101–116.
Kriza zemljoradnje i njena zaduženost u svetlu privredne statistike. Bilten Priviligovane agrarne banke 19, 1935.
Kršev, Boris. *Bankarstvo u dunavskoj banovini*. Novi Sad: Prometej, 1998.
Kršev, Boris. *Finansijska politika Jugoslavije 1918–1941*. Novi Sad: Prometej, 2007.
Kršev, Boris. "Monetarna politika i problem unifikacije novca u Kraljevini Srba, Hrvata i Slovenaca (1918–1923)". *Civitas* 2, No. 1. (2012): 113–124.
Lampe, John R. "The Failure of the Yugoslav National Idea", *Studies in East European Thought* 46, No. 1–2 (1994): 69–89.
Lazarević, Žarko. *Kmečki dolgovi na Slovenskem*. Ljubljana: ZPS, 1994a.
Lazarević, Žarko. "Podjetništvo v slovenskem kmetijstvu". *Prispevki za novejšo zgodovino* 34, No. 1 (1994b): 45–55.
Marcus, Nathan, Nikolić, Stefan, and Straumann, Tobias. "Economic policy, 1918–1939". In *The Economic History of Central, East and South-East Europe*, edited by Morys Matthias,188–215. Routledge, 2020.
Marn, Rudolf. "Gospodarski položaj Dravske banovine danes in pred petimi leti". *Tehnika in gospodarstvo*, No. 10–12 (1935): 169–172.
Mirković, Mijo. *Ekonomska historija Jugoslavije*. Zagreb: Školska knjiga, 1958.
Narodna banka 1884–1934. Beograd (Topčider): zavod za izradu novčanica, 1935.
Nikolić, Stefan. *New economic history of Yugoslavia: Industrial location, Market integration and Finacial Crisis*, 2016 (https://etheses.whiterose.ac.uk/17519/).
Perovšek, Jurij. *V zaželeni deželi: Slovenska izkušnja s Kraljevino SHS/Jugoslavijo*. Ljubljana: INZ, 2009.
Poročilo o delovanju Društva bančnih zavodov v Dravski banovini za dobo 1930–1935. Izdano ob priliki proslave petnajstletnice društvenega obstoja (28. 12. 1921–29. 12. 1936) na dan 29. decembra 1936. Ljubljana, 1936.
Potočnik, Drago. "Donosnost industrije v Sloveniji". *Tehnika in gospodarstvo* 5, No. 11–12 (1939): 245–256.
Shoup, Paul. *Communism and the Yugoslav National Question*. New York and London: Columbia University Press, 1968.
Šink, Fran. "Razvoj trgovine". In *Spominski zbornik Slovenije*, 393–396. Ljubljana: Založba Jubilej, 1939.
Statistički godišnjak Kraljevine Jugoslavije, Beograd: Državna štamparija, 1940.
Tasić, Antonije. "Jugoslovensko bankarstvo između dva rata". *Glas CCCLXVI*, No. 26 (1992): 203–205.
Tomašević, Jozo. *Novac i kredit*. Zagreb: vlastito izdanje, 1938.
Tomasevich, Jozo. *Peasants, Politics, and Economic Chage in Yugoslavia*. Stanford University Press, Oxford University Press, 1955.
Tomasic, Dinko. "Constitutional Changes in Yugoslavia", *Political Science Quarterly* 55, No. 4 (1940): 582–593.
Traven, Janko. "Dvajset let razvoja slovenskega obrtništva". In *Spominski zbornik Slovenije*, 381–390. Ljubljana: Založba Jubilej, 1939a.

Traven, Janko. "Gospodarska kriza v luči statistike pridobitnih podjetij". *Tehnika in gospodarstvo* 5, No. 11–12 (1939b): 257–268.
"Uredba o maksimiranju obrestne mere". *Službeni list kraljevske banke uprave Dravske banovine*, No. 100 (1933): 1153–1154.
"Uredba o maksimiranju obresti". *Službeni list kraljevske banke uprave Dravske banovine*. No. 68 (1934a): 712–713.
"Uredba o zaščiti denarnih zavodov in njihovih upnikov". *Službeni list kraljevske banske uprave Dravske banovine*, No. 100 (1934b): 965–974.
"Uredba o zaščiti denarnih zavodov in njihovih upnikov". *Službeni list kraljevske banske uprave Dravske banovine*, No. 100 (1934c): 968.
"Uredba o zaščiti kmetijskih kreditnih zadrug in njihovih zvez". *Službeni list kraljevske banske uprave Dravske banovine*, no. 100 (1934d): 976–977.
"Uredba o zmanjšanju režijskih stroškov denarnih zavodov pod zaščito". *Službeni list kraljevske banske uprave Dravske banovine*, No. 100 (1934e): 974–976.
"Uredba o zmanjšanju režijskih stroškov gospodarskih podjetij". *Službeni list kraljevske banske uprave Dravske banovine*, No. 100 (1934f): 977–979.
"Uredba o izpremembi uredbe o maksimiranju obresti". *Službeni list kraljevske banke uprave Dravske banovine*, No. 11 (1935a): 101.
"Uredba o izpremembi uredbe o zaščiti denarnih zavodov in njihovih upnikov z dne 23. novembra 1934". *Službeni list kraljevske banske uprave Dravske banovine*, No. 87 (1935b): 819; No. 88 (1936): 806; No. 95 (1937): 921; No. 22 (1938): 205.
"Uredba o občinskih hranilnicah". *Službeni list kraljevske banke uprave dravske banovine*. No. 98 (1938a): 911–916.
"Uredba o ustanovitvi poslovnih rezerv in rezervnih skladov pri zavarovalnih podjetjih, ustanovah socialnega zavarovanja, denarnih zavodih in zadružnih organizacijah, kakor tudi o delnem nalaganju teh rezerv in rezervnih skladov v državne vrednostne papirje". *Službeni list kraljevske banske uprave dravske banovine,* No. 64 (1938b): 681–683.
Vučković, Miloš. "Uticaj svetske privredne krize 1929–1932 na privredu stare Jugoslavije". In *Svetska ekonomska kriza 1929–1934. godine i njen odraz u zemljama Jugoistočne Evrope*, 197–227. Beograd: SANU, 1976.

4 The political economy of currency devaluation and trade balance

Italy, 1930s

Enrico Berbenni and Andrea Viola

4.1 Introduction

The effects of currency devaluation can be approached from different points of view. Some studies have focused, for example, on the relationship between exchange rates and foreign direct investments (Klein & Rosengren 1994) and others more generally on the effects in terms of economic growth (Di Nino et al. 2013; Miao & Berg 2010). This chapter, on the other hand, addresses the link between devaluation and trade balance. It specifically deals with the measures implemented to remedy the imbalances in the Italian balance of payments during the 1930s, a goal that was to be achieved also through the reduction of the trade deficit (see, e.g., the seminal work by Tattara 1993).

Following the theoretical and empirical work of Eichengreen and Sachs (1985), there is broad consensus that the gold standard was a key factor in the Great Depression and the protracted crisis that struck the world economy in the 1930s, stimulating protectionism and the spread of an economic war in advance of a military conflict (Eichengreen & Temin 2000; Eichengreen & Irwin 2010). The 1933 World Economic Conference's failure exemplified the contrasted political and economic climates of those years.

Against this backdrop, countries had greater difficulty in rebalancing their external accounts, if necessary. A vicious circle was set in motion: widespread protectionism made it difficult to rebalance the balance of payments, thus pushing many countries to be even more protectionist (Albers 2020). From a theoretical point of view, the 'trade policy disaster' of those years is explained with the classic open economy trilemma, which provides a powerful interpretative framework according to which policymakers are bound to choose only two of the following policies: fixed exchange rates, free trade, and monetary independence (Obstfeld et al. 2004; Irwin 2012).

Italy in the 1930s represents a perfect case study for examining provisions implemented to defend the country's gold reserves, reconciling the needs of public finance with the ambitions of an increasingly aggressive regime (Guarneri 1953; Berbenni 2021). To be sure, exchange controls affected not only Italy but also a large number of nations (Hirschman 1987; Eichengreen & Sachs 1985; Raitano 1995). Indeed, the coexistence of two risk factors, economic and political, appears

DOI: 10.4324/9781032656199-5

to be a key element, as several studies have highlighted (Wandschneider 2008; Hallwood et al. 2011; Jacks & Novy 2020). Devaluation was one of the main interventions to try to level out a structural deficit in the trade balance, but was it enough? And what other factors were at work to counteract such a readjustment?

The devaluation of the lira, announced in October 1936, marked a turning point in Italian trade policy in the 1920s and 1930s, which shifted from favouring a reduction in imports towards the application of a reciprocity principle to achieve a balance between import and export, leveraging exports as a tool to obtain the currencies necessary to pay for imports[1].

It follows that, despite the regime's autarkic propaganda, Italy needed an international framework which was as open as possible to trade in goods and capital:[2] an increase, rather than a contraction, in international trade would have prevented Italy from exhausting its means of payment to finance the imports, especially of raw materials, necessary to keep its national industry operating (Guarneri 1937, 235–236). However, in a context of widespread protectionism, this was a tricky goal to pursue. Favouring exports in a protectionist context also implied diversifying outlet markets, which was particularly complicated for a country like Italy that traditionally concentrated its exportation to a few countries: in 1929, more than 60.5 percent of Italian exports was absorbed by only eight markets, of which five of them were in Europe[3].

This paper aims to study the composition of the Italian trade balance before and after the realignment of the lira and to demonstrate why monetary leverage could not be enough to rebalance the external deficit. Providing an extension of the main findings presented in Berbenni (2021), we provide further evidence about the absence of the effect of Italian lira devaluation: contrary to the objectives set by the Italian state, the devaluation of the lira failed to yield the anticipated outcomes across the three areas under investigation (imports, exports, and the trade balance). This outcome can be attributed to a multitude of factors, encompassing not only economic considerations, such as the dissolution of the Gold Bloc and concurrent devaluations of the lira and other European currencies, but also geopolitical factors. These geopolitical factors comprised sanctions imposed due to the war in Ethiopia and escalating tensions that ultimately led to the outbreak of the Second World War. The sanctions themselves seem to have exerted a substantial impact on the trends in imports (adversely), exports (also negatively, though with a lesser magnitude than the effect on imports), and the trade balance (positively). In contrast, no significant effect is discerned concerning either the composition of the Gold Bloc or, most importantly, the devaluation of the lira.

4.2 Methodology

Drawing on unpublished archival sources and the writings of some of the major Italian economists of the time, we performed a critical analysis of a valuable source of data, the Italian foreign trade database (hereinafter FTV-SN Bankit [Federico et al. 2011]), placing it within the proper historical framework.[4] The importance of this source is highlighted by the fact that, until the Second World War, the trade balance was the only part of the Italian balance of payments documented to a certain extent, albeit with several weaknesses (Bientinesi 2006, 479).

Based on a mix of quantitative and qualitative sources, the paper reconstructs the historical background that eventually led the Italian government to devalue (third part); it then breaks down the trade balance into its components, specifically addressing imports (fourth part) and exports (fifth part); the sixth section provides an overall analysis of trade balance. The seventh section provides some considerations on the Italian external deficit in the aftermath of devaluation. The last section summarizes our conclusions.

Each section dedicated to imports, exports, and trade balance comprises a qualitative reconstruction informed by the database, along with an analysis of data and trends spanning the period from 1928 – the pre-crisis year – to 1940. The objective is to disentangle the impact of geopolitical events, such as the dissolution of the Gold Bloc, the imposition and lifting of sanctions against Italy due to the Ethiopian war, and the currency devaluation that occurred in 1936. This analysis is conducted using data on imports and exports with key trading partners including the USA, Germany, Austria, France, Switzerland, Russia, Argentina, and Great Britain. By examining both the total value of imports, exports, and trade balance, as well as the relative position with foreign counterparts, we aim to explore how economic relationships were shaped and evolved during the years under analysis, with a particular emphasis on the period following the devaluation of the lira.

4.3 Italy before the devaluation

The Great Depression spread internationally from the United States through two main mechanisms, one of a commercial nature and the other of a financial nature. The value of world trade, pegged at 100 in the reference year 1929, fell to 39 in 1932 (Feinstein et al. 1997). This trend was both cause and effect of the widespread adoption of protectionist economic policies. The second way by which the crisis spread was the drastic restriction of international credit.

Faced with these problems, many countries decided to rebalance their economies with trade restrictions and currency devaluation, that is, by leaving the gold standard (Great Britain in 1931 and the United States in 1933). On the other hand, six countries (France, Belgium, Italy, Switzerland, Holland, and Poland) reaffirmed their intention not to devalue but to maintain parity with gold, signing a collaboration agreement known as the Gold Bloc.

Italy remained anchored to the policy of deflation. However, with the Depression, this strategy was undermined by a progressive worsening of public finance, which was increasingly funded by printing new money. Then, starting from the middle of the decade, war expenses represented another large burden on public finances (Zamagni 1990, 319–320).

Regarding external relations, the Great Depression greatly reduced the openness of the Italian economy (Federico et al. 2011, 7–8).[5] This notwithstanding, reaching a balance in trade was of primary importance to Italy in order to counterbalance the diminishing remittances from emigrants, tourism revenues, and sea freight, as well as to counter the massive capital leaks in the early 1930s (Tattara 1993, 387–388). Narrowing the structural trade deficit was therefore a priority. However, the protectionist measures in those years, compounded by the constraints imposed by the gold standard, made this difficult to achieve (Eichengreen & Temin 2010).

This explains the Italian situation in the early 1930s, when it suffered a dramatic erosion of gold reserves mainly as a result of capital flight. The trade deficit also contributed to the worsening balance. Devaluation was only one possible option and there were a number of reasons that made the authorities reluctant to adopt it. The procurement of capital and raw materials was a priority in a resource-poor country like Italy and, in this context, the precarious confidence of savers and international markets in the country's financial stability turned the gold standard into a real dogma for the regime (Storaci 1993, 454–455). The alternatives were deflation – this was the official policy until 1934 – or exchange rate control along with tighter trade restrictions, later on.

Despite the official stance of the Italian government, the capital flight points to a lack of confidence in the stability of lira. Indeed, the massive capital outflows that took place in the early 1930s showed that the gold peg was no longer sufficient to stabilize the lira if free export of gold and capital was not barred and imports restricted, although this would have meant contradicting the very foundations of the gold standard (Mitchener & Wandschneider 2015). In this perspective, 1934 was a watershed year, because the strong appreciation of the lira (the real exchange rate of the lira was revalued, compared to 1930, by 36 percent against the dollar and 29 percent against the pound) and the consequent expectations of devaluation contributed to aggravating the external accounts through a surge of capital outflows and high trade deficits (Storaci 1993, 464–465; Di Quirico 2001, 75).

The year 1934 also marked a turning point in prices due to increases recorded in the primary sector during the second half of the year, which put an end to the deflationary policy pursued in previous years and forced the population to accept sacrifices that could not be further extended, even by a dictatorial regime, without undermining popular support. The inability to continue deflation forced the implementation of a more rigorous policy to control goods and capital. Therefore, the monetary and currency policy shifted from a substantially liberal approach to dirigisme (Cotula & Spaventa 2003, 303–304; Gagliardi 2007).[6]

But the lira was still not officially devalued, partially because the possible consequences could not be predicted with certainty, prompting nearly all Italian economists, both liberal and corporatist, to oppose it (Pavanelli 1990, 342). It was not obvious that the trade deficit would have benefited substantially in that context of generalized protectionism and given the type of products traded by Italy.

Although the parity was not officially modified, the lira began to depreciate. Several factors contributed to making the Italian currency particularly unstable: price growth, capital outflows, the reduction of the ratio between gold reserves and circulation, and the low interest rates intended to lower the cost of the Ethiopian campaign (Hirschmann 1987, 230–233).

An official devaluation, however, clashed with the needs of the Ethiopian campaign. The imminence of war made any monetary reform too risky (Balogh 1940, 8)[7]. The sanctions imposed on Italy by the League of Nations (November 1935–July 1936) also contributed to accentuating the rigidity of Italian foreign trade, increasing the relevance of bilateral clearing agreements (Banca d'Italia 1938, 244–247). Although sanctions had only been partially effective, they did have large consequences on the ability to hoard foreign currencies through international trade and on the distribution of this trade, which was increasingly oriented towards clearing agreements with Nazi Germany (Tattara 1993, 420–423; Bientinesi 2006, 489–490).

The dissolution of the Gold Bloc had initiated with the exit of the Belgian franc in 1935, soon to be followed by the French franc, the Swiss franc, and the Dutch guilder. Faced with this situation, and after the Ethiopian campaign was accomplished, the time seemed ripe for Italy to officially abandon the 1927 parity. The regime could therefore make all this appear not as a surrender but as a necessary response to changed external circumstances (Senato del Regno 1937, 2555).

In October 1936, the gold parity of the lira was reduced by 40.9 percent compared to *Quota 90*, setting the exchange rate at 19 lire per dollar and 92.4 per pound (Hirschmann 1987, 233–237). This provision aimed to realign the internal price to the international price.

4.4 On the import side

Italian imports declined greatly in quantity after the Great Depression and remained at significantly lower levels than in the previous decade (Figure 4.1). Between 1930 and 1938, the general index averaged around 70 percent of the 1928 value, the pre-crisis year, with a sharp deterioration in 1936, which was affected by the exceptional circumstances of the sanctions. Also looking at Table 4.1, the primary

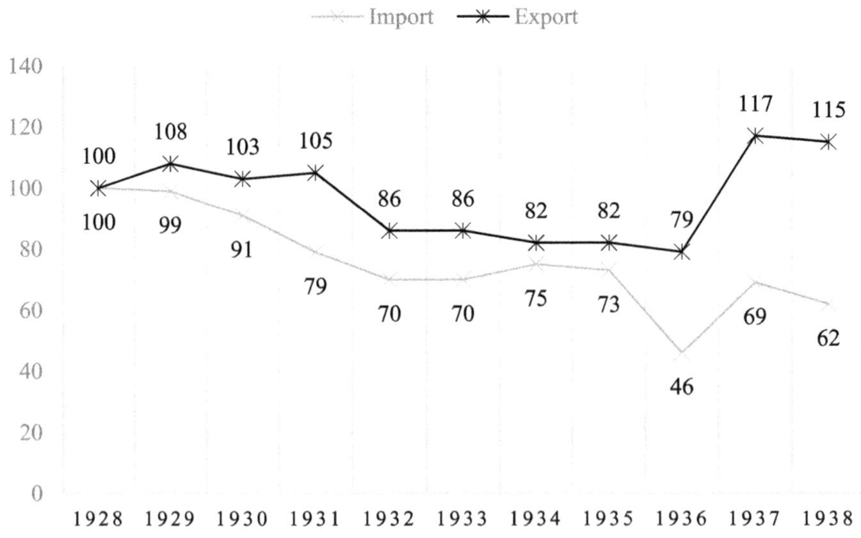

Figure 4.1 Quantity indices of imported and exported goods, 1928 = 100.

Source: Fossati (1939, 664)

Table 4.1 Analysis of Italian imports – Italian lira revalued to 1940

Year	*Austria*	*Belgium*	*France*	*Germany*	*UK*	*Netherlands*	*Russia*	*Switzerland*	*Argentina*	*USA*	*Total (L. 1940)*
1928	2.01%	2.61%	9.00%	12.07%	7.84%	1.27%	0.79%	2.30%	8.35%	17.56%	27,656,626
1929	2.19%	2.37%	9.27%	14.18%	9.24%	1.03%	1.11%	2.49%	6.21%	16.08%	26,327,553
1930	2.30%	2.05%	8.38%	14.10%	9.35%	0.99%	2.73%	3.06%	4.00%	14.15%	22,066,029
1931	2.46%	2.01%	6.98%	14.50%	9.28%	1.16%	4.12%	3.39%	4.77%	11.22%	16,094,681
1932	2.28%	2.42%	5.83%	13.12%	8.92%	1.58%	3.73%	3.62%	4.14%	13.39%	11,567,811
1933	2.36%	3.04%	5.56%	14.85%	9.77%	1.61%	3.04%	3.64%	2.96%	14.95%	11,038,947
1934	2.51%	2.81%	5.69%	15.73%	9.30%	1.76%	2.72%	3.70%	3.54%	12.43%	12,039,463
1935	3.50%	2.72%	6.05%	18.33%	7.30%	1.75%	2.37%	3.15%	3.79%	11.21%	12,020,562
1936	6.15%	1.84%	2.11%	26.80%	0.87%	0.76%	2.56%	3.85%	2.95%	14.76%	8,675,634
1937	4.54%	1.38%	3.52%	18.60%	4.03%	0.85%	0.75%	2.94%	7.57%	11.05%	18,266,444
1938	–	1.55%	2.26%	26.77%	6.46%	1.20%	0.06%	3.33%	2.43%	11.32%	13,728,273
1939	–	1.92%	1.49%	29.51%	5.51%	1.30%	0.64%	3.26%	1.49%	9.50%	12,026,088
1940	–	0.98%	0.75%	36.99%	2.90%	0.62%	0.10%	2.89%	2.65%	8.99%	13,211,231

Source: FTV-SN Bankit

observation that emerges is the overarching trend in Italian imports, which is evident from the early 1930s onwards, predating the devaluation of the lira.

However, the substantial stability of imports of raw materials proves the rigidity of some fundamental imports for Italian industry, which the country was unable to reduce even under full autarky during the second half of the decade. Fascist policy-makers were more successful in reducing imports of finished products – because of import substitution practices – and foodstuffs, which most likely led to a compression of internal consumption (Barberi 1961).

The only years that deviated significantly from the general trend were 1936 (contraction) and 1937 (expansion): in the first case due to the sanctions, and in the second because they were lifted. In part, the strong increase in imports in 1937 reflected the rise in prices, but the main reasons were the need to replenish stocks of raw materials after the sanctions period and the needs of the war industry, as well as the exceptional need for wheat following the poor harvest of the previous year. The autarkic policy itself temporarily increased some imports necessary for strengthening industrial and agricultural production (Mortara 1938, 140). Overall, sanctions appear to have played a significant role in contracting Italian imports, and the subsequent lifting of these sanctions likely contributed to the growth observed in 1937.

Aside from that, devaluation does not seem to have had notable consequences on the distribution of Italian imports by country of origin. While we cannot assert that the monetary provision was completely irrelevant, contemporary historical events allow us to ascribe a more accurate weight to it. The English case, for example, shows that neither the devaluation of the pound sterling in 1931 nor that of the lira in 1936 significantly altered the percentage of imports from Great Britain. Instead, the drastic drop witnessed in 1935 and 1936 may principally be attributed to sanctions, similarly to what was observed in France, against which no asymmetric monetary shock had occurred.

As regards Germany, the significant increase in imports had already begun in 1935, after the clearing agreement was signed between the two countries in 1934. The reasons behind the closest commercial relationships could be traced back to the currency difficulties of Italy, which was driven to regulate increasing shares of foreign trade through clearing agreements. And the political and military events of those years led Italy to turn to Germany as a favoured partner for these agreements: on the one hand, both countries had similar currency problems, on the other Germany did not adhere to the Geneva sanctions and was thus able to operate in spaces off limits to the sanctioning powers. These spaces were later maintained after sanctions had been lifted (Tattara 1993, 416–418). It is worth noting that this growth may be partly attributed to Germany's annexation of Austria (Anschluss) in 1938, which likely absorbed the trade relationship with Austria. However, the significance of this growth extends beyond this event, reflecting an increasingly close economic relationship between Italy and Germany.

Concerning the United States, it lost almost four percentage points in 1937 compared to 1936 – partly due to the devaluation of the lira, which made American imports more expensive – but this brought its share back to that of 1935, after an artificial increase in its relative weight had occurred in 1936 because of sanctions, which the United States did not join.

Without dismissing some possible impact of devaluation, it therefore seems that the trade balance was strongly influenced by political-diplomatic events (sanctions and progressive rapprochement with Germany), as evidenced *inter alia* by relations with France, whose currency further weakened in the second half of 1937 without this translating into a greater weight of French exports into Italy compared to the pre-1936 period. Table 4.1 reports imports from 1928 (the pre-crisis year) to 1940 (when Italy entered the war) and corroborates those findings.

In order to identify the possible impact of lira devaluation, it may also be useful to look at two sub-samples: in the same year, France, the Netherlands, Switzerland, and Italy implemented currency devaluations to a comparable degree. Shortly before, Belgium devalued its currency.[8] Panel A of Figure 4.2 illustrates the trend of Italian imports from countries that devalued their currency in 1936, while Panel B displays the trends of countries that did not implement this policy. Interestingly, both panels exhibit similar patterns. Initially, during the early 1930s, no distinct trend is evident. For instance, despite Britain's exit from the Gold Bloc and the subsequent devaluation of the pound in 1931, there was no significant impact on Italian imports from this country. Additionally, there is no discernible difference based on membership or non-membership in the Gold Bloc. It is important to note that the Gold Bloc was not a trade agreement but rather an arrangement concerning the pegging of currencies to gold. However, a notable trend emerges during the years when Italy faced sanctions due to the war in Ethiopia. During this period, there is a decline in imports from countries that imposed sanctions, such as Great Britain and France, coupled with an increase in imports from countries like Germany and the US, which did not impose such measures. This trend reverses as soon as the sanctions were lifted, with imports returning to previous levels. The absence of distinct trends in the two panels of Figure 4.2 further supports the notion that the devaluation of the Italian lira did not have a significant impact on Italian imports.

4.5 On the export side

Table 4.2 indicates that Italian exports exhibited a distinct trend compared to imports. While a decrease is observed at the outset of the 1930s, there are no apparent signs of contraction during periods of sanctions at the overall level. Following 1936, Italian exports began to increase significantly (Figure 4.1). However, if we look at values rather than quantities (last column of Table 4.2), some decline took place, suggesting that Italian exporters were willing to accept diminishing profits in order to maintain their positions on the international markets.[9]

Even amid the world crisis, the quantity index showed substantial stability, thanks above all to the elasticity of demand for agricultural and food exports, as well as some finished products. This lasted at least until the pound and dollar devaluations in 1931 and 1933, which caused exports to drop, with the greatest

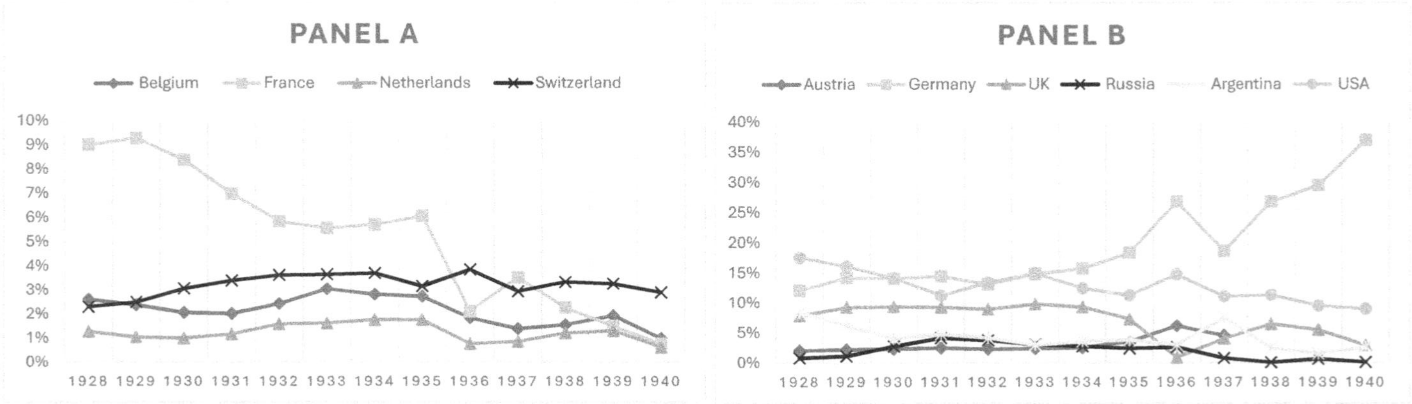

Figure 4.2 Italian imports by counterparty, 1928–1940.

Source: FTV-SN Bankit

Table 4.2 Analysis of Italian exports – Italian lira revalued to 1940

Year	*Austria*	*Belgium*	*France*	*Germany*	*UK*	*Netherlands*	*Russia*	*Switzerland*	*Argentina*	*USA*	*Total (L. 1940)*
1928	2.91%	1.75%	9.21%	12.28%	9.40%	1.03%	0.43%	6.86%	7.92%	10.72%	18,175,346
1929	2.82%	1.86%	8.41%	11.72%	9.57%	1.20%	0.27%	7.08%	7.54%	11.83%	18,283,499
1930	3.07%	2.09%	9.95%	12.58%	9.66%	1.58%	0.80%	7.54%	6.78%	10.77%	15,150,821
1931	3.05%	1.51%	10.86%	10.56%	11.59%	1.46%	2.66%	7.47%	8.03%	10.13%	14,051,581
1932	2.76%	1.82%	7.50%	11.30%	10.30%	2.04%	3.35%	8.30%	5.50%	9.27%	9,612,386
1933	2.19%	2.39%	7.59%	11.93%	11.35%	2.56%	2.15%	7.98%	6.24%	8.75%	8,978,095
1934	2.32%	2.18%	6.68%	15.81%	9.97%	2.55%	2.36%	8.25%	4.08%	7.36%	8,251,685
1935	2.56%	1.95%	5.82%	16.23%	8.22%	1.99%	1.06%	6.44%	3.09%	8.06%	8,094,171
1936	3.48%	0.85%	3.50%	19.55%	2.82%	0.42%	0.16%	6.22%	2.89%	9.90%	7,977,470
1937	2.77%	1.31%	4.19%	14.39%	6.12%	1.24%	0.09%	4.86%	3.85%	7.50%	13,707,130
1938	–	1.28%	3.12%	19.07%	5.59%	1.42%	0.00%	4.72%	3.86%	7.45%	12,795,229
1939	–	1.07%	2.24%	17.55%	4.78%	1.77%	0.65%	5.35%	1.97%	7.14%	12,637,833
1940	–	0.76%	2.45%	29.95%	2.22%	1.58%	0.03%	5.35%	0.42%	3.15%	11,507,596

Source: FTV-SN Bankit

difficulties recorded in 1934 and 1935 (1936 is usually considered exceptional because of the sanctions).

Similar to import quantities, an exceptional expansion in exports took place in 1937. A rise in food exports, for example, was driven by the successful outcome of the agricultural campaign, but there were other contributing factors, in particular: the resumption of trade relations with former sanctioning countries and successful competition of Italian exports with Spanish exports. In fact, the Spanish supply contracted following the civil war, while Italy was able to increase the quantities of foodstuffs exported in those years. This happened just as the German market was opening up as part of the clearing agreements.

According to the Italian economist Mortara, the devaluation of the lira also played a part. However, he was already arguing as early as 1938 that monetary devaluation would not be able to restore the Italian trade balance (Mortara 1938, 127 and 132). Indeed, due to the complexity of the variables influencing Italian foreign trade and the central importance of the political factor, the devaluation of the lira seems to have played a less decisive role than expected in boosting exports. Moreover, a depreciation in the lira preceded the formal decision to alter the gold parity, and in any case, it was a measure taken after other currencies had already been devalued, so there is some doubt as to whether a currency alignment could have resulted in long-term competitive gains (Cavalcanti 2011, 185). It should also be considered that the end of the sanctions provided impetus for exports, even if some of the sanctioning countries were now merely secondary outlets for Italian products.

Finally, the breakdown of Italian exports by country of destination shows substantial similarities with what has already been observed for imports but also some notable differences. Eastern Europe and Latin America (mainly Argentina) provide for a significant contribution, averaging around 40 percent in the late 1930s. However, it is noteworthy that exports to Argentina experienced a significant decrease in the latter years of the 1930s. Table 4.2 also confirms the role of sanctions in redirecting trade to non-sanctioning countries, especially the United States and Germany, against a sudden drop in flows to France and Great Britain (Riccardi 1939, 94 and 132–142).

The remarkable stability of the United States as a destination for Italian exports during the mid-1930s is noteworthy, which seems to indicate an effort by the Italian side to maintain firm trade relations with the dollar area at the expense of the United Kingdom. Political motivations were also behind this decision, given the tensions between Italy and Great Britain in the aftermath of the Ethiopian war.[10]

Exports to Germany grew strongly in the second half of the 1930s. However, the balance was tipped in favour of German exports with Italy recording continuous trade deficits. The particular configuration assumed by the Italian-German clearing – which also included invisible and financial flows as clearing items – reflected precisely the need to reach a balance that would compensate for commercial asymmetry (Tattara 1993, 423–430; Mantelli 1996, 1212).

All the points discussed are corroborated by Figure 4.3, which, as previously, delineates separately the trend of Italian exports to countries that devalued their currency in 1936 (Panel A). Two distinct trends become apparent. Firstly, exports

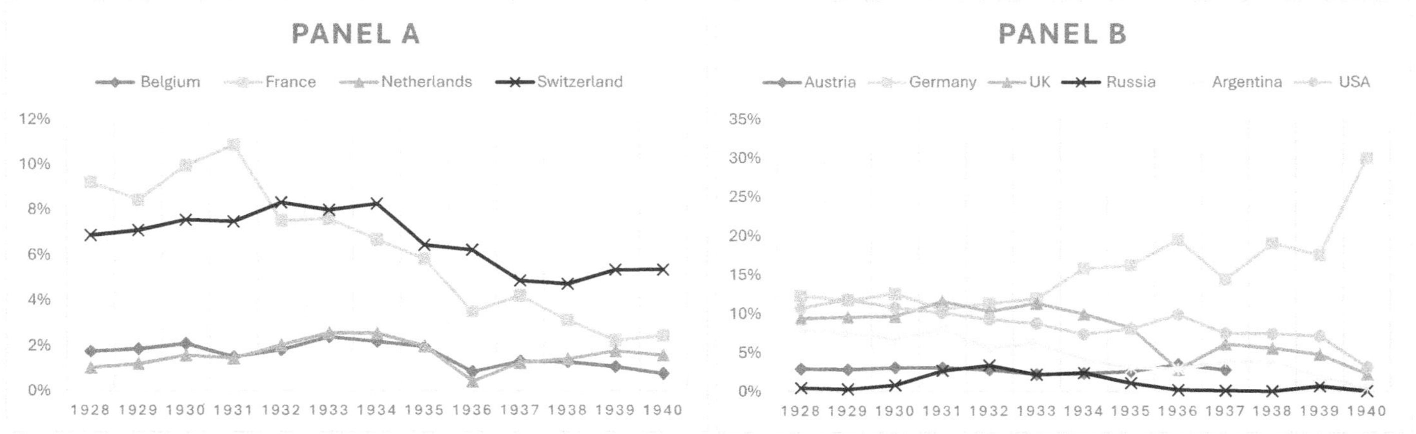

Figure 4.3 Italian exports by counterparty, 1928–1940.

Source: FTV-SN Bankit

to France exhibit a sharp decline during the 1930s, followed by a modest recovery subsequent to the lifting of sanctions. Conversely, the trade relationship with Germany emerges as increasingly significant, mirroring patterns observed in imports.

Furthermore, the graphs underscore the impact of sanctions on trade dynamics. Conversely, there appears to be no discernible effect of the lira's devaluation, even when compared to trade counterparts that did not devalue their currencies simultaneously. For instance, exports to Argentina and the US, countries that did not impose sanctions, showed no growth but rather a decline in the late 1930s.

4.6 The overall trade balance

The real value of international trade increased after the implementation of monetary reforms leading to the dissolution of the Gold Bloc, although in 1937 this was accompanied by an increase in trade deficits in the devaluing countries (Borgatta 1937a, 261–262).

In Italy, the worsening trade balance in 1937 was attributed to the way the currency adjustment took place. Indeed, the parity variation left further margins of intervention in case of need, so that importers were encouraged to advance some purchases to forestall a future worsening of the exchange rate. Other factors also contributed to the deterioration of foreign accounts in the aftermath of the currency reform: the replenishment of stocks, especially of raw materials and fuels, which had been depleted during the sanctions; increasing imports driven by rising internal consumption and the need to stimulate export-oriented production and provisions to the colonies; the need to bolster the military; and unfavourable harvests, especially wheat. Consequently, as expected by theory, the reason for the imbalance lay in the different nature of the domestic demand for foreign products compared to the foreign demand for Italian products, the former being more rigid, whereas the latter more elastic (Borgatta 1937b, 332–333).

Overall, therefore, the total trade balance improved following the devaluation, but only after 1937 (Table 4.3). Nevertheless, the effect of the monetary realignment should not be overstated, not least because a significant part of the exports was absorbed by colonies. The international situation was also more favourable to increasing trade relations. Indeed, the impact of the devaluation and the lifting of sanctions occurred concurrently. For similar reasons outlined earlier, it is reasonable to assert that the primary influence on Italy's trade position initially stemmed from the political détente in this context and, later, from the new worsening of international relations.

Regardless of the lira devaluation, a study of the trade balance and trade by country highlights the shift of Italian trade flows towards the colonies and especially towards Germany in the late 1930s, with opposite effects: an exceptionally high surplus towards the former and a significant, relatively constant deficit towards the latter. Both cases seem emblematic of the sometimes-decisive role that politics assumed compared to pure economic considerations, making interpretative schemes that do not include extra-economic variables misleading (Neal 1979, 391–392). This is also shown in Figure 4.4, which highlights the increasingly close ties with the German counterpart.

Table 4.3 Analysis of Italian trade balance – Italian lira revalued to 1940

Year	*Austria*	*Belgium*	*France*	*Germany*	*UK*	*Netherlands*	*Russia*	*Switzerland*	*Argentina*	*USA*	*Total (L. 1940)*
1928	–26,763	–403,917	–814,896	–1,105,249	–460,329	–164,476	–139,061	612,669	–870,260	–2,907,439	–9,481,281
1929	–60,825	–284,329	–903,067	–1,590,353	–682,405	–52,319	–242,322	637,726	–257,556	–2,071,766	–8,044,054
1930	–42,403	–136,270	–341,383	–1,206,079	–600,386	19,850	–481,035	468,261	143,624	–1,490,051	–6,915,208
1931	33,003	–111,354	403,420	–849,804	134,719	17,681	–289,122	504,489	360,598	–382,623	–2,043,101
1932	2,398	–104,907	45,914	–431,723	–41,117	14,000	–109,354	379,912	49,793	–658,067	–1,955,425
1933	–64,196	–121,214	67,551	–567,682	–59,992	52,176	–142,770	314,202	233,818	–864,675	–2,060,853
1934	–110,507	–158,218	–134,509	–588,487	–296,583	–1,007	–132,810	235,419	–89,176	–890,133	–3,787,778
1935	–212,989	–169,269	–255,936	–889,927	–211,719	–50,173	–198,559	142,571	–205,568	–695,278	–3,926,391
1936	–255,494	–92,012	95,432	–765,295	149,406	–32,558	–209,255	161,932	–25,717	–490,803	–698,164
1937	–449,998	–72,169	–68,999	–1,425,221	103,621	14,304	–125,382	129,219	–854,679	–991,469	–4,559,315
1938	–	–48,301	89,756	–1,235,422	–171,801	16,666	–7,639	146,468	159,753	–600,775	–933,044
1939	–	–95,879	104,488	–1,330,335	–58,329	67,211	5,670	284,075	70,816	–240,648	611,746
1940	–	–41,353	182,783	–1,440,252	–128,211	100,831	–8,991	234,353	–301,040	–825,766	–1,703,635

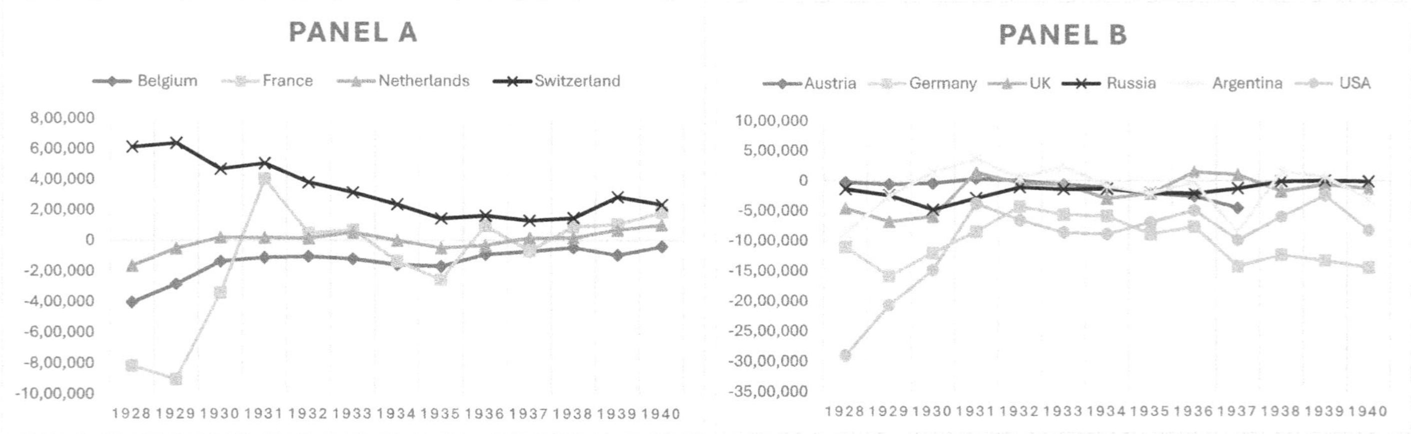

Figure 4.4 Italian trade balance by counterparty, 1928–1940 – Italian lira revalued to 1940.

Source: FTV-SN Bankit

Another primary partner was the United States, whose share of Italian foreign trade remained substantially stable throughout the 1930s, only decreasing as the Second World War approached. Italy always had deficit accounts, but the extent of this imbalance had fluctuated over the years.

Considering Argentina, which initially accounted for over 8% of Italian total trade, identifying a clear trend proves challenging. The trade balance fluctuated around zero throughout the analyzed period, exhibiting a slight decline in 1937 before swiftly reverting to prior levels thereafter.

As for France and Great Britain, their weight as a portion of Italian foreign trade decreased, which seems to be at the basis of the Italian surplus towards the former in the late 1930s, while the deficit towards the latter persisted, with the exceptions of 1936 (due to the sanctions) and of 1937, as a transitory effect of the lira devaluation and the Anglo-Italian clearing agreement. The similarity in trends between these two countries is noteworthy. Despite the heavy devaluation of the lira against the pound (when the UK exited the Gold Bloc in 1931, followed by the devaluation of the pound), France departed from the Gold Bloc almost concurrently with Italy by devaluing the franc.

The remaining countries – representing about half of Italian foreign trade and including not only the Danuban-Balkan countries but also important partners such as Switzerland, Belgium and to a lesser extent Russia – showed a marked turnaround as early as 1936, as a modest surplus emerged favouring Italy.

However, for a country like Italy, whose trade was settled by bilateral clearing agreements for at least half of the amount, trade surpluses and deficits could not be offset on a multilateral basis. This limitation led to accumulating debt and credit positions towards one country or the other, greatly reducing the possibility to preserve, much less expand the small flows.

In summary, the data presented in Figure 4.4 and Table 4.3 reveal notable findings. Firstly, sanctions inadvertently strengthened the trade balance by reducing the openness of the Italian economy, whereas devaluation did not significantly impact the Italian trade balance. As we delve deeper into the subsequent section, we will explore how the tightly controlled nature of trade and exchange rates limited the potential of the 1936 currency reform to reshape the overall composition of trade, which had to be a very desirable goal to allow Italy to increase its reserves of key currencies. This finding contradicts economic theory's predictions following a substantial 40 percent devaluation.

4.7 After the devaluation

After October 1936, currency and trade restrictions could be partially eased and measures were introduced to contain the foreseeable rise in domestic prices (Pavanelli & Nenovsky 2008, 91).[11] According to Ciocca and Ulizzi (1990), the gain in competitiveness was, in fact, significant, but the benefits were only temporary, since the increase in production costs fuelled by the autarkic policy and the devaluation of other currencies soon cancelled the initial advantage, making the lira again overvalued and causing a resumption of capital flight (Cavalcanti

2011, 192).[12] Indeed, the devaluation would have had lasting effects only under three conditions, namely that foreign countries did not impede exports of devaluing countries with additional tariffs; that the main foreign countries did not devalue in turn; and finally, that domestic prices did not grow to the point of damaging exports (Papi 1936, 832–833; di Fenizio 1934, 56). In a highly conflictual international context, however, the simultaneous fulfilment of all three conditions was unlikely.

The trade balance was only one component of the more general problem relating to the Italian balance of payments. But focusing on the balance of trade is crucial to understanding how a complex mesh of economic and political factors affected a broad trend. This could not be explained merely by changes in exchange rates, especially when a considerable part of the trade was regulated by means of clearing arrangements. Against this backdrop, the speed of payment was even more important than the price of the goods (Tattara 1993, 377–378).[13] Indeed, the clearing mechanism undermined the export incentive deriving from a currency devaluation, since – by setting a certain exchange rate and balancing import and export – it did not allow a country with depreciated currency to increase its exports (Renzi 1940, 253). This situation threatened to seriously damage the national economy, as the clearing strategy was not able to rebalance Italian foreign trade, which remained structurally in deficit (Hirschmann 1987, 223–224).

Therefore, the highly controlled nature of trade and exchange rates limited the possibility for the currency reform of 1936 to structurally impact the general composition of trade, contrary to what theory would have predicted following a 40 percent devaluation. On the one hand, the deficit had a permanent nature for the Italian trade balance, which only an adequate influx of invisible items and capital – hardly imaginable in those years – could effectively compensate. On the other, the easing of exchange controls, favoured by the devaluation, did not last long, as the lira began to depreciate again due to the diverging trend in domestic prices (increasing, despite measures aimed at containing inflation), and the decline in world prices (Pavanelli 1990, 328). The autarkic approach and the strong public spending called for by an aggressive foreign policy were among the main factors that contributed to fuelling inflation.

This does not mean that the structure of foreign trade did not undergo some changes in the second half of the 1930s. If we compare 1939 data with those of 1935, Italy had increased trade with various countries, sometimes also improving the trade balance. But these were often countries with whom Italy had a clearing agreement or colonies, for which the price factor was less important and which above all did not make it possible to obtain foreign currency, only indirectly affecting the ability to rebalance foreign accounts. The change in total trade and trade balance during the two years under consideration can be summed up in Figures 4.5 and 4.6, which includes many of Italy's major trading partners. The two maps reveal the evolution of Italian foreign trade, highlighting the countries that experienced significant changes in total trade and trade balance.[14]

As proof of this, the memorandum that the Minister of Trade and Currencies, Felice Guarneri, sent to Mussolini in July 1937, expressed his concern regarding the negative trend in the trade balance and the recovering exodus of foreign exchange reserves.[15] At this juncture, the only alternative was, again, deflation:

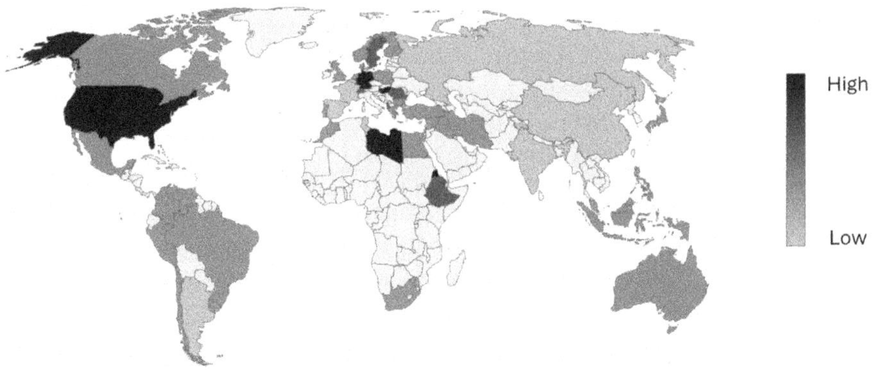

Figure 4.5 Change of total trade* between 1935 and 1939.

Source: Authors' own elaboration on ISTAT (1936, 1951)

Million lire of 1939, current borders. More intense colours correspond to greater variations. Light gray areas are not considered (minor trade partners).

* Total trade = Import + Export.

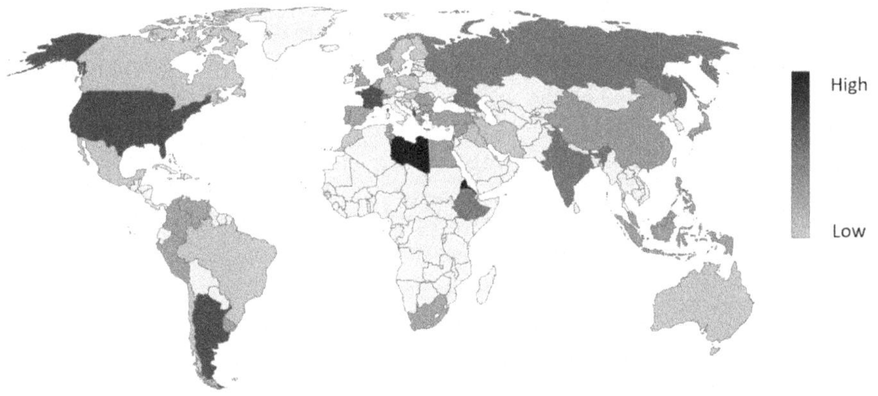

Figure 4.6 Change of trade balance between 1935 and 1939.

Source: Authors' own elaboration on ISTAT (1936, 1951)

Million lire of 1939, current borders. More intense colours correspond to greater variations (i.e. positive change of Italian trade balance). Light gray areas are not considered (minor trade partners).

'it is necessary', Guarneri argued, 'to bring expenditures back to the limit of revenues because a constant deficit policy leads to the debasement of the currency, to the progressive depletion of gold reserves and eventually leads the country to insolvency abroad. Halting and deflating becomes indispensable and cannot be postponed'.[16] However, this path was no longer practicable to the necessary extent, conflicting both with the regime's ambitions (see, for instance, the financial burdens linked to the Italian intervention in the Spanish civil war) and the need to ensure its social sustainability.

4.8 Conclusion

In this chapter, we have set the goal of studying the trend in Italian foreign trade over the decade, explaining why devaluation could not be a decisive intervention. Exploiting the potential of the available database, the study thus contributes to the existing literature, which has emphasized the ineffectiveness of such monetary policy intervention without providing a full explanation of how the structure of the trade balance had transformed in those years with respect to the various outlet markets. In so doing, the paper highlights the particular relevance assumed by purely political motivations in influencing Italian foreign trade in those years.

The trend of the Italian trade balance in the latter half of the 1930s points to an actual improvement in the years preceding the war. This result, although built on annual rather than monthly data, would seem to correspond to theory. However, a number of additional factors, some non-economic, have contributed to this trend. While other empirical investigations may help shed further light on the issue, this analysis, which combines quantitative data on Italian foreign trade with rigorous historical contextualization, strongly suggests that devaluation had no plausible significant effect on reducing the imbalance.

The devaluation, in short, did not solve the structural problems of the trade balance, nor did it make possible – at least not significantly, it not being possible to entirely exclude some facilitating role – a reorientation of Italian exports towards free currency countries. In fact, the geographical composition of Italian foreign trade was heavily affected by the international politics of those years. On the other hand, the very characteristics of commercial policy (entailing problems relating to clearing agreements, multiple exchange rates, quantitative and bureaucratic restrictions, etc.) made the price factor only one of the numerous variables that affected foreign trade, and it is difficult to determine which one was most prevalent.

Archival Sources

Fondazione L. Einaudi (FLE), Archivio Thaon di Revel (AtdR), Turin (Italy):

- Direzione generale del Tesoro: fasc. 76, 138, 280, 608.
- Miscellanea: fasc. 15.

Notes

1 P. Colombo, *Come avviarci verso la soluzione della crisi economica nazionale*, Milano, March 1935, in Fondazione L. Einaudi (FLE), Archivio Thaon di Revel (ATdR), Direzione generale del Tesoro, fasc. 138. For details on the reciprocity principle, see Riccardi (1939, 101).
2 A strong defence of the economic value of autarchy is provided, for example, by De' Stefani (1940).
3 P. Colombo, *Come avviarci verso la soluzione della crisi economica nazionale*.
4 The database, made available to historians only in recent years, is the result of the re-elaboration and standardization of the official statistical sources on Italian foreign trade. The Italian Foreign Trade Database, 1862–1950, is available online at the following website:

https://www.bancaditalia.it/statistiche/tematiche/stat-storiche/stat-storiche-microdati/index.html?com.dotmarketing.htmlpage.language=1 (last accessed: 16 February 2024).

5 The degree of openness measures the sum of exports and imports relative to GDP.

6 P. Thaon di Revel, *Situazione del lavoro e dei salari a seguito dell'allineamento della lira*, Roma, 1936, in FLE, ATdR, Direzione generale del Tesoro, fasc. 608.

7 P. Henzig, *La politica monetaria italiana dopo la composizione del conflitto abissino*, in FLE, ATdR, Miscellanea, fasc. 15.

8 In 1935, Belgium experienced a 28% devaluation due to the adoption of a new definition of gold parity. In 1936, attempts were made to return to the gold bullion standard, which was abandoned in 1940 with the beginning of the German invasion.

9 Indeed, the terms of trade worsened between 1929 and 1937: export prices in 1937 were 23 percent lower than in 1929 for raw and semi-finished materials; 40 percent for finished products; and 29 percent for food. Import prices, on the other hand, only decreased by 11 percent for raw materials; 3 percent for finished products; and 21 percent for food (Mortara, 1938, 140). For similar considerations relating to 1931–1932, see P. Grassi, *Bilancia pagamenti italiana 1927–1932*, Roma, 10 September 1935, in FLE, ATdR, Direzione generale del Tesoro, fasc. 76.

10 P. Thaon di Revel, *Motivi che inducono ad allineare la lira*, Roma, 16 September 1936, in FLE, ATdR, Direzione generale del Tesoro, fasc. 562.

11 For a discussion on the "capital circuit" as a method of price control—an in-depth treatment of which exceeds the scope of this contribution—refer to Della Torre (2001).

12 According to the purchasing power parity (PPP)-based definition, the real exchange rate (r_{ppp}) is defined as the nominal exchange rate (e) multiplied by the ratio of the foreign price level (p_f) to the domestic price level (p): $r_{ppp} = e\frac{p_f}{p}$. An increase in p determines a real appreciation of the domestic currency.

13 In 1937, about 50 percent of Italian imports came from countries with clearing, where about 62 percent of exports were directed (Mortara 1938, 137).

14 The 1939 figure for Germany must be interpreted considering the annexation of Austria the previous year: even so, however, we believe that our conclusions about the structural dynamics of Italian foreign trade are not substantially changed. For additional information on trade variations by country, please refer to Berbenni (2021).

15 F. Guarneri, *Bilancia commerciale e bilancia dei pagamenti. Promemoria per S.E. il Capo del Governo*, 10 July 1937, in FLE, ATdR, Direzione generale del Tesoro, fasc. 280.

16 F. Guarneri, *Bilancia commerciale e bilancia dei pagamenti. Promemoria per S.E. il Capo del Governo*, 10 July 1937, in FLE, ATdR, Direzione generale del Tesoro, fasc. 280.

References

Albers, T.N.H. (2020). Currency Devaluations and Beggar-My-Neighbour Penalties: Evidence from the 1930s. *The Journal of Economic History, 73*(1), 233–257.

Balogh, T. (1940). Foreign Exchange and Export Trade Policy. *The Economic Journal, 50*(197), 1–26.

Banca d'Italia. (1938). *L'economia italiana nel sessennio 1931–1936. Parte prima.* Rome: Istituto poligrafico dello Stato.

Barberi, B. (1961). *I consumi nel primo secolo dell'Unità d'Italia 1861–1961.* Milan: Giuffrè.

Berbenni, E. (2021). External Devaluation and Trade Balance in 1930s Italy. *Structural Change and Economic Dynamics, 57*, 93–107.

Bientinesi, F. (2006). La bilancia dei pagamenti italiana (1890–2000). In C. Pavone (ed.), *Storia d'Italia nel secolo ventesimo. Strumenti e fonti. Vol. I. Elementi strutturali* (pp. 477–506). Rome: Ministero per i beni e le attività culturali.

Borgatta, G. (1937a). Osservazioni sui prezzi e sull'oro. *Rassegna Economica. Pubblicazione mensile del Banco di Napoli, 7*(7–8), 253–262.

Borgatta, G. (1937b). Osservazioni sui prezzi e sull'oro. *Rassegna Economica. Pubblicazione mensile del Banco di Napoli, 7*(9–10), 325–341.

Cavalcanti, M.L. (2011). *La politica monetaria italiana fra le due guerre (1918–1943).* Milan: Franco Angeli.

Ciocca, P., & Ulizzi, A. (1990). *I tassi di cambio nominali e 'reali' dell'Italia dall'Unità nazionale al Sistema monetario europeo (1861–1979).* Rome-Bari: Laterza.

Cotula, F., & Spaventa, L. (2003). La politica monetaria tra le due guerre 1919–1935. In *La Banca d'Italia. Sintesi della ricerca storica 1893–1960* (pp. 209–310). Rome-Bari: Laterza.

Della Torre, G. (2001). La finanza di guerra e il "circuito dei capitali" in Italia, 1935–1943: una valutazione quantitativa. *Rivista di storia economica, XVII*(2), 173–200.

De' Stefani, A. (1940). *Travaglio economico.* Bologna: Zanichelli.

di Fenizio, F. (1934). *Questioni monetarie.* Milan: Aracne.

Di Nino, V., Eichengreen, B., & Sbracia, M. (2013). Real exchange rates, trade, and growth. In G. Toniolo (ed.), *The Oxford Handbook of the Italian Economy since Unification* (pp. 351–377). Oxford-New York: Oxford University Press.

Di Quirico, R. (2001). La crisi valutaria del 1935 e la politica economica dell'Italia fascista. *Passato e presente, 53*, 69–94.

Eichengreen, B., & Irwin, D.A. (2010). The Slide to Protectionism in the Great Depression: Who Succumbed and Why? *The Journal of Economic History, 70*(4), 871–897.

Eichengreen, B., & Sachs, J. (1985). Exchange Rates and Economic Recovery in the 1930s. *The Journal of Economic History, 45*(4), 925–946.

Eichengreen, B., & Temin, P. (2000). The Gold Standard and the Great Depression. *Contemporary European History, 9*(2), 183–207.

Eichengreen, B., & Temin, P. (2010). Fetters of Gold and Paper. *Oxford Review of Economic Policy, 26*, 370–384.

Federico, G., Natoli, S., Tattara, G., & Vasta, M. (2011). *Il commercio estero italiano. 1862–1950.* Rome-Bari: Laterza.

Feinstein, C.A., Temin, P., & Toniolo, G. (1997). *The European Economy Between the Wars.* Oxford: Oxford University Press.

Fossati, A. (1939). Il commercio estero italiano dal 1928 al 1938. *Rivista Internazionale di Scienze Sociali, 10*(4), 647–671.

Gagliardi, A. (2007). *L'impossibile autarchia: la politica economica del fascismo e il Ministero scambi e valute.* Soveria Mannelli: Rubettino.

Guarneri, F. (1937). Italy's Commercial Policy. *The Banker, XLIII*(140), 232–236.

Guarneri, F. (1953). *Battaglie economiche tra le due grandi guerre* (Vol. 2). Milan: Garzanti.

Hallwood, P., MacDonald, R., & Marsh, I. (2011). Remilitarization and the End of the Gold Bloc. *De Economist, 159*, 305–321.

Hirschmann, A. (1987). *Potenza nazionale e commercio estero.* Bologna: 11 Mulino.

Irwin, D.A. (2012). *Trade Policy Disaster. Lessons from the 1930s.* Cambridge, MA: MIT.

ISTAT. (1936). *Commercio estero nell'anno 1935.* Roma: Failli.

ISTAT. (1951). *Commercio con l'estero. Anni 1939, 1946–1949.* Roma: Failli.

Jacks, D.S., & Novy, D. (2020). Trade Blocs and Trade Wars During the Interwar Period. *Asian Economic Policy Review, 15*, 119–136.

Klein, M.W., & Rosengren, E. (1994). The Real Exchange Rate and Foreign Direct Investment in the United States. Relative Wealth vs. Relative Wage Effects. *Journal of International Economics, 36*, 373–389.

Mantelli, B. (1996). Dagli 'scambi bilanciati' all'Asse Berlino-Roma. *Studi storici, 37*(4), 1201–1225.

Miao, Y., & Berg, A. (2010). The Real Exchange Rate and Growth Revisited: The Washington Consensus Strikes Back? *IMF Working Papers*, 10/58.

Mitchener, K.J., & Wandschneider, K. (2015). Capital Controls and Recovery from the Financial Crisis of the 1930s. *Journal of International Economics, 95*, 188–201.

Mortara, G. (1938). Il commercio dell'Italia con l'estero nel 1937. *Giornale degli Economisti e Rivista di Statistica* (2), 118–142.
Neal, L. (1979). The Economics and Finance of Bilateral Clearing Agreements: Germany, 1934–8. *The Economic History Review, 32*(3), 391–404.
Obstfeld, M., Shambaugh, J., & Taylor, A.M. (2004). Monetary Sovereignty, Exchange Rates, and Capital Controls: The Trilemma in the Inter-War Period. *IMF Staff Papers No. 51*, Washington, DC: IMF.
Papi, G.U. (1936). Conseguenza e punto d'arresto del protezionismo: l'allineamento delle monete. *Giornale degli Economisti e Rivista di Statistica, 76*(11), 828–834.
Pavanelli, G. (1990). Gli economisti e la politica economica: le svalutazioni degli anni '30 nel dibattito italiano. *Quaderni di Storia dell'Economia Politica, 8*(2–3), 321–358.
Pavanelli, G., & Nenovsky, N. (2008). Exchange Rate Control in Italy and Bulgaria in the Interwar Period: History and Perspectives. In *The Experience of Exchange Rate Regimes in Southeastern Europe in a Historical and Comparative Perspective* (pp. 80–117). Vienna: OENB.
Raitano, G. (1995). I provvedimenti sui cambi in Italia nel periodo 1919–36. In *Ricerche per la storia della Banca d'Italia* (Vol. VI, pp. 265–335). Rome-Bari: Laterza.
Renzi, A. (1940). *Tecnica degli scambi con l'estero*. Milan: Hoepli.
Riccardi, R. (1939). *Economia fascista. Sanzioni, commercio estero, autarchia.* Rome: Unione editoriale d'Italia.
Senato del Regno. (1937). *Atti Parlamentari. Senato, Discussioni, Legislatura XXIX, 2 sessione, Vol. 3, Sedute dal 14 dicembre 1936 al 25 maggio 1937*. Rome: Tipografia del Senato.
Storaci, M. (1993). L'Italia e il Blocco dell'Oro (1933–1935). In P.F. Asso, A. Santorelli, M. Storaci, & G. Tattara (eds), *Finanza internazionale, vincolo esterno e cambi. 1919–1939* (pp. 441–486). Rome-Bari: Laterza.
Tattara, G. (1993). La persistenza dello squilibrio dei conti con l'estero dell'Italia negli anni Trenta. In P.F. Asso, A. Santorelli, M. Storaci, & G. Tattara (eds), *Finanza internazionale, vincolo esterno e cambi. 1919–1939* (Vol. III, pp. 368–440). Rome-Bari: Laterza.
Wandschneider, K. (2008). The Stability of the Interwar Gold Exchange Standard: Did Politics Matter? *The Journal of Economic History, 68*(1), 151–181.
Zamagni, V. (1990). *Dalla periferia al centro. La seconda rinascita economica dell'Italia (1861–1990)*. Bologna: Il Mulino.

5 The Bank of Italy goes to war

Financing fascist warfare, 1935–1943

Marianna Astore, Mario Perugini, and Valerio Torreggiani

5.1 Introduction

The interplay between finance and warfare continues to raise questions for economic historians seeking to unravel the complexities of wartime economies. Among the various cases that illustrate this relationship, that of the role of the Bank of Italy during the Fascist era stands as an interesting subject of inquiry. Firstly, from 1935 to 1943, Italy, under Benito Mussolini's Fascist regime, embarked on a path of military conquest first in Africa, occupying Ethiopia, and then in Europe, attempting to expand into Greece and the Balkans during the Second World War. Secondly, the period from 1935 to 1943 in Italy has attracted little specific attention from economic historians, largely because its falls between two highly significant periods in Italy's economic history: on the one hand, it follows the upheaval of the Great Depression and the extensive nationalization of key sectors of the Italian economy during the early 1930s; on the other, it is overshadowed by post-war reconstruction and the ensuing economic boom, commonly called the "miracolo economico." Starting from these considerations, this chapter explores the Bank of Italy's involvement in financing fascist warfare and the theoretical debate it generated, aiming to contribute to our understanding of the complex interplay between economic theory and the concrete forms in which wartime financing was implemented in this pivotal period in history.

Wars entail a reorientation of the economic system from private to public consumption, with an accompanying decline in investment not directly bound up with wartime production. They result in a substantial increase in the demand for "public" goods (mainly raw materials and military equipment), driven by the rise in public spending, and a significant, simultaneous contraction in the supply of consumer goods as factories convert to military production (Roselli 2017). Even for opposite reasons, shocks to both supply and demand contribute to upward pressures on prices. Containing these pressures requires more efficient organization of wartime production (and resources from abroad are particularly useful in this respect). It also entails limiting the demand for private goods so as to ensure sufficient resources to finance the increased public expenditure on war-related goods and services. This limitation can be implemented through a combination of policies, namely higher taxation, massive public borrowing, and/or administrative

DOI: 10.4324/9781032656199-6

measures such as rationing, and wage and price freezes. In the absence of a rise in taxation or new public debt, the increment in public spending is financed with the money stock, which affects prices, potentially cancelling out the effect of the measures taken to keep inflation under control. Wartime changes in income and prices hinge on the success or failure of these economic policies.

With this interpretative framework, it is possible to compare the financing of war in Italy during the two world wars (for Italy, 1915–1918 and 1940–1945, respectively). Both growth and inflation were significantly worse during the Second World War. Measured by the consumer price index, inflation rose by 2.6 times during the Great War, with an average annual increase of 41%, compared with 22.9 times during the Second World War, when prices rose on average by 3.8 times per year (Roselli 2017, 130–131). As to economic growth, the increase in real GDP during the period 1915–1918 is estimated at 2%, whereas during the Second World War, real GDP collapsed by 44%, the average annual decline exceeding 7% (Baffigi 2015, 210–211). The moderate increase in real GDP during the First World War came from a significant rise in public consumption, which more than compensated for the decline in private consumption, total investment, and exports. Overall, consumption grew by 20%, while investment and exports shrank by more than 50%. During the Second World War, instead, the plunge in GDP, despite the increase in public consumption, reflected a huge drop in private consumption and investment and a complete halt on exports. The total consumption fell by 38%, investment by 46%, and exports by 97% (Baffigi 2015, 204–205).

How was the substantial increase in war-related public spending financed? As in other belligerent countries, also in Italy the coverage of public expenditure through taxes was relatively moderate in both conflicts (Broadberry and Harrison 2005). The decision to avoid tax increases so as not to antagonize the public restricted the fiscal system's capacity to finance expenditures. In the Italian case, the situation was further complicated by the absence of an income tax (Einaudi 1927). In fact, the percentage of state expenditure covered by taxes was surprisingly similar in the First and Second World Wars: 33% and 30.7%, respectively. Taxes amounted to only 11.9% of GDP in the first conflict and a mere 8.8% in the second, leaving the problem of financing wartime expenditure unsolved (Roselli 2017, 134).

Where differences do emerge is in recourse to public debt as opposed to monetary policy. During the First World War, over 70% of the growth in the deficit was covered by public debt. The cornerstone of this policy consisted of five national loans (Repaci 1962, 280–282). Another factor to consider is reliance on foreign debt. This was significant for Italy during the First World War, given the needs for war matériel, the main creditors being the United States and the United Kingdom (Astore and Fratianni 2019). During the Second World War, by contrast, external financing was lacking, with a net outflow of resources from Italy to its ally Germany (Zamagni 1998a, 183 and 188).

During the First World War, direct financing of the Treasury by the Bank of Italy, through advances, stabilized at around 11% of the debt by the end of 1918. However, the central bank's backing went beyond direct loans to the Treasury, as it purchased large quantities of Treasury bonds in the primary or secondary market, supporting their prices and facilitating their placement. The central bank's balance sheet during the four years of war grew by approximately three and a half times (Banca d'Italia 1993, 749–750).[1] Its exposure to the Treasury, counting both advances and government securities, exceeded 11 billion lire at the end of the war, compared with 1.6 billion at the end of 1914, and equaled 70% of its balance sheet – an unprecedented level (Roselli 2017, 140).

Public financing had a radically different profile during the Second World War. Financing through public debt accounted for just over 42% of the total and was offset by a surge in advances from the Bank of Italy to the Treasury, which peaked at 43% of the total public expenditure in 1944. As Alessandro Roselli remarked, "It appears paradoxical that, having learned from the experience of the great inflation of the First World War, an eminently monetary financing of the conflict was sought during the Second World War to stabilize prices" (Roselli 2017, 144).

This essay argues that to fully understand the relationship between fiscal policy and monetary policy in Italy during the Second World War – and especially the attempt to establish a "circuit of capital" overseen by the central bank – it is crucial both to include an analysis of the years leading up to the war and to frame the concrete forms through which wartime financing was implemented against the background of the economic theory that sought to describe, explain, and guide that process. The period beginning with the Italian invasion of Ethiopia in October 1935 saw the regime emphasize economic self-sufficiency and intensify its military adventures. In fact, the circuit-of-capital theory was developed retrospectively and was explicitly based on practices that had been evolving since the start of the Ethiopian War, as Finance Minister Thaon di Revel said in his speech inaugurating the National Institute of Corporatist Finance in October 1941. The chapter is organized as follows. Section 5.2 presents a brief overview of the main transformations that the Italian economy underwent before and after the launch of economic autarky by the Fascist regime. It also examines a series of fiscal measures implemented with a view to constructing (or at least preparing) the circuit. Section 5.3 focuses on the evolution of the model of intervention of the Bank of Italy, which also developed new practices in response to the pressures exerted by autarky and the wartime economy. In Section 5.4, we outline the key stages of the debate that took place between 1940 and 1942 between economists and policymakers seeking to formulate a theoretical framework for the circuit of capital. The concluding section discusses the definitive rupture of that circuit in 1943, highlighting the gap between the theorization of the circuit and its real-world functioning.

5.2 Italy and the Autarkic economy

By the mid-1930s it was already evident that the fundamental structures of the world economy had undergone profound changes compared with the preceding decade.

Between 1931 and 1933, Britain and the United States had left the gold standard, increased tariffs, and initiated a series of competitive devaluations. As the stage was being set for the failure of the 1933 World Economic Conference in London, the groundwork began to be laid for the creation of regional economic blocs, as exemplified by the imperial tariff concessions within the Commonwealth area, decided at the Ottawa Conference in 1932. In these circumstances, the appreciation of other currencies relative to the Italian lira did not help Italy's economic situation. Despite an initial revision of customs duties, in the early months of 1934 Italy's trade balance, along with exports and the gold reserves of the Bank of Italy, showed clear signs of deterioration (Banca d'Italia 1935; Cotula and Spaventa 1993; Tattara 1993). The Minister of Finance, Guido Jung, decided to address the situation with a comprehensive maneuver aimed at reducing public spending, production costs, prices, and monetary circulation, at instituting stricter exchange controls, and at implementing clearing exchange deals with international partners, of which the most important was the one signed with Germany in September 1934. But these measures failed to yield the expected results. The 1934 trade balance closed with a deficit more than one billion lire greater than in the immediately preceding years and the reserves of the Bank of Italy recorded continuous outflows totaling 619.7 million lire during the second half of that year (Guarneri 1953, 318–332).

Given the severe conditions mentioned earlier, the subsequent turning point took the form of a more aggressive foreign policy, in line with developments in Germany and, as remarked by Rolf Petri, after Italian diplomacy's substantial failure throughout the 1920s to gain recognition of Italy's hegemonic role in the Mediterranean (Petri 2002, 115). In monetary and fiscal terms, signs of this change began to emerge in late 1934 and early 1935, as preparations got under way for the October 1934 invasion of Ethiopia. On December 8, 1934, the shift in Italian trade policy materialized with the reinstatement of the monopoly on foreign exchange operations under the National Institute for Foreign Exchange (Italian acronym: INCE; see Raitano 1995; Astore 2014). The change of course of 1934 could not have been more radical: Italy's exchange controls became, after Germany's, the most comprehensive among those in any capitalist country, extending to all exchange transactions (whether commercial, financial, or tourist-related) and all means of payment.

On January 7, 1935, Paolo Thaon di Revel was appointed Minister of Finance. In February, he imposed a regime of ministerial licensing for all imports. As in Germany, the public monopoly on foreign exchange was coupled with stringent controls on imports by means of a system of quotas and licenses. In February, Italy abruptly turned its back on its traditional allegiance to the policy of the most-favored-nation clause and multilateral trade, fully embracing the principle of balanced trade: after a "partial experiment" with applying this principle during 1934, and facing a dire situation, the Fascist government decided to make a new, larger-scale attempt, hoping that by elevating the principle of balanced trade to a system it would succeed in saving the lira (Guarneri 1953, 350–351). The problem of reorganizing all the services responsible for regulating imports, exports, and foreign means of payment under a single direction and unified command was solved in May 1935 with the creation of the Currency Exchange Supervision Office headed by Felice Guarneri, a representative of Confindustria (Zani 1988; Gagliardi 2006). The imposition of an import control regime and the creation of a General

Directorate for War Production were harbingers of the aggression against Ethiopia in October.

Following Italy's invasion of Ethiopia in 1935–1936, the League of Nations imposed economic sanctions on Italy, triggering an intensified pursuit of national self-sufficiency known as autarky. The "autarkic plans" formulated in the spring of 1936 and autumn of 1937 set domestic production targets for essential raw materials and industrial products to be achieved by 1941 (or 1940 for certain agricultural goods). Concurrently, private corporations were incentivized with subsidies and other financial measures to increase their fixed capital investment. Autarky facilitated the reallocation of resources towards heavy industry and arms production. Light industry, including chemical and human-made fiber production, also received significant benefits from autarky (Bertilorenzi et al. 2022).

Along with the financial commitments necessary for autarkic development plans, wartime expenditures rose steadily. Following the war in Ethiopia, Italy became embroiled in the Spanish Civil War (1936 to 1939), and in 1939 it invaded Albania before officially entering the Second World War in June 1940. Throughout the period from 1935 to 1943, the Finance Minister Thaon di Revel identified escalating inflationary pressure stoked by public spending as a primary concern. To address the risk of runaway inflation, the regime implemented measures in two principal directions. Firstly, it tried to prevent the formation of excessive demand through wage and price controls. With Italy's entry into the Second World War in June 1940, this discipline became a general wage freeze. Secondly, the minister sought to contain price growth through rationing and other measures designed to curb private consumption and investment.

These two approaches were implemented with a series of fiscal measures put in place in the period stretching from 1935 through the war years. In 1935, a special tax of 10%, later raised to 20%, was imposed on income from bearer securities. In 1941, the tax was extended to newly introduced registered shares. The limit on distributed profits was set at 6% in 1935; after a few years of experimentation with a progressive tax on dividends, the limit was reinstated in 1940 and set at 7%. On that occasion, a tax was also introduced that effectively blocked transfers of reserves to share capital by subjecting them to a 100% tax rate. Starting in 1935, the formation of new companies and the issuance of shares and bonds required ministerial approval. In October 1936, the lira was pegged to the dollar through a devaluation of 41%. A forced loan was imposed on property owners, who were also subject to an extraordinary tax earmarked to service the loan. In February 1937, the conversion to capital and distribution of revaluation gains resulting from the lira alignment were also prohibited. Finally, war-related increased profits were subjected to a progressive tax in 1940, with rates ranging from 10% to 60%. The portion of increased profits not absorbed by the tax was earmarked in 1942 for investment in Treasury bonds bearing 3% interest. In conjunction with the devaluation of the lira, the government introduced an extraordinary tax of 10% on the capital of joint-stock companies. Capital gains arising from real estate transactions, compared with pre-war values, were taxed at a rate of 60% starting in 1940. In 1941, capital gains from stock transactions were subjected to a progressive tax, which was soon changed to a flat rate of 20%. The securities trading tax underwent two increases in 1935 and then in 1940. The second increase was accompanied by a surcharge equal to 4% of the value of the securities traded. The surcharge was raised to 5% in 1942. From that year onwards, companies were obligated to invest one-fifth of the capital raised through equity issues in Treasury bonds bearing 3%. Buyers of shares were compelled to invest in these bonds in an amount equivalent to their share purchases (Baffi 1965, 226–228).

While the large increase in public spending contributed to an upturn in Italian economic growth in the second half of the 1930s, the shift to an autarkic economy had a major impact on the relationship between the Bank of Italy and the Treasury, to the detriment of the former's operational autonomy. From December 1935 onwards, the obligation for the Bank of Italy to hold gold or equivalent reserves equal to at least 40% of its sight liabilities was suspended. For the first time in the Bank's history, there was no formal limit on the increase in circulation. Furthermore, the government gained unrestricted access to central bank credit. In December 1936, two months after the devaluation of the lira, extraordinary advances to the Treasury were reintroduced without any cap on their amount. With this step, the Fascist government essentially asserted its right to resort to the monetary instrument to cover its financial needs whenever and to whatever extent it deemed appropriate. Overall, the severing of the link with gold was associated with the creation of an institutional framework that subordinated monetary policy to the needs of the Treasury (Gelsomino 1992, 105).

The Bank of Italy provided a similar interpretation of the situation: "The currency, partially freed from the traditional rules of the gold reserve game, is now entrusted not to automatic control but to the wise management of monetary and financial policies" (Banca d'Italia 1937, 61). The primary mandate of the Bank of Italy was no longer to maintain the fixed exchange rate under the gold standard but to ensure the full development of autarkic policies while limiting their inflationary effects. The chief outcome was the creation of a direct link between money creation and industrial capital accumulation, the former being responsible for actively promoting the latter, in accordance with the production priorities established by the Fascist regime through the autarkic plans.[2]

As Bank of Italy Governor Vincenzo Azzolini argued in a speech delivered in September 1938:

> [T]he implementation of the autarkic plans will subject our production apparatus to a complete overhaul. Problems will arise with the expansion of production and often also with the transformation of existing technical processes. The need to provide the national territory with the raw materials needed in some sectors of the economy, the employment of new labour forces and the technical overhaul of production facilities require that an additional mass of capital flow into production. It is up to the financing institutions to solve the problem of the most suitable technical instruments to facilitate the formation of savings and to direct the flow of savings towards autarkic initiatives.[3]

In the same speech, Azzolini emphasized the importance of preserving a clear distinction between bank credit for day-to-day business operations and medium-term to long-term credit for enduring investments, and stated that only in private savings could there be a "secure source of financing for new initiatives." As we show in the next section, this aspiration was destined to go largely unfulfilled.

5.3 The Bank of Italy and the monetary financing of war

Starting in autumn of 1937, the Bank's leaders began to focus more closely on the new institutional mandate, paying special attention to the German example. Governor Azzolini received insights into the "principles of doctrine and practice guiding the autarkic policy of the National Socialist regime,"[4] most notably from Antonino Cimino, the Bank's delegate in Berlin, and Giuseppe Di Nardi, a young economist in its Research Department. The similarities with the German experience were striking. On the one hand, there were the government's pursuit of economic self-sufficiency, the necessity to step up production for domestic needs, difficulties in accessing international credit, and scarcity of gold reserves. On the other hand, the country was run by a highly centralized economic organization, with a banking system operating under direct public control.

The increase in public spending on public works and rearmament in Germany after 1933 had been financed through the discounting of special bills presented to banks by public-works contractors and producers of war matériel. This short-term bank credit was later consolidated into long-term loans funded by private savings. The key elements characterizing Germany's success in the years 1933–1936 were, in summary, price and production controls, the halt of private loan issues in favor of state-contracted loans and rationing of credit and raw materials. According to Cimino's detailed communication to Governor Azzolini, the pivotal role played by the German central bank in funding the autarkic plan through the discounting of bills from the Metallurgischen Forschungsgesellschaft (MEFO: Metallurgical Research Company) was crucial. Conceived by the president of the Reichsbank, Hjalmar Schacht, the MEFO was a financial vehicle wholly owned by the central bank and responsible for financing military provisioning of different types:

> The operation of this institution concerning the creation of securities would roughly unfold as follows. The supplier would issue the draft, also affixing its signature. Subsequently, a signature would be provided by a specific entity closely associated with the Reich, established in the form of a limited liability company [. . .], essentially serving no other purpose than to provide the guarantee of the Reich. Packaged in this way, the commercial drafts would be accepted by the banks, which, when necessary, could discount them at the Reichsbank.[5]

The MEFO bills yielded 4% annual interest and had short (three- or four-month) maturities. However, they could be renewed for up to five years. Industrial firms accepting MEFO bills in payment could choose either not to renew them or to discount them with the Reichsbank, receiving German marks. About half of the MEFO bills were not discounted and remained in the hands of the private sector. This was attributed to their ready discountability and the 4% interest rate they guaranteed. By means of this mechanism, the MEFO – indirectly representing the Reichsbank and, essentially, the state – could not only collect funds but also defer payments for industrial orders. In other words, it could support public spending, finance production, and stimulate demand. Its operations were kept confidential in order to conceal German rearmament efforts (Schacht 1955, 317–318; James 1999, 34).

The difference between the German and the Italian cases lay in the economic context in which the autarkic experiment unfolded. At the advent of Nazism in 1933, Germany's primary economic challenge was pronounced underutilization of existing industrial capacity, which had been renewed and expanded in the second half of the 1920s owing to foreign loans. The solution achieved through the MEFO bills scheme generated the financial liquidity necessary to restart the production cycle using the factories available, thereby stimulating economic activity. With the economic recovery, GDP and savings started to rise again. Savings, in particular, "through the subscription of Treasury bonds, funded the State's spending . . . for its ambitious programs of public works and armaments".[6]

In Italy, the starting point for implementing autarky was different and, accordingly, the intervention of the central bank had to be managed with greater caution. The economy was already expanding and there was no significant margin of spare capacity; the challenge, rather, was to create new plant capacity. As early as the summer of 1938, the debate within the Bank of Italy acknowledged that it was substantially impossible for the credit system to absorb the increased demand for financial capital without affecting the money stock. In the comments on a document prepared by Di Nardi in 1938 on the financing of autarkic plans, the following observation was made:

> Everything suggests that the financing of autarkic plans may have to rely partly on inflation. In other words, the funding will require the utilization of future savings, which the issuing institution will be called upon to advance. The risks of the operation could be mitigated if the state, minimizing expenses and avoiding future direct appeals to the market for purposes other than autarkic ones, allows future savings to be directed towards autarkic enterprises. This would enable these enterprises to repay the advances received.[7]

However, the country's wartime needs were pressing, as was the push to finance them through money creation: Italy's experience of financing autarky and above all the war ended up resembling Germany's. As in the German case, the state's war contracts were financed through the direct creation of new currency by the central bank ("extraordinary advances" to the Treasury) and, partially, through "special operations" of the Consorzio Sovvezioni per Valori Industriali (CSVI), whose bills, which were supposed to finance private business, were rediscounted by the central bank itself.

The CSVI was a financial vehicle created by the Italian government in 1914 as an exceptional and temporary entity in view of Italy's probable involvement in the First World War. It was later used by the Bank of Italy to carry out bank rescues during the banking crisis of 1921–1922 (Gigliobianco 1993), and it continued to operate under successive legislative extensions in the following years. During the 1920s, the CSVI solidified its role as an industrial credit institution, becoming an example of a new model for financing infrastructure and major industrial enterprises. This model was firmly established in Italy during the 1930s and was based on a quasi-public bond circuit linking savings with fixed capital investment under the protection of a state guarantee. In 1924, the CSVI obtained the right to rediscount its portfolio of credits not only with issuing banks but also with other banking institutions (Astore and Perugini 2024). In addition, it was empowered to issue interest-bearing certificates. As the Italian banking system underwent restructuring in the early 1930s, with banks focusing on short-term ordinary credit after the banking reform of 1936, the CSVI's role evolved to complement Istituto Mobiliare Italiano (IMI), the new specialized institution for long-term financing of businesses. This restructuring was formalized with the banking reform, which made the CSVI an autonomous section of the IMI, while the presidency of both entities continued to be entrusted by law to the governor of the Bank of Italy.

As Governor Azzolini explained, IMI, established because of the bank rescues in the early 1930s, operated by "granting financial assistance to industrial business, mainly for the reorganization and expansion of plants," while the CSVI facilitated "with its special operations, the execution of the most important state orders," including military ones (Banca d'Italia 1942, 86). The use of the CSVI seemed naturally to fit its characteristics and its special connection with the bank of issue: it was indeed "[well-suited] for agile emergency public spending . . . to support the most dynamic industrial sectors, and familiar with resolving business financial matters with state assistance" (Caracciolo 1992, 68–69). Another purpose of the "special operations" of the CSVI was to "hide" from the public a substantial share of the advances granted by the Bank of Italy to the Treasury. The CSVI's financing was indeed guaranteed by the state, and the Bank could discount CSVI bills beyond the discount limits fixed by the standard regulation. In this way, the CSVI effectively established a "deferred" creditor position vis-à-vis the Treasury, with a potentially unlimited time horizon. The mechanism of "special operations," very similar to that of the MEFO bills, allowed the Bank of Italy to finance military procurement from the end of 1935 onwards and was also increasingly used to finance a variety of public expenditures, including public works, agricultural reclamation, and the extraordinary expenses of the Ministry of the Interior (Caracciolo 1992, 70–71).[8]

As shown in Figure 5.1, "special operations" significantly surpassed the CSVI's regular activities from 1939 onwards, constituting nearly the entirety of CSVI's operations during the Second World War. The bulk of the overall funding for the CSVI's special operations came from monetary circulation, that is, from the Bank of Italy. The share of total Treasury debt consisting of debt towards the Bank of Italy – including the CSVI's special operations – trended considerably upward between 1936 and 1945

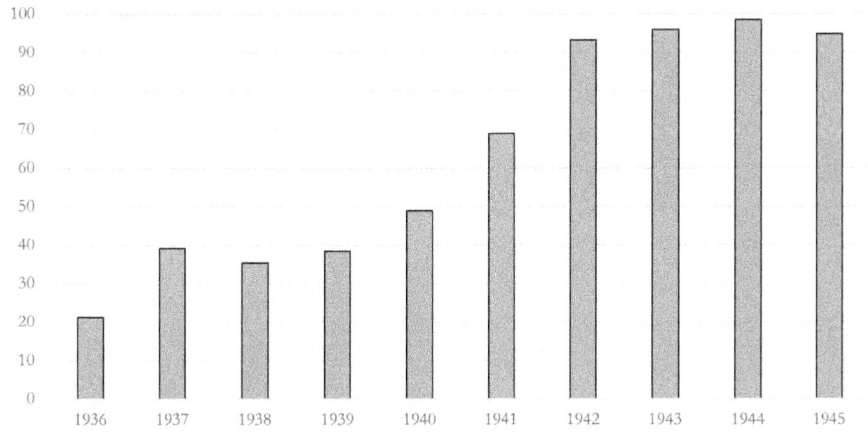

Figure 5.1 CSVI special operations/CSVI total operations (%, 1936–1945).

Sources: For details on CSVI special operations, see Caracciolo (1992, 138) and Zamagni (1998b, 227); for details on CSVI total operations, see Archivio Storico Banca d'Italia (ASBI), Carte Baffi, Servizio studi, pratt., n. 58, fasc. 6, p. 10

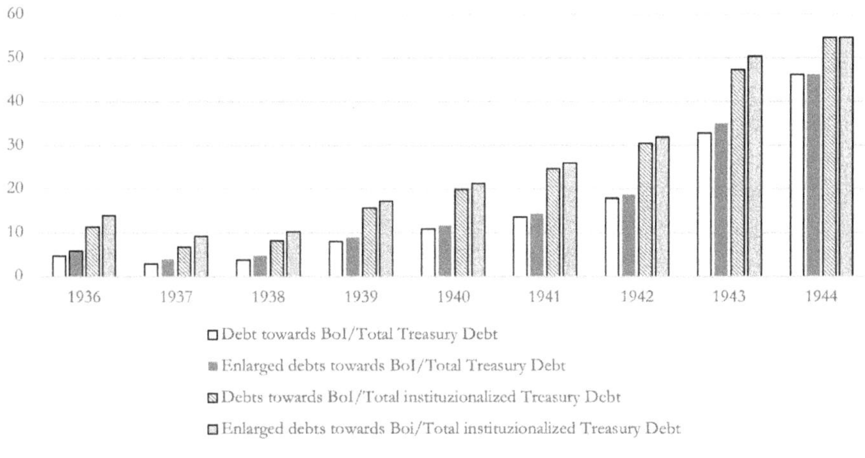

Figure 5.2 Debt towards the Bank of Italy (with or without bonds) as a percentage of Treasury debt and "institutionalized" Treasury debt.

Sources: For details on debt towards Bank of Italy, see Zamagni (1998b, 227); for details on total Treasury debt and total institutionalized Treasury debt, see Della Torre (2001, 185); and for data on government bonds held by the Bank of Italy, see Della Torre (2000, 21)

Note: In this chart we do not consider banknotes and coins, but the "State circulation" was not an insignificant form of Treasury financing in a still relatively underdeveloped financial system similar to that of Italy during the interwar period (Salvemini and Zamagni 1998, 159).

Figure 5.3 CSVI special operations as percentage of the debt towards the Bank of Italy.

Source: The two series of CSVI special operations and of the debt towards the Bank of Italy are available in the work of Zamagni (1998b, 227)

(Figure 5.2). This trend grew more pronounced starting in 1939, with the share increasing from 7.97% to reach 46.10% in 1944. The numbers are even higher when we look at the ratio between the debt towards the Bank of Italy and the institutionalized debt of the Treasury. The latter refers to the portion of the debt held by public institutions or institutions influenced by economic policy authorities.[9] In this case, the percentage of the debt towards the Bank of Italy reached a peak of 54.58 % in 1944. We can observe similar trends, although with a slightly upward shift, if we include in the debt towards the Bank of Italy medium-term and long-term government bonds held by the Bank of Italy ("enlarged debt towards the Bank of Italy," as shown in Figure 5.2).

More generally, the importance of public-monetary institutions grew from the mid-1930s until the armistice. As a result, the portion of debt held by the private sector fell drastically, while the expansion of "institutionalized" debt demonstrates the hegemonic role played by public institutions in financing the Treasury during the war (Della Torre 2001, 186).[10]

If, on the other hand, we consider the trend of special operations in relation to the debt towards the Bank of Italy alone, the series exhibits greater variability (Figure 5.3) and seems to be strictly correlated with spending on armaments (Minniti 1978).

The debt towards the Bank of Italy comprised various components besides government securities. In addition to the special operations with the CSVI, it also included the following: state banknotes and coins in the Bank of Italy's vaults, advances to the Treasury, other assets related to the Treasury, and, starting from 1937, the rediscount of stockpiling bills.[11] As can be seen from Figure 5.3, advances to the Treasury were the principal component of the debt to the central bank. After the restoration of the convertibility of the lira with *Quota Novanta*, the possibility for the Treasury to request extraordinary advances was abolished, and temporary advances, up to an amount of 450 million lire, were instituted. In 1936, the constraints on Treasury financing were essentially dismantled: not only was the ceiling on temporary advances increased to one billion lire, but it was also stipulated that for extraordinary needs the Bank would make additional funds available based on a simple agreement

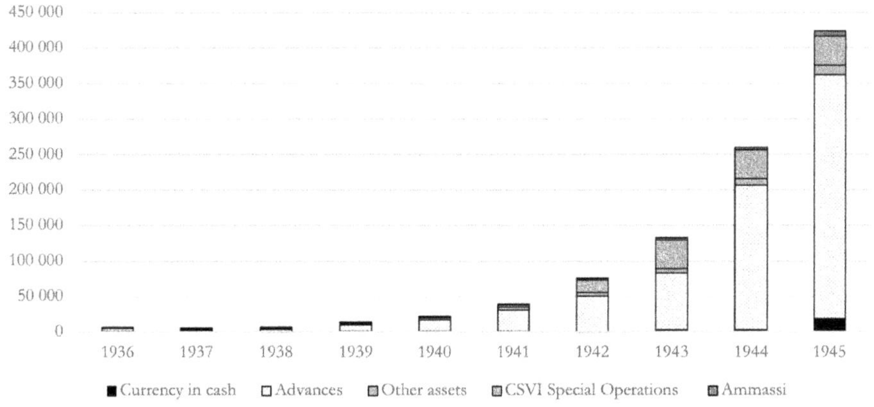

Figure 5.4 Components of the debt towards the Bank of Italy (millions of lire).
Source: Zamagni (1998b, 227)

between the Ministry of Finance and the governor, against the issuance of special Treasury bonds as collateral (Salvemini and Zamagni 1998, 161–162). This option was utilized from 1936 onwards throughout the wartime period.

In 1940, Ezio Vanoni, an economist collaborating with the Bank of Italy, argued that in order to contain inflation this increase in monetary financing needed to be accompanied by administrative measures (e.g., price and wage controls and rationing), along with the channeling of savings towards public securities (and a crackdown on speculation), at the expense of peacetime investments (Vanoni 1940, 103–104).[12] In accordance with this scheme, which represented one of the early public disclosures of the practices developed by the Bank of Italy in the preceding years, the excess monetary savings resulting from the restraint on private consumption imposed by rationing and price increases were supposed to be invested in public debt securities. In other words, the excess monetary savings were supposed to flow into the banking system in the form of deposits. The banks, in turn, would subscribe public debt securities to cover the additional expenditure. The liquidity thus created by the central bank, for the part flowing to the banks, would constitute, through the deposit multiplier, the "basis for the pyramid-like expansion of the banks' investments in Treasury securities" (Baffi 1965, 228). The public debt securities were to be subscribed by institutional investors controlled by the state: publicly controlled banks, Cassa Depositi e Prestiti, and pension and insurance institutions. As for the business sector, the redirection of investment towards military purposes and the reduction of private investment in peacetime goods were to be achieved through a series of tax measures and anti-inflation policies which, as we have seen in the previous section, had already been implemented starting in 1935 by the Finance Minister Thaon di Ravel.

5.4 The theoretical debate on the "circuit of capital"

After 1940, the financial policy model remained unchanged with respect to the preceding years. The practice that the Bank of Italy initiated in 1935, analyzed in the preceding section, began to be referred to in the regime's documents as the "circuit of capital." Between 1940 and 1942, efforts were made in both academic and policy-making circles to provide a theoretical foundation for it (Mancini 1948; Baffi 1965; Faucci 1975; Gattei and Dondi 1990; Fratianni and Spinelli 1991; Della Torre 2008; Toniolo 2022; Pavanelli 1993; Roselli 2001, 2014, 2017).

The main forum for debate was the newly established National Institute of Corporatist Finance (NICF). The NICF, headquartered in the Rome offices of the Bank of Italy, began operations on October 1, 1941. The decision to finance the war – initially expected to be short – through the circuit of capital increased the role of the Bank of Italy in managing economic policy, although, according to Toniolo, it was not comparable to the role the Bank had played during the First World War (Toniolo 2022, 695). As the Governor Vincenzo Azzolini explained during the inaugural ceremony of the NICF, "In the context of wartime finances, the investigations carried out or promoted by the Institute will aim to establish some of the conditions for the operation of the circuit of capital, upon which today's financial policy must focus" (Azzolini 1941, 223). On the same occasion, Minister Paolo Thaon di Revel clarified the nature of the relationship between financial theory and practice in the Fascist regime, and provided some indications as to the origins of the circuit (Thaon di Revel 1941, 228):

> In the twenty years of the Regime, fascism always gave precedence to practice over theory, to practicality over doctrine. Even in the financial field, the same method was employed. Therefore, as we prepare to execute the Duce's order, it seems that the time has come to draw together the threads of a financial experience that has now spanned nearly two decades and has undergone the test of exceptional events such as the war in Ethiopia and the sanctions, colossal armaments, and the current conflict. I believe there is no doubt about the opportunity to proceed with the assertion of principles that simultaneously represent the result of this twenty-year experience and the guiding norm for the future.

According to the economists of the NICF, the circuit of capital could be conceptualized as a search for a delicate equilibrium, essentially dynamic in nature, between a financial constraint, relating to the best way to procure and maintain extraordinary purchasing power for a state at war without causing undesired inflationary consequences, and a real constraint, relating to the most effective methods for productive capital allocation during wartime (Gattei and Dondi 1990, 360; Della Torre 2008, 488–489). More broadly, as Thaon di Revel affirmed, among the expected contributions of the Institute was the elaboration of "a third Charter of Fascism, chronologically following those of Labor and Education: the Charter of Finance," which "should be a systematic and logical expression of Fascist thought" (Thaon di Revel 1941, 228).

The Institute has an interesting history that deserves brief mention. It originated in a collaboration between the academic world, primarily the Institute of Finance of the University of Pavia – what Sergio Steve called "the workshop" (Steve

1990) – founded by Benvenuto Griziotti in 1929[13] and the Bank of Italy, through Governor Vincenzo Azzolini; and the political world, with Finance Minister Paolo Thaon di Revel, whose friendship with Griziotti dated back to their time as colleagues at the International Institute of Agriculture (Caracciolo 1992, 50–51). The first plans to create a national institute of corporatist finance surfaced in the spring of 1938, driven by Griziotti's initiative[14] to establish a body whose goals had to be set "in the interest of the public finances and the advancement of studies,"[15] thus combining a political purpose with an academic one.

More than three years had elapsed, however, when the Institute finally commenced its operation between October and December 1941, when the first two meetings of its board of directors appointed its executive bodies and advisory board and drafted its activities plan.[16] The basic philosophy of the circuit of capital took as its starting point the evidently exceptional situation of public and private finances during the war. Economic and financial structures appeared to be crucial for winning the war. In Grazioli's words, "In the modern world, in a long-lasting war, it's economic strength that prevails" (Grazioli 1939, 275). And Griziotti Kretschmann, an economist and the wife of Benvenuto Griziotti,[17] argued that "economic resilience and financial security are the best guarantees of a final victory" (Griziotti Kretschmann 1939, 283). The extraordinary demands of war made it necessary for the state to draw on both ordinary production and capital assets. From a financial perspective, they required the use of both future and present savings. Overall, as Thaon di Revel put it, warfare was "a matter of transforming the colossal expenses generated by the war into wealth, albeit fictitious, by mortgaging and monetizing in part the assets corresponding to past savings investments and partly discounting the future income of the nation" (Thaon di Revel 1942a, 204).

Influenced both by Keynesian principles and by German financial policy (Roselli 2001, 272),[18] the initial engine of the circuit was the increase in monetary circulation whereby the state could pay for goods it urgently needed. This increased nominal availability was the central issue that the technique of the circuit of capital was called upon to solve. In fact, as Arena wrote in 1942, "if these monetary availabilities were left in the hands of the public, since production increases much less than monetary income, there would be a dangerous imbalance between the total of monetary incomes and the total of available goods, with inflationary effects from unregulated price increases" (Arena 1942, 381). Inflation would have had devastating economic, political, and social consequences. Inflation was "the crusher of the most deserving social classes, the true backbone of the Nation; . . . the devourer of assets and savings possibilities; . . . a threat to financial stability due to the rising state expenses that follow price increases and require ever-new issues, precisely creating the spiral of inflation; . . . the destruction of the tax system" (Arena 1942, 382).

The main way to halt any inflationary process was to control consumption by rationing and reining in non-military production investment with fiscal measures that reduced the return on capital, such as higher taxes on dividends and capital or the channeling of war profits into the Treasury. Secondly, wage and price controls, applied as early as 1935 through the corporatist system and transformed into a general freeze with Italy's entry into war in 1940. Finally, any form of speculation was targeted as the chief driver of the feared inflationary process. In particular, in addition to the 60% tax on the appreciation of real estate calculated from January 1, 1939, until the moment of sale, enacted in 1940, stock market trading – labeled "the last stronghold of economic liberalism" (Thaon di Revel 1942a, 210) – was hit in October 1941 with a trading surtax of 4%, raised to 5% the following year, and in June 1942 with the reintroduction of mandatory registration of stock certificates (Baffi 1965, 226–228).

All the measures mentioned here aimed at ensuring that the increased monetary purchasing power that the state had to introduce into the system to pay for those essential military goods would not be used in ways contrary to the directives of the Fascist government: "[P]rivate savings must be directly or indirectly channeled, to the greatest extent possible, into State coffers. For this to happen, all escape routes must be closed through a series of measures that prevent savings from being used for purposes other than the fundamental one – lending to the State – which is essential for the country's interest" (Thaon Di Revel 1942a, 98). At the same time, these measures also served to ensure social stability insofar as, for the political and monetary authorities, the wartime effort had to guarantee a "balance of the respective situations of the various social groups regarding the distribution of the cost of the war" (Arena 1942, 379). This was especially important considering the lingering memory of injustice related to the enrichment of small segments of society during the Great War. As the Finance Minister wrote in this context, "[W]ith the fiscal, economic, and social policy pursued by the Fascist government in this war, it is necessary to achieve the goal of eliminating from the memory of the past war the mentality of enrichment due to war" (Thaon di Revel 1942b, 217).

According to the theory, to have a perfectly closed circuit of capital, the monetary surplus generated by the combination of the expansion of monetary circulation, price and wage controls, and the restriction of investment opportunities – what Thaon di Revel called "a monetary mass of wandering or vagabond means" (Thaon di Revel 1942b, 222) – had to flow back into the state's coffers. The greater the amount of monetary circulation recovered by the state, the greater the closure of the circuit and the better the state's ability to ensure the much-desired financial balance. No one thought it would be possible to achieve a complete recovery, and thus a perfect closure. Accordingly, the Bank of Italy suggested thinking of the circuit of capital "not as a method to transform into a circular motion what is actually a long spiral motion," but, rather, as a way "to ensure that at least the curve evolves steadily and that its development is as narrow as possible" (Banca d'Italia 1942, 23; Griziotti 1942, 3).

The forms that this reabsorption of monetary circulation should take were the subject of heated debate, especially regarding the question of whether it should be achieved mainly by resorting to public debt or through increased taxation. Issuance of public debt securities had the undeniable advantage of absorbing monetary surpluses more rapidly compared with new taxation and without provoking a social or political backlash. On the other hand, since purchases of public debt securities at issue were voluntary, it was impossible for the state to predict the amounts that would come in. More serious, according to many economists, was the inherent risk of the public debt becoming unstainable as the war continued. Some observers saw resorting to public debt as a way to "defer the solution" until after the war: peacetime, with the abatement of tension, would be the right time to devise new forms of taxation enabling the state to repay the debts it had incurred during the conflict.

Interestingly, Minister Thaon di Revel was actually in agreement with this perspective, as he believed that taxes were naturally preferable because they represented a definitive recovery of the purchasing power exceptionally granted by the state, without imposing any burdens on the state other than collection expenses. Nevertheless, he ultimately rejected this idea on the grounds that increasing the tax burden beyond a certain limit would end up affecting "not just income but capital" and thus have an impact "on the productive capacity of the market, which should, instead, be boosted and stimulated to the maximum" (Thaon di Revel 1942a, 98). These were, after all, the principles that had guided the work of the NIFC from the outset, despite proposals by Griziotti, which were promptly rejected by the advisory board, to develop schemes for forced loans, extraordinary taxes on wealth increments, or, in general, the imposition of new taxes.[19]

5.5 Conclusion

This chapter investigated the practice and theory of wartime financing in Fascist Italy between 1935 and 1943, examining both the interrelation and any potential discrepancies between the two levels. As highlighted by the debate described in the preceding section, the perfect functioning of the circuit of capital would have required that the initial creation of monetary circulation be reabsorbed by the Treasury through taxation and the issuance of government securities purchased by the private sector. The "closure" of the circuit was "direct" if the expansion of the excess of public spending resulted in the growth of the stock of government bonds held by the public. Conversely, its closure was "indirect" if the monetary base remained in circulation or if it flowed back into the Treasury's coffers through forms of debt monetization by the banking system and the Cassa Depositi e Prestiti, inasmuch as reabsorption of the monetary base was achieved by increasing liquid assets in circulation (postal and bank deposits).

Some studies have found that the indirect circuit worked more or less effectively until 1942–1943 (Mancini 1948, 13–18; Fratianni and Spinelli 1991, 400–409; Toniolo and Ganugi 1992, 123–126). Others, instead, have expressed a more negative view, contending that "the monetary circuit operated rather weakly in Italy – unlike in Britain and Germany – even in the early years of the war" (Confalonieri 1986, 54) and that "the objective of reabsorbing monetary surpluses, neutralizing their effects in terms of increased demand for consumer goods, was achieved only in part, and exclusively in the two years 1940 and 1941" (Pavanelli 1993, 192).

Owing to a quantitative reconstruction of the financing of the Italian public debt in the period 1930–1943, Giuseppe Della Torre has shown that the circuit of capital worked until 1942 (Della Torre 2001). From the beginning, it was essentially an "indirect" circuit, as shown by the share of public debt absorbed by institutional investors. By the end of 1934, the Cassa Depositi e Prestiti (the entity managing postal deposits) alone already absorbed more than 20% of the total Treasury debt, while "institutional investors" (including the Bank of Italy) accounted for 36% of the aggregate. These percentages increased in 1938 to 24.5% and 51%, respectively (Della Torre 2000, 15–16, 2001, 185).

However, as the circuit was "indirect," there was the challenge of keeping the public sufficiently inclined to hold bank deposits rather than cash. The weak link of the circuit was thus represented by the maintenance of public trust in the banking system and, ultimately, in the political destiny of the Fascist state. Bank deposits expanded in the early years of the war, owing to the forced compression of consumption and reduced investment opportunities, but this increase was hardly sufficient: "[T]he overall trend was upward for both banknotes and deposits, but in moments of crisis, there were sudden conversions from deposits to banknotes. The rate of expansion was in the long run higher for banknotes than for deposits" (Baffi 1965, 229). The public, in fact, shifted from deposits to cash: for precautionary reasons, the public tended to accumulate reserves of banknotes, which, in the case of enterprises, were also hoarded to hide illegal profits. The flight from bank deposits was particularly significant in the autumn-winter of 1942–1943. According to Azzolini, this was partly due to the evacuations of cities, which made it advisable for individuals to leave with ample cash reserves, and to fear of restrictive measures, but mainly depended on the lack of reinvestment by enterprises. The Bank of Italy was also convinced that one of the main causes was a shortage of bank lending, which was blocking the recirculation of liquidity. This created tensions and misunderstandings between the central bank and the major banks (Toniolo 2022, 701–702). Whatever the cause may have been, the shift from deposits to cash constituted the weak link in the circuit and hindered bank lending (Roselli 2017, 149). Purchases of government securities by institutional investors began to contract already in 1940 and their place was taken by monetary financing by the Bank of Italy. Between 1940 and 1942, the latter increased from 11% to 20% of the total Treasury debt and then surged in the following two years, reaching 60% in 1944. Over the period 1938–1945, the balance sheet of the central bank ballooned from 26.1 billion lire in 1938 to 504.7 billion in 1945, an increase of over 19 times (Della Torre 2001, 185). The most dynamic asset items were advances to the Treasury (growing 38 times), CSVI rediscounting, through which war contracts were financed (76 times), and the portfolio of government securities (53 times). At the end of the war, the Bank of Italy's exposure to the Treasury was equal to more than 95% of its balance sheet (Roselli 2017, 142).

The "circuit of capital" demonstrated its wartime resilience almost until the end of 1942, when the increasing expansion in public spending, widening the gap between expenditure and the fiscal reabsorption of purchasing power, accentuated the state's recourse to the central bank (Mancini 1948). Between 1942 and 1943, military defeats in North Africa and Russia, the fall of Fascism, and the political fragmentation of Italy's territory led to a collapse of the monetary situation. The crisis of the circuit of capital erupted in 1943, with a 138% increase in circulation and a 50% rise in prices. Following the circuit's final breakdown, a purely inflationary approach to war finance was adopted, as evidenced by the circulation/bank deposits ratio, which was 37% in 1939 and exceeded 108% by the end of 1944 (Roselli 2017, 149–150).

In conclusion, the debate surrounding the efficiency of the monetary circuit underscores the complexity of keeping inflationary pressures under control during the war. While some studies suggest the indirect circuit functioned adequately until 1942, others paint a more contradictory picture, focusing on its inherent effectiveness, particularly in comparison to other wartime economies. Giuseppe Della Torre's quantitative analysis provides insights into the functioning of the circuit of capital, emphasizing the challenge of sustaining public confidence in the banking system amid increasing demand for cash. The escalation of military expenditure and subsequent reliance on the central bank marked the circuit's breakdown by 1943, precipitating a severe monetary crisis and inflationary spiral. Ultimately, the examination of wartime financing in Fascist Italy from 1935 to 1943 exemplifies the complex interplay between economic policy, military exigencies, and political instability, shedding light on the management of the economy during wartime – a topic that, unfortunately, is still relevant today.

Sources

Archivio Storico della Banca d'Italia (ASBI), Banca d'Italia, Direttorio Azzolini
Archivio Storico della Banca d'Italia (ASBI), Banca d'Italia, Studi
Archivio Storico Banca d'Italia (ASBI), Carte Baffi, Servizio studi

Notes

1 The reference here is to all three issuing banks (Bank of Italy, Bank of Naples, and Bank of Sicily), among which the Bank of Italy had absolute predominance in terms of its size and its exclusive power to conduct monetary policy.
2 For details on autarkic plans, see Bertilorenzi, Cerretano, and Perugini (2022).
3 Azzolini's report to the Welfare and Credit Corporation, 20 September 1938, in ASBI (Archivio Storico della Banca d'Italia), Banca d'Italia, Direttorio Azzolini, folder 90, file 11, document no. 2.
4 Finanziamento di piani autarchici in Germania, anonymous note, undated, in ASBI, Banca d'Italia, Direttorio Azzolini, folder 90, file 6.
5 Letter from A. Cimino to V. Azzolini, October 11, 1937, in ASBI, Banca d'Italia, Direttorio-Azzolini, folder 90.
6 G. Di Nardi, Il finanziamento dei piani autarchici, in ASBI, Banca d'Italia, Direttorio-Azzolini, cart. 90, fasc. 6, 1938.
7 G. Di Nardi, Il finanziamento dei piani autarchici, in ASBI, Banca d'Italia, Direttorio-Azzolini, cart. 90, fasc. 6, 1938.
8 According to Ristuccia, when considering the military procurement financed by the CSVI, we should also add to the special operations 1,153 million lire in 1939 and 637.5 million lire in 1940. Royal Decree No. 1873 of 15 November 1938, authorized the CSVI to discount the credit certificates issued by the Ministry of the Navy to its industrial suppliers. These figures were recorded in the Bank of Italy's accounts as "operazioni ordinarie con il CSVI" (ordinary operations with the CSVI), and not as "operazioni speciali con il CSVI" (special operations with the CSVI). See Ristuccia (1998, 36–37). For further details on the CSVI, refer to Cianci (1977) and Astore and Perugini (2024); and for details on the naval credit and the role of the CSVI, see Giulianelli (2017).
9 Following Della Torre's reconstruction, these include Cassa Depositi e Prestiti and the institutes it administered, the major public banks, the National Social Security Institute

(INPS), the National Workplace Accident Insurance Institute (INAIL), the National Insurance Institute (INA), the Bank of Italy, and the banking system (Della Torre 2001, 183).

10 Institutionalized public debt refers to the debt held by the public sector and the central bank. Confalonieri (Confalonieri 1952, 276) estimates that of the total public debt at the end of 1939 12.1% was held by credit institutions, 20.3% by the Cassa Depositi e Prestiti, and 6.4% by the Bank of Italy.

11 With the enactment of Royal Decree-Law No. 273 on June 15, 1936, free trade in wheat was terminated. The introduction of obligatory stockpiles for agricultural products (wheat initially, and other agricultural products starting in 1939) aimed at keeping prices low for these commodities, particularly bread. Farmers had to store their harvests in designated warehouses, receiving monetary compensation in return. Storage entities sought financing from the banking system, which provided credit through commercial bills backed by real collateral – namely, the agricultural products stockpiled in the warehouses. Owing to the distinctive nature of the collateral, these bills became known as "Carta ammassi" (Stockpile Paper). Subsequently, banks could present them for discounting at the Bank of Italy (Strangio 2012).

12 For details on Vanoni's contribution to the design of the circuit of capital, see Della Torre (2008).

13 While the Institute of Finance of the University of Pavia served as the engine and the center of the initiative, other university departments soon joined, such as the Royal Higher Institute of Economics and Commerce of the University of Venice, directed by Agostino Lanzillo, and the Institute of Finance of the University of Trieste. The process took up the entire year of 1939. See the following documents: Letter from Griziotti to Azzolini, February 19, 1939; Letter from Azzolini to Griziotti, April 26, 1939; Letter from Griziotti to Azzolini, May 27, 1939; Letter from Azzolini to Griziotti, June 1, 1939; and Letter from Griziotti to Azzolini, June 4, 1939, all in ASBI, Direttorio Azzolini, Pratica 25, folder 3. In the end, the academic founders of the Institute numbered twelve. See minutes of the second meeting of the Board of Directors of the National Institute of Corporatist Finance, December 29, 1941, in ASBI, Studi, Pratica 307, folder 3.

14 See the following documents: Letter from Azzolini to Griziotti, May 18, 1938; Letter from Griziotti to Azzolini, June 4, 1938; Letter from Griziotti to Azzolini, July 9, 1938; Letter from Griziotti to Azzolini, September 3, 1938; and Letter from Griziotti to Thaon di Revel, December 16, 1938, all in ASBI, Direttorio Azzolini, Pratica 25, folder 3.

15 Letter from Griziotti to Thaon di Revel, December 16, 1938.

16 Vincenzo Azzolini was appointed director and Celestino Arena general secretary. The advisory board was composed of Bruno Tenti (a general director of the Ministry of Finance), Benvenuto Griziotti, Gino Borgatta, Francesco Coppola d'Anna, and Celestino Arena. See Minutes of the 1st Session of the Board of Directors of the National Institute of Corporatist Finance, October 6, 1941; and Minutes of the 2nd Session of the Board of Directors of the National Institute of Corporatist Finance, December 29, 1941, in ASBI, Studi, Pratica 307, folder 3.

17 For the biography of Jenny Griziotti Kretschmann, see Parisi (2007).

18 For a comparison of the Italian, British, and German experiences of war finance, see Roselli (2014)

19 For more details, see the minutes of the meetings held on January 16 and then on March 4 and 5, 1942, in ASBI, Studi, Pratica 307, folder 3.

References

Arena, Celestino. "La politica finanziaria e la guerra." *Civiltà Fascista*, no. 6 (April 1942), p. 381.

Astore, Marianna. "Beneduce, l'Ince e l'evoluzione della politica valutaria italiana da Caporetto all'autarchia." *Imprese e Storia* 41–2 (2014), pp. 35–58.

Astore, Marianna, and Michele Fratianni. "'We Can't Pay': How Italy Dealt with War Debts after World War I." *Financial History Review* 26, no. 2 (2019), pp. 197–222. doi: 10.1017/S0968565019000039.
Astore, Marianna, and Mario Perugini. "La Banca d'Italia nel periodo fascista tra gruppi d'interesse e intervento industriale." *Studi storici*, no. 1 (2024), pp. 55–77.
Azzolini, Vincenzo. "L'Istituto Nazionale di Finanza Corporativa. Il programma." *Rivista di diritto finanziario e scienza delle finanze* V, part I (1941).
Baffi, Paolo. "L'evoluzione monetaria in Italia dall'economia di guerra alla convertibilità (1935–1958)." In *Studi sulla moneta*. Milan: Giuffrè, 1965, pp. 225–316.
Baffigi, Alberto. *Il PIL per la storia d'Italia: Istruzioni per l'uso*. Venice: Marsilio, 2015, pp. 210–211.
Banca d'Italia. *Adunanza generale ordinaria degli azionisti tenuta in Roma il giorno 30 marzo 1935-XIII*. Rome: Tipografia della Banca d'Italia, 1935.
Banca d'Italia. *Adunanza generale ordinaria degli azionisti tenuta in Roma il giorno 31 marzo 1937*. Rome: Tipografia della Banca d'Italia, 1937.
Banca d'Italia. *Adunanza generale ordinaria degli azionisti tenuta in Roma il giorno 30 marzo 1942*. Rome: Tipografia della Banca d'Italia, 1942.
Banca d'Italia. *I bilanci degli istituti di emissione 1894–1990*. Roma-Bari: Laterza, 1993.
Bertilorenzi, Marco, Valerio Cerretano, and Mario Perugini. "Between Constraints and Opportunities: Big Italian Business and Autarky, 1934–1943." *Rivista di storia economica/Italian Review of Economic History* 3 (2022), pp. 303–336. doi: 10.1410/104414.
Broadberry, Stephen, and Mark Harrison. "The Economics of World War I: an overview." In *The Economics of World War I*, edited by S. Broadberry and M. Harrison. Cambridge: Cambridge University Press, 2005.
Caracciolo, Alberto. "Introduzione." In *La Banca d'Italia tra l'autarchia e la guerra, 1936–1945*, edited by A. Caracciolo. Rome-Bari: Laterza, 1992.
Cianci, Ernesto. *Nascita dello Stato imprenditore in Italia*. Milan: Mursia, 1977.
Confalonieri, Antonio. "Aspetti della politica del debito pubblico." *Moneta e Credito* V, no. 19–20 (1952).
Confalonieri, Antonio. "La politica del debito pubblico in Italia e in alcuni paesi europei, 1919–1943." In *La politica del debito pubblico in Italia 1919–1943*, edited by A. Confalonieri and E. Gatti, vol. I. Milan-Rome-Bari: Cariplo–Laterza, 1986.
Cotula, Franco, and Luigi Spaventa (eds.). *La politica monetaria tra le due guerre, 1919–1935*. Rome-Bari: Laterza, 1993.
Della Torre, Giuseppe. "La finanza di guerra e il 'circuito dei capitali' in Italia, 1935–1943: una valutazione quantitativa." *Quaderni. Università degli Studi di Siena. Dipartimento di economia politica*, no. 301 (2000).
Della Torre, Giuseppe. "La finanza di guerra e il 'circuito dei capitali' in Italia, 1935–1943: una valutazione quantitativa." *Rivista di storia economica/Italian Review of Economic History*, no. 2 (2001), pp. 173–200. https://doi.org/10.1410/9907.
Della Torre, Giuseppe. "Una nota su Ezio Vanoni, l' "officina" Griziotti e l'Istituto nazionale della finanza corporativa, 1937–1943." In *Ezio Vanoni tra economia, politica, cultura e finanza. Atti del Convegno nazionale di studi, Salerno-Amalfi, 11–12 ottobre 2006*, edited by D. Ivone. Naples: Editoriale Scientifica, 2008.
Einaudi, Luigi. *La guerra e il sistema tributario italiano*. Bari: Laterza, 1927.
Faucci, Riccardo. "Appunti sulle istituzioni economiche del tardo fascismo, 1935–1943." *Quaderni storici* 10, no. 29–30 (1975), pp. 607–630.
Fratianni, Michele, and Franco Spinelli. *Storia monetaria d'Italia. L'evoluzione del sistema monetario e bancario*. Milan: Mondadori, 1991.
Gagliardi, Alessio. *L'impossibile autarchia. La politica economica del fascismo e il Ministero scambi e valute*. Soveria Mannelli: Rubbettino, 2006.
Gattei, Giorgio, and Annalisa Dondi. "La teoria della 'economia di guerra' in Italia (1939–1943)". *Quaderni di storia dell'economia politica* 8, no. 2/3 (1990), p. 360.

Gelsomino, Cosma O. "La politica monetaria italiana tra il 1936 e la fine della Seconda guerra mondiale." In *La Banca d'Italia tra l'autarchia e la guerra, 1936–1945*, edited by A. Caracciolo. Rome-Bari: Laterza, 1992, pp. 103–142.
Gigliobianco, Alfredo. "La Sezione speciale autonoma del Consorzio sovvenzioni per valori industriali." In *La Banca d'Italia e il sistema bancario 1919–1936*, edited by G. Guarino and G. Toniolo, Collana Storica della Banca d'Italia, Serie Documenti, vol. VII. Rome-Bari: Laterza, 1993.
Giulianelli, Roberto. *Armatori, banche e Stato. Il credito navale in Italia dall'Unità alla prima crisi petrolifera*. Bologna: il Mulino, 2017.
Grazioli, Francesco Saverio, "Prospettive economiche e finanziarie della guerra nella recente letteratura straniera." *Rivista di diritto finanziario e scienza delle finanze* III, part I (1939).
Griziotti, Benvenuto. "Controinflazione e circuito dei capitali." *Rivista di diritto finanziario e scienza delle finanze* VI, part I (1942).
Griziotti Kretschmann, Jenny "Aspetti economici e finanziari della guerra." *Rivista di diritto finanziario e scienza delle finanze* III, part I (1939).
Guarneri, Felice. *Battaglie economiche tra le due grandi guerre, vol. I, 1918–1935*. Milan: Garzanti, 1953.
James, Harold. "The Reichsbank, 1876–1945." In *Fifty Years of the Deutsche Mark*, edited by D. Bundesbank. Oxford: Oxford University Press, 1999.
Mancini, Marcello. "Il mercato monetario, il finanziamento del Tesoro e gli impieghi bancari per rami di attività economica." *Moneta e Credito*, no. 1 (1948).
Minniti, Fortunato. "Il problema degli armamenti nella preparazione militare italiana dal 1935 al 1943." *Storia contemporanea*, no. 1 (1978).
Parisi, Daniela. "Una lunga vita da economista. L'itinerario biografico e scientifico di Jenny Kretschmann Griziotti (1884–1980)". *Il Politico*, no. 2 (2007).
Pavanelli, Giovanni. "Note sul 'circuito monetario' e finanza di guerra nel dibattito economico italiano (1940–43)." *Società e storia*, no. 59 (1993).
Petri, Rolf. *Storia economica d'Italia*. Bologna: il Mulino, 2002.
Raitano, Gabriella. "I provvedimenti sui cambi in Italia nel periodo 1919–36." In *Ricerche per la storia della Banca d'Italia*, vol. VI. Rome-Bari: Laterza, 1995.
Repaci, Francesco Antonio. *La finanza pubblica italiana nel secolo 1861–1960*. Bologna: Zanichelli, 1962.
Ristuccia, Cristiano. *The Italian economy under fascism: 1934–1943, the rearmament paradox*. DPhil Dissertation, University of Oxford, 1998.
Roselli, Alessandro. *Il governatore Azzolini*. Rome-Bari: Laterza, 2001.
Roselli, Alessandro. "Gli economisti e il finanziamento della seconda guerra mondiale: ideologie politiche e dottrine economiche." *Rivista di storia economica*, no. 1 (2014), pp. 71–90.
Roselli, Alessandro. "L'Italia e il finanziamento delle due guerre mondiali." In *Economia e Diritto in Italia durante il fascismo: Approfondimenti, biografie, nuovi percorsi di ricerca*, edited by P. Barucci, P. Bini, and L. Conigliello. Firenze: Firenze University Press, 2017. https://books.fupress.com/catalogue/economia-e-diritto-in-italia-durante-il-fascismo/3369
Salvemini, Giancarlo, and Vera Zamagni. "Finanza pubblica e indebitamento tra le due guerre mondiali: il finanziamento del settore statale." In Banca d'Italia, *Ricerche per la Storia della Banca d'Italia. Problemi di finanza pubblica tra le due guerre*, 1919–1939, vol. II. Bari: Laterza 1998.
Schacht, Hjalmar. *My First Seventy-six Years*. London: Allan Wingate, 1955.
Steve, Sergio. "L''Officina' di Benvenuto Griziotti." *Rivista di diritto finanziario e di scienza delle finanze* 49, no. 4 (1990), p. 47.
Strangio, Donatella. "La politica degli ammassi del grano e la sistemazione degli oneri a carico dello Stato italiano nel secondo dopoguerra." *Rivista di storia economica/Italian Review of Economic History* 3 (2012), pp. 453–486. https://doi.org/10.1410/38526.

Tattara, Giuseppe. "La persistenza dello squilibrio dei conti con l'estero dell'Italia negli anni Trenta." In *Ricerche per la storia della Banca d'Italia, vol. III, Finanza internazionale, vincolo esterno e cambi, 1919–1939*. Rome-Bari: Laterza, 1993.

Thaon di Revel, Paolo. "L'Istituto Nazionale di Finanza Corporativa. Il programma." *Rivista di diritto finanziario e scienza delle finanze* V, part I (1941).

Thaon di Revel, Paolo. "La finanza di guerra." *Rivista italiana di scienze economiche* XIV, no. 3 (March 1942a).

Thaon di Revel, Paolo. "Brevi note sul circuito dei capitali." *Rivista di diritto finanziario e scienza delle finanze* VI, part I (1942b).

Toniolo, Gianni. *Storia della Banca d'Italia*, tomo I. *Formazione ed evoluzione di una banca centrale, 1893–1943*. Bologna: il Mulino, 2022.

Toniolo, Gianni, and Piero Ganugi. "Il debito pubblico italiano in prospettiva secolare, 1876–1947." In *Il disavanzo pubblico in Italia: natura strutturale e politiche di rientro*, edited by Ente per gli studi monetari, bancari e finanziari Luigi Einaudi. Bologna: il Mulino, 1992.

Vanoni, Ezio. "Primi indirizzi della finanza di guerra in Italia." *Rivista di diritto finanziario e scienza delle finanze*, no. 4 (1940).

Zamagni, Vera. "Italy: How to Lose the War and Win the Peace." In *The Economics of World War II: Six Great Powers in International Comparison*, edited by M. Harrison. Cambridge: Cambridge University Press, 1998a.

Zamagni, Vera. "Il debito pubblico italiano 1861–1946: ricostruzione della serie storica." *Rivista di storia economica*, no. 3 (1998b).

Zani, Luciano. *Fascismo, autarchia, commercio estero. Felice Guarneri un tecnocrate al servizio dello "Stato nuovo"*. Bologna: il Mulino, 1988.

6 Banca Commerciale Italiana and the re-establishment of Italy's international economic relations after the sanctions, 1936–1940

Federico Castelli

6.1 Introduction

This chapter emphasises the international outreach of the Italian banking system during the interwar period. The focus of this contribution will be on the Banca Commerciale Italiana (Comit) foreign network, which was the most extensive worldwide as compared to Banco di Roma and Credito Italiano (Credit), with a focus on its branches in London and New York, between 1936 and 1940. These three former universal banks[1] played a crucial role in fostering Italy's economic growth during the late nineteenth and early twentieth centuries. They provided essential funding for key sectors of the Italian industry, including shipbuilding, steel, telecommunications, petrochemicals, electricity, and textiles (Brambilla 2011; Confalonieri 1994; De Rosa 1982). Comit's foreign network outperformed that of the other two banks, as it was more embedded in the international financial circuits since it was present in South America with its affiliated banks,[2] but above all in London, where Banco di Roma did not have its own branch, and in New York, where Credit only had a representative office. Furthermore, the chosen timeframe is intended to offer new and preliminary insights into the impact of the implementation of economic and financial sanctions by the League of Nations on the Italian banking sector, through the perspective of a multinational bank (Brambilla 2002, 437–448). In November 1935, Italy declared war on the Ethiopian Kingdom, despite both nations being members of the League of Nations, an international organisation led by the United Kingdom and France. Trade restrictions were imposed on the export and import of goods, particularly military equipment, and munitions, to and from Italy. Notably, Germany and the United States refrained from participating in the sanctions, the latter due to its non-membership of the League. Moreover, the discounting of bills of exchange in London on behalf of Italian banks was hindered, thereby obstructing the potential for short-term financing in trade between Italy and other nations (Arnold 2016; Strang 2013; Clavin 2013; Hufbauer et al. 1990; Ristuccia 2000). This contribution aims to unravel the intermediary role of Comit's London branch through its director, Carlo Lovioz, in keeping export and import flows open from and to Italy. In addition, this study will assess to what extent Comit, through its network of domestic and foreign subsidiaries, has granted loans to Italian shipping companies to purchase merchant vessels, vital for the carriage

DOI: 10.4324/9781032656199-7

of goods and raw materials. In this context, the archival sources kept in the historical archive of Intesa Sanpaolo will be employed. This inquiry will involve an examination of the collections of correspondence between the managing director of the Comit, Raffaele Mattioli, and Lovioz. In addition, this chapter will analyse the minutes of the Head Office Committee (*Comitato della Direzione Centrale*), as these documents provide insight into determining the extent of credits given to support one of the key sectors of the Italian economy (of 'national interest'), namely, the shipping and shipbuilding industry.

Following the Crisis of 1929 and the subsequent banking crisis that severely hit Europe in 1931, which had profound repercussions on the European financial sector, the Fascist government of Italy intervened to bail out the three Italian universal banks, including Comit. These banks experienced widespread deposit withdrawals, intensifying an already precarious situation, due to the difficulties arising from the reduction in long-term loans from the United States, which were crucial for the recovery of the war-affected European economy (Cassis 2011; Feinstein et al. 2008; Eichengreen 1996). In conjunction with Comit, Credit and Banco di Roma underwent nationalisation, becoming state-controlled banks through a government holding company, namely, Istituto per la Ricostruzione Industriale (IRI). Raffaele Mattioli, the new Comit managing director, collaborated with the executives of the IRI in the comprehensive reorganisation of the bank. This restructuring initiative encompassed salary reductions, workforce downsizing, and a thorough reassessment of the bank's branch network. Notwithstanding these adjustments, the profit margins derived by Comit from the collection and exchange of foreign hard currencies suffered a substantial decline (Di Quirico 2008, 138), particularly following the decision to anchor in 1931 lira to the Gold Bloc instead of pursuing devaluation in tandem with sterling (Eichengreen 1996, 302). In other words, sterling was a strong currency and through Italian banks, it allowed the financing of Italian trades with other countries via acceptance credits. The exit of sterling from the gold-exchange standard led to the dissolution of the international monetary system (the dollar opted out in 1933), creating currency areas guided by highly industrialised countries, thereby marginalising those under-industrialised states, such as Italy, which could not import goods without settling payments in hard currencies (Di Quirico 2008, 141–142; Storaci 1993, 441–456).

In the two years before the Ethiopian invasion, which led to important changes in European diplomacy and Italy facing sanctions as a 'rogue' state, Mussolini and the Fascist regime elite focused on establishing the IRI. They also worked on drafting a banking law in 1936 to restrict banks from simultaneously providing both long- and short-term financing. Concurrently, preparations for the invasion of Negus Haile Selassie's kingdom were being finalised, increasing the imports of essential raw materials crucial for the logistical and supply requirements of Italian Army forces, particularly crude oil and coal (Ristuccia 2000, 90). Upon the imposition of sanctions by the League of Nations, in November 1935, the Italian banking sector encountered limitations in accessing the financial hubs of London and New York. This restriction extended to the utilisation of acceptances[3] for funding short-term trade. Within a few months – bills of exchange had already started to be no longer accepted from the end of September 1935 – all British clearing banks stopped accepting bills of exchange drawn on London by Italian banks, thereby rescinding their acceptance credits. Even after the removal of sanctions in July 1936 from the London financial market, it was still difficult to find a clearing bank willing to extend an acceptance credit to an Italian bank.

6.2 Comit's role in the normalisation of Anglo-Italian financial relations

The removal of sanctions in July 1936 did not lead to an immediate resumption of Anglo–Italian financial relations. Indeed, the Italian banks in London suffered from the impossibility of redeeming bills of exchange at British banks, which were vital for financing short-term trade. The latter hesitated in reinstating acceptance credits, waiting for the settlement of trade relations between Italy and the United Kingdom. The re-normalisation of trade dealings, even though for a short time, also passed through the meetings and talks of Comit's London manager – alongside Mattioli – the City's banking elite. Carlo Lovioz was born in 1887 in the Swiss town of Biel and, after obtaining his classical diploma at the town's *gymnasium*, he arrived in Genoa while working for a kitchenware manufacturing company (probably as a sales representative). In 1908, he was hired at Calame & Matthey, a company that dealt with the sales of coal and had dealings with Comit.[4] Hired at its London branch in 1912, Lovioz was widely recognised as a valid interlocutor, as testified by the following excerpt from an article in the *Financial Times*: 'Mr Lovioz has contributed to the friendly trading and financial relations between Great Britain and Italy. [he] came to London when his bank was first established here in 1913 [*sic*] and has a profound knowledge of every branch of British banking. His popularity in financial circles in the City testifies to ability and charm of manner'.[5] Lovioz became the director of the branch in 1934 and began active involvement after the lifting of sanctions, coinciding with the reopening of acceptance credits from autumn 1936 to winter 1937. In his discussions with London bank managers, Lovioz had been arguing since the end of August that there was an unexplained delay in the resumption of acceptance credits for Italian banks. Consequently, he sought permission from Mattioli (which he later obtained) to address this concern with Midland's manager, Arthur Jackson, as follows:

> I would like to request your [Mattioli] consent to discuss the matter of credits, maintaining a strictly confidential approach. Specifically, I aim to convey that American banks have shown a more considerate attitude, suggesting that Midland should not expect a request for assistance from B.C.I. [Comit] in case of urgent needs. Furthermore, Midland should not choose to present itself or await clearings from other banks to reinstate credits in favor of another Italian bank. . . . Naturally, I would communicate to Jackson that certain colonial banks have already approved 120-day credit facilities without reservations. . . I have a suspicion that these individuals may be devising another excuse to shield themselves and prolong the reinstatement of Italian credits indefinitely.[6]

The blockade resulted from a disagreement between the Italian and British governments regarding the resumption of trade. Given the regulations of that period, the exporter of the United Kingdom had to pay an Italian bank for goods before they left Italy. Whitehall, however, had forbidden such payments and had stipulated that they should be made to the Bank of England for the Anglo–Italian clearing office. Notably, the only goods that were freely exportable from Italy were those of a perishable nature, such as fresh fruits and vegetables.[7] Furthermore, the Anglo–Italian clearing office was an institution created to settle the commercial exchanges between Italy and the United Kingdom after the introduction of protectionist policies in 1931, which were issued to avoid speculation on the purchase of goods (Tattara 1985, 119–120; de Bromhead et al. 2019). It was established on 10 July 1936, "with a view to ensuring that the sterling derived from Italian exports to the United Kingdom should be used to meet Italian liabilities to the United Kingdom. . . . the sterling received by the Clearing office should be placed to a reserve account pending the conclusion of negotiations with the Italian government" (Parliament, House of Lords 1943). Thus, Whitehall insisted on the repayment of outstanding debts from the pre-sanctions period, while Rome maintained that it could not afford to clear all such debts at once. Therefore, the Fascist government permitted exports from Italy only on the condition of payment in advance of the shipment of goods.[8] The situation in the context of Anglo–Italian trades persisted until November when outstanding Italian debts and all the commercial arrears of both countries began to be settled because of the ongoing negotiations between the two countries. This development ended with the ratification of the new Anglo–Italian clearing agreement on 27 November 1936 – which would have later morphed into the 'Gentlemen's Agreement', in 1937[9] – a symptom of a diplomatic and economic reconciliation between the two countries.[10] In short, the clearing agreement between the United Kingdom and Italy existed in two accounts, a lire account in Italy and a sterling account in the United Kingdom, in which the payments had to be made. In the sterling account were also included the outstanding financial debts and the commercial arrears for the freight exported from Italy before March 1935, between March and November 1935, and during the period of sanctions (Tattara 1985, 132). Therefore, it is not by chance that Lovioz returned to the door of the Martins Bank's[11] foreign branch manager to inquire once more whether his bank and his British colleagues had any news on the restoration of loans to Italian banks, as reported below:

> I inquired whether he was aware of any colleagues who had reinstated loans to Italian banks, mentioning that I had received this information from Italy. He firmly dismissed this possibility for two reasons: firstly, no such request had been made from Italy yet, and secondly, despite positive sentiments, the loans could not be reinstated until the status of our issuing institution had been officially disclosed. He emphasized that the loans had been cancelled previously due to the increasingly precarious situation at that time. In a jovial manner, I then remarked 'if you wait for the Italians to come and knock at the door, you will get grey hair . . .' he told me that, quite recently and influenced by their representative in Paris, he had informally raised the issue with

> his Board. . . . He noted that he had obtained a reassuring evaluation of our financial condition, specifically concerning gold and dividends, from a trustworthy source. He shared this optimistic assessment with his board members and expressed regret that our situation still remained shrouded in mystery.[12]

In early February 1937, Lovioz inquired with Frederick Bunker, the overseas branch manager of Midland Bank, about the delayed resumption of post-sanctions acceptances. Bunker responded, indicating that the reconsideration of re-establishing credit relations in Italy through Comit had been deliberated by the board, prompting him to undertake another journey to Italy for a current assessment to present to the board with the intention of recommencing relations. Afterwards, Mattioli wrote a memorandum on the Italian economic landscape for Bunker, revealing that following Italy's economic alignment with the exchange rate of sterling, prices had indeed increased compared to the 1927 value of the lira but to a lesser extent. Furthermore, two validating factors served as indirect confirmation of the currency's readjustment. First, no hoarding of gold has taken place, though it was legal to detain gold in Italy and deals in gold were not forbidden. Second, the prices of securities with fixed interest, issued both by the State and by industrial concerns, have improved after a small decline immediately after the monetary adjustment and have remained very steady.[13]

Mattioli pointed out that only in 1935 the Italian balance of payments was in deficit due to sanctions. In fact, the net balance in November 1936 had a surplus of 55 million lire (₤). In contrast to Italy's official statistics, the balance of payments in 1936 showed a deficit of ₤497 million, although it was still lower than the preceding year's figure of ₤2,552 million.[14] Therefore, the data provided by Mattioli to Bunker is inaccurate in quantitative terms, yet it proves correct when considering the improvement in the Italian balance of payments in 1936. The second meeting between Lovioz and Bunker, after the latter's return to London, ended positively. The impression Bunker got from his trip was that of «a country that works, that goes about its business without worrying too much about what is happening and what is said abroad».[15] Mattioli's efforts were rewarded as, on 1 March, Bunker conveyed the news that Midland's board had authorised the reinstatement of former credit facilities amounting to £250,000. This allocation could be employed for initiating new lines of credit for goods intended for Italy. Furthermore, as reported by Lovioz: 'Bunker told us that in compliance with previous promises, this was the first credit that Midland Bank restored in Italy'.[16]

Formerly, Lovioz engaged with the foreign manager of Martins Bank, who was aware of Bunker's trip to Italy to re-establish acceptance credits in favour of Comit, for similar purposes.[17] Bolstered by previous discussions with Bunker, he successfully secured the reopening of a credit line amounting to £50,000. Lovioz's awareness of the difficulties in reinstating acceptance credits dates back to September 1936, as he engaged in talks with the Midland's managers. He initiated meetings with both the Midland and Martins Banks' managers, particularly following the introduction of the new Anglo–Italian clearing agreement. Consequently, in early 1937, although the prevailing trend might have leaned towards a recovery of commerce, through acceptances, Comit-London's manager indisputably put pressure on the negotiation process (to some extent trying also to hasten it), recognising from the outset the importance of this financial instrument.[18]

The major London clearing bank, the Midland, demonstrated over compliance in undertaking financial sanctions against Italy, given the reluctance to promptly reinstate acceptance credits to Italian banks once the sanctions had been removed. Moreover, the Midland pre-emptively interrupted acceptances to Italian banks, when the threat of war intensified following Hitler's ultimatum to the Czechoslovak government, demanding the relinquishment of the Sudetenland territory to the Third Reich (Di Nolfo 2015; Bouverie 2019; Zagare and Kilgour 2023). In light of the political alliance between Czechoslovakia and France–United Kingdom, the prospect of a new European conflict loomed, temporarily averted – by only a year – due to Chamberlain's policy of appeasement towards Hitler. Nevertheless, the mere anticipation of war led the Midland's board of directors to opt for the suspension of acceptance credits to Comit (and Credit). Lovioz (with Mattioli's aid) pursued the reinstatement of acceptance credits at the Midland Bank after the crisis and the Munich Conference. Indeed, the Midland only agreed acceptance credits against cash; therefore, there was not a real credit: the drawer of the bill was supposed to have already paid the amount corresponding to the value of the bill before its acceptance. This request also applied to the bills already accepted and those still in force.[19] Therefore, Lovioz made an urgent plea for a review of this decision both on the grounds of general policy and in terms of the particular relations between Comit and the Midland. Bunker himself described Comit as one of his institution's oldest friends (Green 2017). During a meeting with the managing director of the Midland, Lovioz contested the request for cover, asserting that it ran counter to the established practices between the two institutions. Indeed, suspending those credits could have endangered the nearly 30-year bond of mutual trust and esteem between the two banks. Conversely, the Midland's managers highlighted the political nature of their decision, citing the alignment in Mussolini's speeches in Padua and Verona with Hitler's ultimatum to Czechoslovakian Premier Edvard Benes. This thorny situation was settled owing to Mattioli, who wrote a letter to the Midland's chairman, Reginald McKenna, emphasising the urgent need to maintain unimpaired business relations[20] (Farese 2020, 19). Lovioz reiterated his stance in another meeting with McKenna, during which he claimed that "Italy's foreign debts were trifling, and banking credits were altogether moderate and used in an orthodox manner, in accordance with the traditions of the London market and not, as was the case with the huge German credits, for the purpose of creating internal finance and for all sorts of illicit purposes".[21] The chairman acknowledged the Comit claims and acceptance credits were finally re-established at the beginning of November 1938.

Comit-London, bolstered by the director's frequent meetings, became a respected interlocutor within City's banking elite. This contributed to the normalisation of Anglo–Italian financial relations, particularly on the subject of bank acceptances. Concurrently, with the endorsement of the bank's central management in Milan, the branch played a leading role in financing the acquisition of merchant vessels, alongside two other Comit branches, namely Genoa and New York.

6.3 Comit's role in supporting Italy's mercantile fleet

Comit's intervention in financing Italy's shipping industry in the latter half of the 1930s inevitably aligns with the broader theme of Fascist government involvement in the economy, during the 'final season' of the Mussolini's dictatorship. Although the recent economic historiography on fascist economy has broadened the view about state intervention in Italian industrial sectors regarding the ties between Italian industries and the propagandistic slogan of autarky (Bertilorenzi et al. 2022; Cerretano 2022), the perspective has remained on the domestic side of the Italian economy, not considering some international aspects of the banking sector.[22] As previously stated, scholars have focused their efforts on analysing how the Fascist government intervened in the Italian economy, nationalising those sectors crucial for rearmament on the eve of the invasion of the Ethiopian Kingdom. The shipbuilding industry was actively financed by Italy, in the first half of the twentieth century, for the establishment and expansion of a merchant and war fleet (Giulianelli 2016). In the late 1920s, Alberto Beneduce,[23] under Mussolini's orders, ousted the Italian universal banks from their role in financing shipping companies. This move led to the creation of the state-owned Istituto per il Credito Navale (ICN),[24] in 1928, in response to *Il Duce*'s aspirations to restore the prestige of the Italian navy, severely hit by the previous economic policy brought forward by the Minister of the Treasury, Giuseppe Volpi (De Ninno 2017, 129). His economic policy, following Mussolini's directives in setting the lira–sterling exchange rate at 90, led to a deflationary spiral, diminishing export capabilities and imposing constraints on industrial wages. As a result, the shipbuilding sector suffered considerably, experiencing a steep decline in the tonnage of ships launched from 1926 to 1928, falling from 218,000 tons to 58,000 tons (Ciocca Toniolo 1976, 127–131; Giannetti 1993, 446). Furthermore, Beneduce opted to establish the ICN for two further reasons. First, to dismantle the monopoly held by Italian universal banks in financing shipping and shipbuilding companies, thereby enabling access to international markets to finance that sector. Second, Beneduce aimed to stimulate private savings investment in the maritime sector by issuing long-term bonds (Giulianelli 2016, 341–342). In the early thirties, due to the economic and banking crisis that had severely hit the shipbuilding and shipping companies and the Italian universal banks to which the latter were tied, the bailout of the maritime sector was necessary. Initially established to face the banking crisis of 1931 by relieving the mixed banks of their stakes in Italian industries, the IRI evolved into a permanent, state-driven institution by the second half of the 1930s (Castronovo 2012, 28–35; Fausto 2007, 25–26). The institution eventually gained substantial influence over the Italian economy. Between 1933 and 1937, the IRI undertook a restructuring of the maritime sector by establishing a sub-holding to enhance the coordination of maritime traffic and eliminate inefficiencies. In 1936, the existing agreements were revoked, leading to the dissolution of the four major shipping companies (Italia-Flotte Riunite, Lloyd Sabaudo, Tirrenia, and Adriatica di Navigazione). They were replaced by other entities designated as 'of major national interest', under the control of Finmare (Società Finanziaria Marittima), an industrial sub-holding controlled by the IRI. These newly formed entities assumed responsibility for managing all subsidised services, although no new agreements were concluded before 1939[25] (Doria 2011, 341–342; Giulianelli 2015, 176). Overall, the government's support for the Italian shipbuilding sector primarily centred on enhancing the war fleet and producing passenger ships (notably, two ocean liners, Rex and Conte di Savoia, launched between 1928 and 1931). Although the Fascist government gave priority to the army in the ministerial budgetary lines (and to a lesser extent to the air force), as far as the Italian navy was concerned, a large part of the funding was earmarked for the production of new destroyers, oceanic submarines, and corvettes, while the financing and the launching of cargo and passenger ships, through companies controlled by the IRI, was downsized until 1934[26] (Giulianelli 2015, 137; Fragiacomo 2012, 91–93; Mallett 1998, 59–61). In 1939, the ICN exhibited renewed activity – its final resurgence before being dissolved in April 1940 – by extending a loan of ₤161,000,000 to Società Italiana di Armamento (Sidarma) and the Cooperativa Garibaldi (two shipbuilding companies) for the production of ten freight vessels. The state-controlled institution's response aligned with the government's call for an accelerated expansion of the national merchant navy during that period (Giulianelli 2015, 178).

In this context, Comit and its branches, in London, Genoa, and New York also played an active role in giving credit to Italian shipping companies for the purchase of tankers and steamships. After the removal of economic and financial sanctions, in addition to the provision of raw materials, there was also a necessity for mercantile ships to support the logistical transportation of goods (Savoretti 2013, 143). Before their acquisition and utilisation for both military and civilian applications, raw materials required transportation to Italy and its colonies. Considering this necessity, the London branch of Comit extended its endorsement for the purchasing of tankers and steamships, often prepaying portions of the amounts owed by Italian shipping companies. For instance, in July 1937, the private shipping company Nivose Società Anonima di Navigazione bought a steamship for £70,000.[27] The owners of the company negotiated with Comit-London – on behalf of the Naples branch – a guarantee of £28,000, reimbursed within seven months from the rental fees of a vessel in their fleet and through a counter-guarantee of government bonds pledged to the Naples office. In August 1937, Comit's New York branch was authorised by the Head Office in Milan to extend a credit of $96,000 for the purchase of a US steamship, in favour of the private shipping company Garibaldi Società Anonima Cooperativa di Navigazione.[28] In the autumn of the same year, the Consorzio industriali demolitori navi per acquisto di navi estere per demolizione (Cidnave, or Shipbreaking industrial consortium for the purchase of foreign ships for dismantling) contacted Comit to obtain the wherewithal to participate in an auction of 25 US steamships.[29]. For amount of $800,000, Cidnave had already requested (and obtained) from Banco di Napoli a credit of $100,000, and then reached out to Comit's Genoese branch for the remaining part ($600,000). The negotiations ended positively as this latter extended a credit of $300,000, which would have been increased to $600,000 if Cidnave had pledged the entire foreign currency coverage of the initial steamers purchased at the auction. Another example which shows the entanglement between parastatal and private companies dates back to mid-December 1937. Owing to the requests of the state-owned company Azienda Generale Italiana Petroli (General Italian Oil Company) regarding increases in mercantile tonnage, the Venetian office of Compagnia Industrie Marittime & Affini (Cimar, a private shipping company) formally requested Comit-London's aid in acquiring an English tanker with a cargo capacity ranging from 8,000 to 10,000 tons in mid-December 1937,[30] for £60,000. Comit – through its London branch – and Cimar agreed on the advance payment, in cash. This prepayment was contingent upon depositing an equivalent amount in the Anglo–Italian clearing account, along with an additional sum equivalent to 10% of the previously deposited amount. In July 1938, 1 year later the previous guarantee, Comit granted a 1-year-credit of £27,000 for the purchase of a steamship to the Nivose. As a guarantee, Nivose pledged government bonds to the value of ₤1,500,000.[31] In this episode, as evident from the minutes, it is noteworthy that Comit initially extended a credit of £40,000 to Nivose. However, Comit central managers made the necessary adjustments because Nivose did not receive permission from the Ministero per gli Scambi e Valute (Ministry of Trade and Currency), which authorised the purchase of merchant vessels for £27,000. In September of that year, once again in favour of Garibaldi, Comit-London extended another credit of £10,000 (against the total of £25,000) to acquire a US steamer. The repayment was facilitated through the freight income generated by one of Garibaldi's fleet of steamships.[32] In February 1940, just a few months before Italy entered the war, the New York branch of Comit granted a credit of $150,000 to another shipping company, Società Anonima Leonardo Arrivabene-Trasporti Marittimi e Fluviali (Venice).[33] As with prior credits of this nature, the company planned to reimburse the Comit loan using the freight revenues generated by the newly acquired tanker. The entire credit was authorized in advance by Scambi e Valute, to which the company needed to furnish evidence of generated freight, and upon the repayment of the financing, it was obligated to waive the earnings from the tanker's operations in favour of Istituto Nazionale per gli Scambi con l'Estero (INCE). Overall, all the aforementioned transactions received prior approval from Scambi e Valute, because of exchange controls implemented in 1934 to defend the lira from speculative activities and to stop capital outflows from Italy. Any international financial operation required approval from both INCE and Scambi e Valute (Raitano 1995, 323–326; Toniolo 2022, 612–614).

Despite its secondary significance (as it was not a direct loan for purchasing a cargo ship), the following episode is representative of the assistance provided by the Comit branch of Genoa to the shipping company Garibaldi in June 1937. To avoid the seizure of one of its fleet's steamships resulting from a collision with a German ship (which subsequently sank), the Garibaldi Company sought and secured a bank guarantee of 600,000 Reichsmark (₤4,580,400) from Comit's Genoa branch.[34] In December 1937, the latter extended another bank guarantee of £33,000 (₤3,135,000) in favour of Unione Italiana Sicurtà Marittime (an Italian ship insurance company) to release an Italian steamship stranded in German waters due to an accident.[35] Once again in January 1939, in Garibaldi's aid,

Comit-London assisted this company in a shipping accident in Dutch waters.[36] The vessel Montesanto from the aforementioned society was seized by a British shipping company in the Dutch port of Vlissingen after colliding with one of their steamers. The owners of the British company demanded a bank guarantee of £17,500 (£1,557,150) for the release of the Montesanto, to be paid through a Dutch bank. Consequently, Lovioz was directed by Comit's central management to mediate with the two partner banks in the Netherlands, namely, the Rotterdamsche Bankvereeniging and the Amsterdamsche Bank, to facilitate the payment of the 'fine' for the release of the Montesanto. Overall, from 1937 to 1939, Comit played an active role in supporting Italian shipping companies. This involvement also included assisting stranded steamships in foreign waters following accidents with other steamers, enabling their release, and allowing them to proceed to their ports of arrival. This assistance was facilitated through the provision of bank guarantees totalling £9,272,550.

Although the maritime sector had become of national strategic interest and was controlled almost in its entirety by the fascist establishment, it is interesting to make some comparisons between the credits granted by Comit, acquired through its intermediation, and the ones granted by governmental bodies, along with the associated figures (Table 6.1). Certainly, the loan figures between the ICN and Comit are not directly comparable on a quantitative basis. However, if we examine the number of ships launched owing to the ICN and contrast them with those purchased through credits extended by Comit, a remarkable contribution from the latter becomes evident. Indeed, over its 10-year span of activity, the ICN contributed to the construction of 29 ships, encompassing 220,000 of gross register tonnage for both merchant and passenger vessels (including notable ones, such as the Rex and the Conte di Savoia). In contrast, Comit acquired 17 ships within the 3 years under analysis, with 18,000 tonnes.[37] Delving into a more microscopic level (Table 6.2), when comparing the figures of the Italian merchant fleet with the ships acquired through Comit, it is noteworthy that in 3 years from 1936 to 1939, the latter played a substantial role, contributing 10.96% to the growth of merchant vessels (excluding the one purchased on behalf of Società Anonima Leonardo Arrivabene

Table 6.1 ICN and Comit loans to shipping and shipbuilding companies (million lire).

	ICN (bonds on the market)	*Comit (loans)*
1937	356,000,000	21,574,760
1938	314,000,000	3,443,360
1939	312,000,000	1,557,150
1940	–	2,970,000

Sources: Giulianelli, 'Ship financing in Italy', 343; Asi-Bci, VCD. In total, 3.01% of the loans were granted by Comit compared to those extended from ICN.[38]

Table 6.2 Total Italian commercial fleet compared to the number of ships purchased by Comit on behalf of shipping companies.

	Total	*Cargo ships obtained through Comit*
1936	1072	–
1939	1227 (+155)	17 (+17)

Sources: Marco Doria, "I trasporti marittimi, la siderurgia", in *Storia dell'IRI, Volume I. Dalle origini al dopoguerra, 1933–1948*, edited by Valerio Castronovo (Bari-Roma: Laterza 2012, 335). In total, 10.96% of the overall number of vessels that joined the Italian fleet between 1936 and 1939 were obtained through Comit's brokerage.

in February 1940). Compared to the other two banks of 'national interest', Credit and Banco di Roma, the case of Comit's domestic and foreign branches is a unique example in terms of the quantity of ships acquired on behalf of Italian shipping and shipbuilding companies. Although Credit and Banco di Roma were involved in financing the Italian shipping industry through various means such as promissory notes, overdrafts and sureties, it is noteworthy that they did not rely on their foreign subsidiaries in the two primary centres of the global economy to guarantee loans.

6.4 Conclusion

After the devaluation of sterling in September 1931, the overall tendency indic ated a constant reduction in the share of international trade financed through bank acceptances (Accominotti 2012), but not their disappearance. This financial instrument was affected by further damage after its suspension to the detriment of Italian banks in London, because of the economic sanctions imposed by the League of Nations to Italy between October 1935 and July 1936, after its invasion of the Ethiopian Kingdom. Therefore, the manager of the Comit-London branch, Carlo Lovioz, and Comit's managing director, Raffaele Mattioli, directed their efforts to sustain and to reinstate the financing of short-term trade through bank acceptances. In pursuit of this objective, Lovioz began to play an active role in August 1936, leveraging his connections at Midland and Martins Bank[39] and engaging in lobbying efforts to persuade its board of directors to reinstate acceptance credits. Furthermore, Midland Bank showed excessive caution in implementing financial sanctions against Italy, showing reluctance to promptly restore acceptance credits to Italian banks even after the removal of sanctions in July 1936. This financial countermeasure was reinstated in September 1938 – although for one month – as the spectre of war loomed larger, prompted by Hitler's ultimatum to the Czechoslovak government, insisting on the cession of the Sudetenland territory to the Third Reich. Amidst heightened political tensions between European democracies and nazi-fascist dictatorships, the economic and financial sector of Italy was hit by recurrent standstills in trade agreements and blockades in financial operations. Consequently, the presence of a solid and acknowledged figure in the London's economic hub, namely, Carlo Lovioz, aided in normalising the Anglo-Italian financial relations after the sanctions of 1935–1936. Through sustained meetings, negotiations, and, most of all, dialogue with the members of London's banking elite, Lovioz played an important role in keeping open the economic relations between Italy and the United Kingdom, to the benefit of Italian importers and exporters and, indirectly, to the advantage of the fascist dictatorship.

With the nationalisation of a substantial portion of war-related industries, Mussolini and his clerks redirected production towards the rearmament of Italy. Initially, this was aimed to conquer the Kingdom of Ethiopia, then to support Francoist troops in Spain, and since September 1939 to prepare Italy's entry in the Second World War. This overarching framework resulted in the subordination of the fascist economy to the requirements of the Italian army, neglecting the navy and the aviation (Mallett 1998, 59; De Ninno 2017, 229–230). Scrutiny of the correspondence exchanged between the Comit's managing director, Raffaele Mattioli, and the director of the London branch, Carlo Lovioz, alongside examination of the minutes from the *Comitato della Direzione Centrale* (Head Office committee), unveiled the pivotal role played by the bank's international network in financing various Italian shipping companies with necessary funds for the acquisition of merchant vessels, specifically encompassing steamships and oil tankers. Indeed, following the lift of economic sanctions, Italy faced a shortage of raw materials, prompting the necessity of imports, mostly by sea. Therefore, while the primary focus of the government budget was directed to rearmament, the fascist dictatorship found it necessary to allocate efforts in supporting its merchant navy. Consequently, between 1936 and 1939, the number of cargo ships saw a rise of 155, there was an upswing in demand of merchant vessels, and, in 1939, the ICN resumed financing the construction of cargo vessels (Giulianelli 2015, 177–178). In this sense, AGIP also took proactive steps in response by aiming to expand its fleet of oil tankers (Savoretti 2013, 143). In addition, the conquest of Ethiopia necessitated the transportation of both military equipment and civilian supplies from Italy to its colonies. From October 1937 to February 1940, 17 ships were acquired with a cumulative value of £29,545,270 for Cimar, Cidnave, Nivose, Garibaldi, and Leonardo, through Comit's brokerage. Over the course of 2.5 years, merchant vessels and tankers were provided to the Italian commercial fleet and indirectly to the fascist dictatorship. Furthermore, Comit branches also played a proactive role in assisting Italian shipping and insurance companies, facilitating the release of steamers through bank guarantees; therefore, allowing them not to lose the cargo of goods they were carrying.

Overall, this chapter has explored two facets associated with the financing of an economy under dictatorship by a multinational bank through financial markets and its network of branches. Comit actively contributed to the normalisation of financial relations between Britain and Italy after the lift of the economic sanctions.

Moreover, this Bank played a pivotal role in providing financial support to Italian shipping companies – acquiring tankers and merchant vessels – and in helping in cases where one of their steamers faced accidents with other steamships.

Archival sources

Historical archive of Intesa Sanpaolo, heritage of the Banca Commerciale Italiana, fonds:

'Personale, Matricola', file Carlo Lovioz;
'Contabilità della Direzione Centrale', ledger of 1910;
'Carte di Raffaele Mattioli', folders 155, 157, 193;
'Verbali del Comitato della Direzione Centrale', folders 34–36, 39, 41, 45.

Notes

1 They continued operating as universal banks (in short, ordinary, and long-term credit institutions) until the banking law of 1936, in which the fascist authorities prohibited banks from holding shares in companies. See Conti (2011), Berbenni (2021), and Conti and Schisani (2011).
2 Namely, Banque Française et Italienne pour l'Amérique du Sud (jointly with Banque de Paris et de Pays-Bas), Banco Italiano di Lima, and Banco italiano di Guayaquil. See Brambilla, Costa, and Dettoni (2017).
3 For more comprehensive information, see Accominotti, Lucena-Piquero, and Ugolini (2021).
4 Historical archive of Intesa Sanpaolo, heritage of the Banca Commerciale Italiana (henceforth Asi-Bci), 'Personale, Matricola', file Carlo Lovioz; 'Contabilità Direzione Centrale', ledger of 1911.
5 Asi-Bci, 'Carte di Raffaele Mattioli' (hereafter CM), folder 159, file. 2, no. 43/a.
6 Asi-Bci, CM 155, f. 2, n. 12.
7 Asi-Bci, CM 155, f. 2, n. 10/all. 3, article from the *Financial Times*, 19 August 1936.
8 Asi-Bci, CM 155, f. 2, no. 22/all. 4, article from *The Times*, 4 September 1936.
9 The Gentlemen's Agreement, signed on 1 January 1938, was a pact between Great Britain and Italy aimed at reconciling differences in their Middle Eastern policies and ensuring unimpeded passage through Lake Tana and the Suez Canal. Subsequently, it was reaffirmed in the Easter Accords in April of the same year. See "The Anglo-Italian agreement", *Bulletin of International News* 15, no. 8 (1938), 11, http://www.jstor.org/stable/25642244.
10 However, the situation was far from naive, as reported by Gualtieri (2005). Overall, in the 1930s, Italy exhibited firm import demand, coupled with exports that were readily replaceable in the global market. In addition, the deficiencies of the Italian manufacturing sector were evident in the commodity composition of both imports and exports (Tattara 1993; Berbenni 2021).
11 Another clearing bank.
12 Asi-Bci, CM 155, f. 2, n. 49.
13 Asi-Bci, CM 155, f. 3, no. 15/all.
14 Istituto centrale di statistica del Regno d'Italia, *Annuario statistico italiano. Anno 1938 – XVI*, (Roma: Istituto Poligrafico dello Stato, 1938, 130).
15 Asi-Bci, CM 155, f. 3, no. 19.
16 Asi-Bci, CM 155, f. 3, no. 24.
17 Asi-Bci, CM 155, f. 3, no. 14.

18 Acceptance credits were finally re-established in early 1937. The difficulties in their reinstatement are also demonstrated by the decrease in the number of credits issued by Italian banking system between 1936 and 1937, which were £1,150 and £1,080 million lire (Di Quirico 2008, 156 and 162).
19 Asi-Bci, CM 157, f. 3, no. 2/all. 1.
20 Asi-Bci, CM 193, f. 13, no. 2
21 Asi-Bci, CM 157, f. 3, n. 7/all.
22 Few scholars focused on this topic, for instance, Astore (2011), Farese (2009, 92–106), and Gagliardi (2006).
23 Beneduce played a key role in advocating for state intervention in the economy and was the architect behind the establishment of institutes dedicated to funding public works and Italian industries (including the two discussed in this chapter, namely the IRI and the ICN). The distinctive feature and success of these institutes were rooted in the concept of long-term financing facilitated by gathering public savings, with the assurance backed by the issuance of state bonds. See Dell'Orefice (2007, 252–253), Magnani and Franzinelli (2009), and Armani et al. (1985).
24 Alberto Beneduce founded and chaired the ICN, which played a crucial role in supporting the maritime industry between 1928 and 1940. Established in late 1928, the ICN aimed to financially assist shipping companies in building new vessels, thereby fostering the modernisation of the national fleet. Nevertheless, during the latter half of the 1930s, the ICN's contribution to the rejuvenation of the shipping sector waned because of conflicts with the Italian Treasury, the unstable framework of the shipping industry, and ongoing reorganisation processes within the sector. See Giulianelli (2015, 170–171, 178)
25 In 1936, a committee established by IRI annulled the conventions of the shipping companies, placing them into liquidation. Subsequently, four new entities (Italia, Tirrenia, Lloyd Triestino, and Adriatica) assumed control, and it was only in 1939 that they stipulated a new agreement with the Italian government for the provision of maritime transport services.
26 This economic policy towards the shipping industry was undoubtedly influenced by external factors affecting the entire inter-war period, namely the reduction in international trade, as reported in Mellinato (2017).
27 Asi-Bci, 'Verbali del Comitato della Direzione Centrale' (hereafter VCD), volume 35, assembly of the 21/07/1937.
28 Asi-Bci, VCD 35, assembly of the 13/08/1937.
29 Asi-Bci, VCD 36, assembly of 19/10/1937. The headquarters of the consortium was located in Genoa.
30 Ivi, assembly of 14/12/1937.
31 Asi-Bci, VCD 39, assembly of 19/07/1938.
32 Ivi, assembly of 21/09/1938.
33 Asi-Bci, VCD 45, assembly of 13/02/1940.
34 Asi-Bci, VCD 34, assembly of 01/06/1937.
35 Asi-Bci, VCD, vol. 36, assembly of 31/12/1937.
36 Asi-Bci, VCD 41, assembly of the 20/01/1939.
37 The tally only includes ships whose tonnage is explicitly indicated in the documents. In the case of the 12 steamships of Cidnave, precise data are unavailable; therefore, it was deemed inappropriate to include even approximate figures in the count.
38 Comit loans have been converted into lire by utilising the historical series of exchange rates between the lira, dollar, and sterling, as provided on the Bank of Italy website: https://tassidicambio.bancaditalia.it/terzevalute-wf-ui-web/timeSeries.
39 Those relationships dated back to the immediate post-World War I period when the director of Comit-London was Alessandro Joel, son of Otto, one of the founders of the bank (Green 2017; Farese 2019).

Bibliography

Accominotti, Olivier, "London merchant banks, the Central European Panic, and the Sterling crisis of 1931", *The Journal of Economic History* 72, no. 1 (March 2012), 1–43, doi:10.1017/S0022050711002427.

Accominotti, Olivier, Lucena-Piquero, Delio, Ugolini, Stefano, "The origination and distribution of money market instruments: Sterling bills of exchange during the first globalization", *The Economic History Review* 74, no. 4 (November 2021), 892–921, doi:10.1111/ehr.13049.

Armani, Pietro, Cassese, Sabino, Saraceno, Pasquale, Bonelli, Franco, Villari, Lucio, *Alberto Beneduce e i problemi dell'economia italiana del suo tempo. Atti della giornata di studio per la celebrazione del 50° anniversario dell'istituzione dell'IRI: Caserta, 11 novembre 1983*, Roma: Edindustria, 1985.

Arnold, Aaron, "The true cost of financial sanctions", *Survival* 58, no. 3 (June–July 2016), 77–100, doi:10.1080/00396338.2016.1186981.

Astore, Marianna, "Beneduce, l'INCE e l'evoluzione della politica valutaria italiana da Caporetto all'autarchia", *Imprese e Storia* 41–42, nos. 1–2 (January–December 2011), 35–68, doi:10.1400/226559.

Berbenni, Enrico, "External devaluation and trade balance in 1930s Italy", *Structural Change and Economic Dynamics* 57, no. 2 (June 2021), 93–107, doi:10.1016/j.strueco.2021.02.001.

Bertilorenzi, Marco, Cerretano, Valerio, Perugini, Marco, "Between constraints and opportunities: Big Italian business and autarky, 1934–1943", *Rivista di Storia Economica* 38, no. 3 (October 2022), 303–336, doi:10.1410/104414.

Bouverie, Tim, *Appeasement: Chamberlain, Hitler, Churchill, and the Road to War*, New York: Tim Duggan, 2019.

Brambilla, Carlo, "Italian multinational banking: Banca Commerciale Italiana and Credito Italiano between 1930s and 1940s, in *Transnational Companies. 19th−20th Centuries*, edited by Hubert Bonin, 437–448. Paris: Éditions Plage, 2002.

Brambilla, Carlo, "Banche ed economia nazionale (1861–1914), in *Le banche e l'Italia. Crescita economica e società civile 1861–2011*, edited by Leandro Conte, 63–100. Roma: Bancaria Editrice, 2011.

Brambilla, Federica, Costa, Barbara, Dettoni, Maura, *Una vocazione internazionale. Le radici di Intesa Sanpaolo nel mondo (1905–2006*), Milano: Nexo, 2017.

Cassis, Youssef, *Crises & Opportunities. The Shaping of the Modern Finance*, Oxford: Oxford University Press, 2011.

Castronovo, Valerio, "Un profilo d'insieme", in *Storia dell'IRI. Volume I. Dalle origini al dopoguerra, 1933−1948*, edited by Valerio Castronovo, 3−78. Bari−Roma: Laterza, 2012.

Cerretano, Valerio, "Autarky, market creation and innovation: Snia Viscosa and Saici, 1933–1970", *Business History* 64, no. 6 (September 2022), 1110–1130, doi:10.1080/00076791.2020.1750599.

Ciocca, Pierluigi, Toniolo, Gianni, *L'economia dell'Italia fascista*, Bologna: Il Mulino, 1976.

Clavin, Patricia, *Securing the World Economy. The Re-invention of the League of Nations, 1920–1946*, Oxford: Oxford University Press, 2013.

Confalonieri, Antonio *Banche miste e grande industria in Italia 1914–1933. Volume I. Introduzione – L'esperienza della Banca Commerciale Italiana e del Credito Italiano*, Milano: Banca Commerciale Italiana, 1994.

Conti, Giuseppe, "Fallimenti di mercato e fallimenti di regolazione prima della legge bancaria del 1936", *Mercato Concorrenza Regole* 39, no. 3 (December 2011), 521–548, doi:10.1434/35973.

Conti, Giuseppe, Schisani, Maria Carmela, "Crisi di governance e crisi di liquidità. La fine del modello di banca mista nel periodo tra le due guerre", in *L'intervento dello stato nell'economia italiana. Continuità e cambiamenti (1922–1956)*, edited by Alberto Cova e Gianpiero Fumi, 165–191. Milano: FrancoAngeli, 2011.

D'Antone, Leandra, "Da ente transitorio a ente permanente, in *Storia dell'IRI. Dalle origini al dopoguerra, 1933–1948*, edited by Valerio Castronovo, 168–228. Bari-Roma: Laterza, 2012.
de Bromhead Alan, Fernihough, Alan, Lampe, Markus, O'Rourke, Kevin Hjortshøj, "When Britain turned inward", *The American Economic Review* 109, no. 2 (February 2019), 325–352, doi:10.1257/aer.20172020.
De Ninno, Fabio, *Fascisti sul mare. La Marina e gli ammiragli di Mussolini*, Bari-Roma: Laterza, 2017.
De Rosa, Luigi, *Storia del Banco di Roma. Volume I*, Roma: Banco di Roma, 1982.
Dell'Orefice, Anna, "La politica industriale del fascismo", in *L'intervento pubblico e la politica economica fascista*, edited by Domenicantonio Fausto, 201–326. Milano: FrancoAngeli, 2007.
Di Nolfo, Ennio, *Storia delle relazioni internazionali. Dalla pace di Versailles alla conferenza di Postdam, 1919–1945*, Bari-Roma: Laterza, 2015.
Di Quirico, Roberto, *Building on Borrowed Bricks. Italian Banks and International Finance During the Inter-War Period*, Florence: European Press Academic Publishing, 2008.
Doria, Marco, "I trasporti marittimi, la siderurgia", in *Storia dell'IRI. Volume I. Dalle origini al dopoguerra, 1933–1948*, edited by Valerio Castronovo, 329–419. Bari-Roma: Laterza, 2012.
Eichengreen, Barry, *Golden Fetters: The Gold Standard and the Great Depression, 1919–1939*, Oxford: Oxford University Press, 1996.
Farese, Giovanni, *Dare credito all'autarchia: l'IMI di Azzolini e il governo dell'economia negli anni Trenta*, Napoli: Editoriale Scientifica, 2009.
Farese, Giovanni, "Banche, circolazione delle *élites*, organizzazione degli uffici studi. La formazione della cerchia internazionale degli economisti di banca e il ruolo della Comit negli anni Trenta", *Storia e Politica. Annali della Fondazione Ugo La Malfa* 39 (2019), 323–340.
Farese, Giovanni, *Mediobanca e le relazioni economiche internazionali dell'Italia: atlantismo, integrazione europea e sviluppo dell'Africa, 1944–1971*, Milano: Mediobanca, 2020.
Fausto, Domenicantonio, "L'economia del fascismo tra Stato e mercato", In *L'intervento pubblico e la politica economica fascista*, edited by Domenicantonio Fausto, 1–47. Milano: FrancoAngeli, 2007.
Feinstein, Charles H., Temin, Peter, Toniolo, Gianni, *The World Economy Between the World Wars*, Oxford and New York: Oxford University Press, 2008.
Fragiacomo, Paolo, *L'industria come continuazione della politica. La cantieristica italiana 1861–2011*, Milano: FrancoAngeli, 2012.
Gagliardi, Alessio, *L'impossibile autarchia: la politica economica del fascismo e il Ministero Scambi e valute*, Soveria Mannelli: Rubbettino, 2006.
Giannetti, Renato, "I fattori del successo delle costruzioni navali mercantili italiane nel periodo tra le due guerre mondiali: mercato, tecnologia, organizzazione", in *La penisola italiana e il mare. Costruzioni navali, trasporti e commerci tra XV e XX secolo*, edited by Tommaso Fanfani, 443–453. Napoli: Edizioni Scientifiche Italiane, 1993.
Giulianelli, Roberto, "The state and the sea. Economic policy for the shipbuilding and the marine-equipment industry in Italy between the two world wars", *The Journal of European Economic History* 44, no. 1 (April 2015), 151–181, https://www.jeeh.it/articolo?urn=urn:abi:abi:RIV.JOU:2015;1.151&ev=1.
Giulianelli, Roberto, "Ship financing in Italy in the first half of the twentieth century", *The International Journal of Maritime History* 28, no. 2 (May 2016), 335–355, doi:10.1177/0843871416630263.
Green, Edwin, *Calling London. Travels by British Bankers, 1904–63*, Croydon: Threadgold Press, 2017.
Gualtieri, Roberto, "Da Londra a Berlino. Le relazioni economiche internazionali dell'Italia, l'autarchia e il Patto d'acciaio (1933–1940)", *Studi Storici* 46, no. 3 (July–September 2005), 625–659, doi:10.7376/71421.
Hufbauer, Gary Clyde, J. Schott, Jeffrey, Elliott, Kimberly Ann, *Economic Sanctions Reconsidered. History and Current Policy*, Washington, DC: Institute for International Economics, 1990.

Istituto centrale di statistica del Regno d'Italia, *Annuario statistico italiano. Anno 1938–XVI*, Roma: Istituto Poligrafico dello Stato, 1938.
Magnani, Marco, Franzinelli, Mimmo, *Beneduce: Il finanziere di Mussolini*, Milano: Mondadori, 2009.
Mallett, Robert, *The Italian navy and fascist expansionism, 1935–1940*, London: Frank Cass Publishers, 1998.
Mellinato, Giulio, "Il sistema internazionale della mobilità commerciale fra le due guerre: Deglobalizzazione e involuzione", in *Attraverso i conflitti. Neutralità e commercio fra età moderna ed età contemporanea*, edited by Daniele Andreozzi, 111–129. Trieste: Edizioni Università di Trieste, 2017.
Parliament, House of Lords, *Clearing Office (Italy) Amendment Order, 1943* (HL 1943 (129)), London: Hansard, 1943.
Raitano, Gabriella, "I provvedimenti sui cambi in Italia nel periodo 1919–36", in *Ricerche per la storia della Banca d'Italia. Volume VI*, edited by Gian Carlo Falco, Giorgio Fodor, Alberto Monticone, Gabriella Raitano, 265–335. Bari-Roma: Laterza, 1995.
Ristuccia, Cristiano Andrea, "The 1935 Sanctions against Italy: Would coal and oil have made a difference?", *European Review of Economic History* 4, no. 1 (April 2000), 85–110, doi:10.1017/S1361491600000150.
Savoretti, Angelo, "La marina mercantile italiana durante il Ventennio fascista", *Bollettino d'Archivio dell'Ufficio Storico della Marina Militare* 3, no. 4 (December 2013), 129–165, https://www.marina.difesa.it/media-cultura/editoria/bollettino/Pagine/2013_dicembre.aspx.
Storaci, Marina, "L'Italia e il Blocco dell'oro (1933–1935)", in *Finanza internazionale, vincolo esterno e cambi. 1919–1939*, edited by Pier Francesco Asso, Andrea Santorelli, Marina Storaci, Giuseppe Tattara, 441–486. Bari-Roma: Laterza, 1993.
Strang, Bruce (editor), *Collision of Empires. Italy's Invasion of Ethiopia and Its International Impact*, Surrey: Ashgate, 2013.
Tattara, Giuseppe, "An example of countertrade: The Anglo–Italian clearing", *Rivista di Storia Economica* 2, International Issue (January 1985), 115–154.
Tattara, Giuseppe, "La persistenza dello squilibrio dei conti con l'estero", in *Ricerche per la storia della Banca d'Italia, volume III. Finanza internazionale, vincolo esterno e cambi 1919–1939*, edited by Pier Francesco Asso, Andrea Santorelli, Marina Storaci, Giuseppe Tattara, 367–440. Bari-Roma: Laterza, 1993.
The Institute of International Affairs, "The Anglo-Italian agreement", *Bulletin of International News* 15, no. 8 (April 1938), 11–13, http://www.jstor.org/stable/25642244.
Toniolo, Gianni, *Storia della Banca d'Italia. Tomo I. Formazione ed evoluzione di una banca centrale, 1893–1943*, Bologna: Il Mulino, 2022.
Zagare, Frank C., Kilgour, Marc D., "Modeling threats and promises: Explaining the Munich crisis of 1938", *Journal of Peace Research* 60, no. 4 (July 2023), 661–674, doi:10.1177/00223433221089729.

7 Support the devil

The involvement of German banks in the NS politics from the occupation to the final solution

Anna Veronica Pobbe

7.1 Banks and NS regime: profits and interests

More than two decades ago Christopher Simpson reported, in his *The War Crimes of the Deutsche Bank and the Dresden Bank: the OMGUS Report*, how Anglo-American authorities, as early as 1946, had identified such co-dependence between some German banks and the National Socialist regime that they suggested, as the only solution likely to maintain a lasting peace, an immediate liquidation of these banks (Simpson 2002). Soon after Simpson's study was published, several other researches highlighted the link between certain banks and the darkest pages of Nazi policy: Rudolf Herbst and Thomas Weihe published a study on Commerzbank's involvement within the expropriations against Jews (Herbst and Weihe 2004); Klaus Henke highlighted how the Dresdner Bank was one of the institutions most directly involved in financing facilities such as the Auschwitz-Birkenau concentration camp (KL) and extermination camp (Henke 2006); and Ingo Loose conducted a study on German Credit Institutes within the occupied territories in Poland between 1939 and 1945 (Loose 2007). In the scenario outlined by these studies, it is possible to identify a question implied but not always completely evaded by the data presented to us: what prompted German banks to support, sometimes enthusiastically, the projects first of conquest and then of extermination proposed by the National Socialist Party (NSDAP)?

In order to attempt to answer this question, it is necessary, first, to trace the historiographical debate that has attempted to describe the relationship between the business world and the Nazi Party. In Raul Hilberg's narrative of the so-called *Nazi cosmos*, the business world is described as one of the main "bureaucratic galaxies," consisting essentially of managers, bankers, freelancers and executives of large industrial groups; among these it was mainly managers and bankers who supported the NSDAP from the very beginning, in contrast to the executives of large industrial groups, who viewed the proposals of the party led by Hitler with skepticism, at least initially (Hilberg 1999, 61). Exerting an irresistible attractive force for businessmen was, according to Timothy Snyder, the idealization of the war experience into a kind of conquest in the East borrowed on the model of the conquest of the American Wilde West (Snyder 2015, 11–28).

DOI: 10.4324/9781032656199-8

Parallel to the studies on the involvement of banks, some scholars have delved into the issue of *personal enrichment*: in fact, it has been seen how economic theories such as that of the *tabula rasa*, proposed by Helmut Meinhold, served as an ideological basis for practical financial experiments in the occupied territories as early as 1939 (Aly and Heim 2002, 143); or, as argued by Frank Bajohr, precisely personal enrichment was a non-unique factor, thus acting sometimes as an accelerator, others as an inhibitor of certain practices (even genocidal ones) (Bajohr 2005, 119–125). But how could this *hunger* for personal enrichment be combined with the economic ideology proper to Nazism, which was based on the exaltation of national interest, at the expense of personal interest, and which defined "finance and economics as mere instruments within the battle for the survival of the German people?" (Overy 2012, 51). The answer to this question lies in the evolution that the concept of profit underwent precisely within the Nazi economic context. . . .

The topic of profit was, in fact, for years branded as uninteresting by economic historians, as it was considered worthless within the Nazi legislative universe (Spoerer 2000, 53): one of the earliest attestations concerning this definition is by Arthur Schweitzer who, as early as 1946, described how the effects of profit in the general German economy were replaced by the Nazis with the government's economic plans, through what was officially called the policy of *profit fixing* (Schweitzer 1946). Opposed to this view is the reading proposed by historian Dietrich Eichholtz who, in his monumental work *Geschichte der deutschen Kriegswirtschaft* (Corni 1998), recognized the union of interests between financial capital and the state (Corni 2017). The latter interpretation has suffered from the general devaluation suffered by the historiography of the former GDR (Corni 1998, 336); so much so that, despite the fact that Eichholtz had already pointed out how economic and political interests interacted not without deep internal rifts, and a decisive factor was the enormous possibilities for expansion that military conquests offered to private German companies and banks, still in the 1990s historian Richard Overy supported the position expressed years earlier by Schweitzer, calling the control of profits carried out by the party very tight and, for this reason, highly compromising towards the freedom of action of businessmen (Overy 1994). But it was at the turn of the old and the new millennium that historian Mark Spoerer, through an analysis of data on the profits of joint stock companies, countered the now-established view of profit in the Nazi context by asking, "but if that was really the case, why did the stock market grow in such a way that the Nazis felt compelled to actually close the stock exchanges in early 1943 (Spoerer 1996)?" Indeed, Spoerer's thesis presents profit as an *incentive* used by the Nazis towards the managerial and industrial world so as to achieve the change in the German industrial structure necessary to achieve the political goals set by the party. Despite the substantial differences that exist between an economic system placed in peacetime and the wartime economy, Spoerer is not alone in arguing a thesis based essentially on the Nazi regime's *fascination* with managers and industrialists (Kater 1983, 129).

The "carrot-and-stick" theory, used until the end of the last century to describe the relationship between the regime and business, is contradicted, again according to Spoerer, by the booming profits of private firms, which the Nazis made no attempt whatsoever to block. What ensued was thus not a downsizing of profit, which retained its distributive function, but a change in risk that moved from a microeconomic level (competition) to a macroeconomic level (possibility of expropriations) (Spoerer 1996, 218–219). In this sense, businessmen (including bankers) were able to transform a series of ethical problems, such as the exploitation of Jewish labor, into a series of business-oriented problems, where morality and ethics (which are not economic parameters) were expressed in terms of calculating risk (Loose 2013, 89).

7.2 The development of an enrichment system

If, from the ideological point of view, the promise of profit was thus the main vehicle that allowed an alignment between the interests of the banks and those of the Party; from the practical point of view, starting in 1938, the Nazi regime implemented a series of reforms so that the profits, especially from expropriation operations, were obtained in the shortest possible time. This practice became particularly evident if one analyzes, as an exemplum, the case relating to the Polish territories occupied from 1939 onwards, which in part were directly annexed to the Third Reich and in part were placed under the management of the General Government. In fact, "immediately after German troops occupied Poland, before a new regime was established, local military commanders and civilian administrators ration issued the first orders to register the property of Jews and Poles in preparation for eventual confiscation . . . the property of Jews, in particular, was considered to be free for the taking" (Bräu 2016, 431). Precisely within these territories the regime, in attempting to match economic interest and war aims, moved within a three-way direction.

The first way concerned *method*: as far as the occupied territories from 1939 onward were concerned, expropriations were implemented according to the "Austrian model" (also referred to as the "Viennese model") used during the *Anschluss*, which was designed as a response to the period of "unrestrained Aryanization" (wilde Arisierung) that involved Austrian society immediately after annexation (Goschler 2013, 195). This model involved a division of labor within the Nazi hierarchy: one part of the personnel assigned to these operations was in fact engaged in devising legal avenues through which to implement the expropriation of property from Jews (and others), while another part of the personnel was concerned exclusively with forced emigration (Goschler 2013). For the Nazis, Austria became a test case for the administration of the territories to the east, owing largely to the acceleration that expropriation practices underwent; in particular, the theft of Jewish property, which developed over years in Germany, was completed within months on Austrian soil (Simpson 1993). But despite the implementation of this model, the Nazi government was unable to fully control the dynamics related to expropriation processes and, from time to time, was forced to issue retroactive sanctions against local initiatives already in place (Simpson 1993; Bajohr 1997).

The second guideline is related to the institutions and professionals involved in the expropriation process: if, again, we look at the scenario given by the occupied territories, it is possible to see how, in the case of the Warthegau region (Western Poland), there is the presence of offices such as the *Haupttreuhandstelle Ost* in Posen (the regional capital) (Bräu 2016, 432), which worked with such diligence and speed that, according to the study conducted by Jeanne Dingell, the value that the embezzlement operation carried out by the Nazis in the territory in question had reached RM 500 million, the latter figure referring only to the first months of the war (September–December 1939) (Dingell 2003, 124; Pobbe 2023a, 991).

Finally, a third, but no less important way within the discourse being presented here, is that of the financial instruments that facilitated the link between economic and party interests. Within the R2 (Ministry of Economics and Finance) archival fond at the Bundesarchiv Lichterfelde in Berlin, there is a document that identifies the Wehrmacht as the beneficiary of a loan of as much as RM 50 million a few days after the start of the invasion operations of Polish territories.[1] At the same time as issuing cash for the armed forces, the major German credit banks opened branches in almost all occupied territories as early as the late fall of 1939: "Polish banks were expropriated and liquidated or taken over by German banks. The Germans imposed mandatory exchange rate of 2 zloty: 1 Reichsmark. Poles were allowed to exchange a maximum of RM 250; the Germans seized all cash assets beyond that limit. Prices and wages in the affiliated eastern territories were set by administrative fiat" (Bräu 2016, 433).

Apparently, therefore, the union of interests knew how to find different modes of expression within the policies of occupation; however, there was no shortage of even large losses: as far as economic exploitation is concerned, it has been calculated that in the Nazi-occupied Polish territories anti-Jewish policies caused the loss of more than 10 percent of the labor force, and that the policy of forced labor, which began in late 1940, proved profitable only when it was applied to the agricultural and mining sector (Klemann and Kudryashov 2012, 131–132). In this sense, the legislative instrument through which an attempt was made to define European economic exploitation declined in favor of German interests was the Four-Year Plan, presented by Göring through a decree in the summer of 1940,[2] which, however, did not affect the war economy of the occupied territories (Klemann and Kudryashov 2012, 173). And it was precisely here that, despite the massive use of figures such as trustees (Treuhänder) so that the interests of private firms would collide with those of the party (Milward 1980, 159), it was seen how the Nazis possessed no idea how to use the newly obtained industrial capacity to their advantage (Klemann and Kudryashov 2012, 173).

In light of all this, some historians have recently redefined the economic policy of the Third Reich not so much as part of an exploitation aimed to physical destruction (Aly and Heim 2002), but rather as a protracted activity of theft (Klemann and Kudryashov 2012, 178; Overy 2012, 136). There is also another element to be emphasized within this discourse: while on the one hand, in fact, the documents tell us a story within which the appropriation of assets and the transfer of property had an acceleration after the Anschluss; on the other hand, it is still the documents that testify how, still in mid-1941, the liquidation of the Polish credit institutions (absorbed, in most cases, by German banks) was far from complete and, indeed, needed new resources to be completed.[3]

7.3 The Litzmannstadt case study

In the peculiar context of the territories occupied by the Nazi regime, the following contribution will focus on the events that involved one specific city: Lodz. Although the reasons behind this choice are many, here I will list only a few. First of all, it is a city that was not bombed in the course of the war and that preserves, even today, a mass of documents regarding its past, hardly comparable to other contexts.[4] Secondly because a Jewish ghetto was established in this city (December 1939), which became the second largest and longest-lived of those established by the Nazis during the war (fall 1944); around this ghetto, especially starting from mid-1940s, an "economic" discourse developed (Levi 1981, 68). The third reason concerns the special interests, which the city and its ghetto were able to attract, that only recently have been framed within a complex "game of mirrors" characterized essentially by ideology and a strong hunger for profits (Schnaus et al. 2017).

Lodz before the Second World War was commonly referred to as the "Polish Manchester," because of the numerous textile industries located on its urban territory. Once occupied, the city was included within those territories directly annexed by the Third Reich, becoming part of the Warthegau region, headed by Reichstatthalter Arthur Greiser (Epstein 2011). Lodz was then Nazified and renamed as Litzmannstadt after which, in December 1939, Regierungspraesident Friedrich Uebelhoer gave the order to establish a Jewish ghetto, in the areas near Baluty Square, located in the northwestern part of the city (an area with no sanitary facilities or electricity) (Eisenbach 1946, 27–31; Hilberg 1961, 226–227). Within six months, the Jewish ghetto became the crossroads of a considerable number of interests: with the arrival of a young manager from Bremen, Hans Biebow, the ghetto was transformed, in fact, into a vast *archipelago of Ressorts*,[5] dedicated to the production of clothing for the army and the German market; Gauleiter Greiser was so enthusiastic that he even called a film production company to record the evolution "of Lodz into Litzmannstadt"[6] towards the end of 1940 nearly sixty ghettos were established in the Litzmannstadt and Hohensalza Regierungsbezirken (regional districts), many of which had within them textile workshops directly connected to the Litzmannstadt *Gau-ghetto* (Megargee and Dean 2012). Despite the terrible living conditions inside the ghetto, which were documented as early as the winter of 1941 and which worried some regional Nazi authorities,[7] the ghetto was included within Goring's Four-Year Plan, thus officially entering the Nazi war economy.[8] A peculiar *narrative* concerning the Litzmannstadt ghetto as a model ghetto thus came to be consolidated, where Jews produced goods for the Third Reich at very low cost due to an agreement made by the Nazi authorities that tied Jewish subsistence to productivity.[9]

According to the historian Christopher Browning, the peculiar management of the Litzmannstadt ghetto was the result of a minority approach towards the Jewish question, which could be described as *productivist*, as opposed to the far majority, the *attritionist* approach, which instead did not involve economic exploitation of the labor locked up in the ghettos (Browning 1992). On the value that the Nazi regime placed on the exploitation of forced labor what we can say, to date, is that from the point of view of the Nazi authorities what could be derived from the labor of Jews and prisoners of war (POWs) was considered, at least until the end of 1941, to be extremely marginal vis-à-vis the war economy (Custodis 2016). It is therefore even more interesting, in my opinion, to note how in such a scenario, a specific narrative (of the Litzmannstadt ghetto) is consolidated, based on an equally specific source of profit (Jewish forced labor).

There was no shortage of contradictions here as well; indeed, *Amtsleiter* Biebow's choice to operate in a short-term context (the ghetto) and the detour of production within the ghetto to wartime needs (the Four-Year Plan) were symptoms of two phenomena, especially emphasized by historians of "anti-profit" theory: the first concerns the end of the "honeymoon" between businessmen and the party, especially when managers realized that the Nazis did not have the structures necessary to achieve long-term goals (Overy 1994, 94); the second phenomenon concerns the strong conditioning of profits, achieved through the use of stimuli oriented towards a government demand (in our case represented by the demand for clothes formulated by the Wehrmacht) (Merlin 1943, 180–183). But at the same time the tactics used to attract investment and especially the response of local authorities to the proposals made by Biebow (and managers like him) show how there was a shared basis, among businessmen and party men, regarding the profits that could be extracted from a particular situation such as the one being described here (Pobbe 2023b, 68). This communion of purpose just described was not interrupted even when, starting in late 1941, the systematic destruction of the Jewish communities, which lived within the territories occupied by the Nazi regime, began.

7.4 The *Sonderkontos 12300* and 3030–358

One of the banking tools most widely used by the Nazi regime were the *Sonderkontos*: these were special bank accounts that were opened within most German credit institutions and enabled Nazi institutions to capitalize, first on the expropriation actions and then on the killing actions carried out systematically from the fall of 1941. It is well known, for example, how *Sonderkonto S* was used by the so-called "Keppler Circle" to finance specific SS actions; or how *Sonderkonto R* was used by Odilo Globocnik to deposit the profits of Operation Reinhardt (Moehrle 2014), the bloodiest of the killing operations carried out by the Nazis, involving the death camps of Treblinka, Sobibor and Belzec (Berger 2013). The information that we have about these bank accounts are, in most cases, indirect; however, precisely in the case of Litzmannstadt, we are in the peculiar position of having access to almost all of the banking documentation that was produced in conjunction with the beginning of the deportations and killing operations.

It was in this city that, probably in January 1942 (the date is not certain), a Sonderkonto with serial number 12300 was opened at the Savings Bank (Stadtsparkasse), expressly dedicated to the collection of "profits" from the deportations and to the payment of expenses related to,[10] as evidenced by early documented transactions to pay Sonderkommando Lange and Gestapo operations.[11]

According to the statements made by Adolf Eichmann during his trial in Jerusalem, in the fall of 1941 the Obersturmbannführer was sent (by order of Heinrich Müller[12]) first to Kulm[13] (Browning 2003) and then to Litzmannstadt, with the aim of establishing the suitability of these places for possible use in the plan concerning the solution of the Jewish question in the Warthegau region.[14] Confirming the shift from a pattern of "secondary destruction to one of total destruction," as historian Christopher Browning called them (Browning 2004, 173–196), there are the first liquidations in the Warthegau region that took place in the Kreis (districts) Konin and Turek. Among the first victims of this new phase were the Jews of the Hinterberg (Zagórów) ghetto, who were killed in October 1941 inside the Kazimierz Biskupi forest by Sonderkommando Lange (Dąbrowska and Wein 1976, 103; Epstein 2011, 180).[15] This special unit, headed by Herbert Lange (Friedlander 1997, 138; Aly 2013, 59–71), in 1940 had been primarily concerned with the killing of psychiatric patients and disabled persons through the use of mobile structures, within which carbon monoxide was used (Montague 2012, 188–190). In December, Lange was promoted to the rank of captain and put in charge of a new facility, dedicated solely to the killing of deportees destined there: the extermination camp (Vernichtungslager or Todeslager) at Kulmhof (Chełmno), near the Ner River about 60 km from Litzmannstadt. Here the Gaswagen were installed,[16] inspired by the mobile structures used by Lange himself in operations related to Aktion T4, the Nazi killing program against the mentally ill and handicapped:

> Chełmno did not look like a camp. It did not possess barbed wire or facilities that resembled barracks. There was only a park, a gate, and a Villa. It was staffed, at peak times, by 20 SS men and a few policemen from Litzmannstadt. A dozen local Poles were occasionally engaged in cleaning work.[17]

The solutions that were first applied at Kulmhof, such as the use of the principle of geographical proximity for the organization of transports (Stone 2019), later became part of the *modus operandi* of every *Vernichtungslager* (Głowacka-Penczyńska 2015, 321–323). Kulmhof was not only a model but also an experiment, from which practice the Nazis drew less logistically "cumbersome" and more quantitatively effective modes of mass killing (Głowacka-Penczyńska 2015, 324), as evidenced by the orders for "improvements" to be made to the technology used in the Gaswagens beginning in the summer of 1942.[18] Indeed, the capacity of Chełmno never exceeded 1,000 deaths per day (Głowacka-Penczyńska 2015, 324) in contrast to the nearly 15,000 daily death rates recorded in the extermination centers of the General Governorate during Aktion Reinhardt (Stone 2019, 9; Arad 1989; Berger 2013), which led within a few months to the killing of half a million Polish Jews (Pohl 2008, 89–111). Extermination operations were inaugurated at Kulmhof on December 8, 1941, when the first convoy of Jews from the Koło ghetto arrived (Megargee and Dean 2012, 62–63). Initially the bodies were buried in mass graves within the Rzuchowski Forest, but with the arrival of the summer season an underground furnace was built:

> The furnaces were built underground, . . . the surface area was 6x10 m, with a depth of 4. At the bottom of the furnace was a 1.5x2 m ash collector. The grates were made from train tracks. . . . The capacity of the furnace was about 100 bodies.
>
> (Bednarz 1946, 154–155)

The deportations developed along a vertical line, from north to south, starting from Regierungsbezirk Hohensalza (Inowrocław) to Kreis Welungen (Wielun) (Głowacka-Penczyńska 2015, 346–347). The extermination camp activity was concentrated purely in the ten months between December 1941 and September 1942, reaching its peak between the spring and summer seasons, within which more than one hundred thousand victims were killed.

By looking at the banking records, it is possible to trace the entire genocidal process step by step. Beginning, for example, with the role of the secret police (Gestapo), which was paid large sums in the first six months of 1942, probably due to the task it held during the deportations, namely that of confiscating money and luxury goods still in the possession of Jews before their departure for Kulmhof.[19] In continuity with what happened in the rest of the Warthegau, in Litzmannstadt, too, the Gestapo in fact assumed the role of *armed arm* vis-à-vis the civil administration, which always remained at the head of the organizational structure behind the deportations, in a concert of institutions that involved the region's chancellery (Reichsstatthalter), the provincial divisions, and the *Gettoverwaltung* (the Nazi administration of the Litzmannstadt ghetto) (Mix 2017; Alberti 2006). The Gestapo not only was the beneficiary of several transfers made in its favor but also paid out large sums from the *Aktionen* (deportations), especially from the month of September,[20] in the face, therefore, of its particularly active role, the secret police monitored the banking activity connected with the Litzmannstadt ghetto from the very beginning, following directives that started with Müller himself as early as the beginning of 1942[21] and exposing a critical stance on the cronyism now prevailing within the Biebow's administration.[22]

The Sonderkonto was from early on (April 1942) the beneficiary of several payments from account 3030–539, which was established at a small branch in Kulmhof, where an extermination camp had been set up in December 1941. Here Sonderkonto 3030–539 was used by the Sonderkommando to disburse the money seized upon the arrival of the deportees.[23] Some *Belege* (pieces of paper) relating precisely to the deposit of money in the Kulmhof branch show Biebow's signature, proving the Bremen manager's presence there during some deportation procedures.[24] And, again as evidence of the Amtsleiter's involvement with regard to the management of the deportation proceeds, the lists of bank movements also bear the signature of the Bremen manager at the bottom.[25]

Thanks to the massive amount of bank statements (Bankauszüge) and their supporting pieces (Belege) kept at the State Archives in Łódź,[26] it is also possible to describe the capital increase of Sonderkonto 12300: bank movements up to June were quite limited, with the exception of a payment of 400,000 RM in favor of Friedrich Hausler,[27] head of Greiser's accounting office; later, beginning in August, a dizzying increase in capital took place until it reached the sum of almost 3.5 million RM in October (Montague 2012, 35). The deportations from Litzmannstadt to Kulmhof took place within a route (the Litzmannstadt-Kutno-Koło) under the direct responsibility of the Reichsbahn, which at the end of each deportation submitted documentation of the costs incurred for the transport and the number of people involved. Owing to these pieces of evidence, which were probably kept as actual receipts within the expenditure budget related to the Sonderkonto, we can see how, during the deportations concerning Western Jews, the Reichsbahn charged an *ad personam* fare for both the outward and return journey, totaling more than RM 30,000 in reference to the activity between May 4 and 15, 1942.[28] In the case of the journey from Litzmannstadt to Kulmhof, the fare differed according to the type of passenger: RM 2.95 for Jews, while RM 5.6 for members of the police or SS. While for the return journey the only item of expense was for members of the police.

It was at the turn of July and August 1942 that the first payments implemented at the hands of the *Amtskommissaren*, in charge of managing the small ghettos scattered around Litzmannstadt, made their appearance.[29] The transfers not only confirm the thesis concerning the type of management of the deportations in the Warthegau but also indicate the close connection between these local administrators and the Amtsleiter of Litzmannstadt, Biebow, who signed the Belege relating to the various Aktionen[30] and the authorization for payments relating to the expenses incurred by the various administrators during the liquidations,[31] such as those relating to the personnel employed, who were paid at rates on a daily basis.[32]

Between mid-August and the end of September, Sonderkonto's capital increase was mainly due to the accumulation of various down payments related precisely to settlement activity in the region, with disbursements that, again, started from a few RM,[33] up to hundreds of thousands of RM.[34] Beginning in September several movements also appear in connection with the purchase of alcohol and cigarettes as a "reward" for the activity carried out by members of the Sonderkommando and civil servants involved in the deportations (Klein 2009, 482–486); cigarettes and tobacco in particular were purchased from two stores in Litzmannstadt, one of which was owned by a certain Fischer, while the other was called Boelke&co.[35] Also in the same month some disbursements of several thousand RM were motivated as relating to payment for the work done at the Kindler factory, under the control of the VoMi (Volksdeutschen Mittelstelle, Coordination Center for the Volksdeutschen), an SS organization which had the task of preserving the interests of the Volksdeutschen in the occupied territories.[36]

The capital increase of the Sonderkonto 12300 reached its peak during the first months of 1943, exceeding RM 4 million; after that the bank account was subject to a series of withdrawals: from January until March 1943 five withdrawals were made (every twenty days) of RM 50,000 each; then on April 17 from the account, which had reached the figure of almost RM 300,000, more than RM 200,000 were withdrawn, and again on September 4, when the account had almost RM 600,000 in it, half a million was withdrawn. Although we do not have the Belege as a reference, with regard neither to the withdrawal of February 24 nor to those that followed, the financial movements here too, as was the case in 1942, reflect the changing situation that characterized the territory in question (Warthegau) and, more generally, the entire Nazi system (Pobbe 2023b, 1002). Indeed, at the dawn of 1943, the German Ministry of Economics decided to cut the funds earmarked for the Warthegau to the tune of about RM 500,000 per month, the reason for this decision being the profits Greiser had managed to make from the exploitation of deportations and forced labor within his region (Pobbe 2023a, 1002; Klein 2009, 501; Epstein 2011, 257).

There are no records testifying to any kind of limitation when it comes to deposits and withdrawals made within the Sonderkontos, despite the fact that, over the years, the special account had become a veritable receptacle for various "criminal" benefits such as profits from labor camps, which had been established mainly in the areas in front of Posen.

The data that has been presented during this essay are only a small part of the banking documents preserved at the State Archive of Lodz and, consequently, the image that was portraited is partial. Nevertheless, by looking at the freedom that the Nazi institutions had over the management of the *Sonderkontos* or by looking at the speed that certain expropriation operations had between 1938 and 1941, we can add new nuances to the co-dependency defined by Simpson twenty years ago. The escalation that the destruction process underwent from the end of 1941 was in fact supported by a series of financial tools (like the special bank accounts) that mutually reinforced the hunger of profits and the ideological aims of the Party.

Notes

1 BArch (Bundesarchiv Lichterfelde, Berlin): R2/14578, p. 98
2 *Documents on German Foreign Policy*, Her Majesty's Stationery Office, London, vol. 10, 1957, n. 278.
3 BArch: R2/14577, p. 351.
4 Most of the documents relating to the history of Lodz during World War II are still preserved at the Lodz State Archives (APL): this is a collection that, for the documentation produced by the Nazi authorities alone, includes almost 1 million papers and is available online at https://www.szukajwarchiwach.gov.pl/en/strona_glowna
5 Definition used by the Litzmannstadt ghetto Jews in order to define the factories of clothes.
6 BArch: Filmarchive, Magazin-N.3578: *Aus Lodz wird Litzmannstadt.*
7 BArch: R 58/954, Bl. 189–191; YVA (Yad Vashem Archive, Jerusalem): TR. 3–1410; BArch: N 2503/1275, pp. 112–113, correspondence between Höppner and Eichmann of July 16, 1941;
8 BArch: R2/56159, 10 June 1941.
9 According to this agreement, 35 percent of the profits given by Jewish labor would be used to purchase foodstuffs, while the remaining 65 percent would flow into a bank account managed directly by the *Reichstatthalter* Greiser. See also YVA: O.53–78, 9 November 1940.
10 APL (State Archive of Lodz, Lodz): 39/221–29664, Bank-Auszüge
11 APL: 39/221–29664, Bank statements of February 28 and March 14, 1942.
12 Heinrich Müller (1900–1945), head of the Gestapo, starting from 1939.
13 It refers to Chełmno, where Eichmann was sent at the end of 1941.
14 State of Israel Ministry of Justice, *The Trial of Adolf Eichmann*, vol. 1, sess. 10; see also document T-244, which shown during the trial is related to the correspondence between Eichamnn and Müller regarding the "Warthegau" *issue.*
15 Barch: NS 19–2576, pp. 3–4, payment towards Lange.
16 Literally "bus of gas" were duly modified trucks, where the body part was used as a rudimentary gas chamber inside which the victims were first picked up and, once the door was sealed, carbon monoxide was injected.
17 From the General Prosecutor Władysław Bednarz, head of the investigations related to the Kulmhof (Chelmno) death camp, AŻIH (Archive of the Jewish Historical Institute – Emanuel Ringelblum, Warsaw): 344/1, Trial against Hans Biebow, 4th day of trial, p. 136; see also YVA: O.53–12, list of the Kulmhof employee.
18 BArch: R 58/871, June 23, 1942.

19 APL: 39/221–29668, *Belege* 301–400, #326–327.
20 APL: 39/221–29664, bank statement September 2, 1942.
21 BArch: R 49–2656, 022 Müller correspondence for 1941; 020–060, bank statements related to January and February 1942.
22 YVA: O.51–13, 315–42, Bradfisch report (head of the SD) regarding the ghetto situation.
23 APL: 39/221–29664, bank statement April 3, 1942.
24 APL: 39/221–29665, #70, p. 100.
25 APL: 39/221–29665, p. 195, list of bank movements (month of March).
26 The sample used for this essay is about 5,000 documents.
27 APL: 39/221–29664, bank statement May 1, 1942; APL: 39/221–29665, #42, p. 166.
28 APL: 39/221–29665, #78, *Belege* related to the bank statement of May 19, 1942, payment for special trains to Warthbruchen (Koło), p. 82.
29 APL: 39/221–29664, bank statement July 7, 1942, income related to an *Aktion* in the ghetto of Grabow.
30 APL: 39/221–29668, #301–400, p. 100, check on *Aktionen* Bełchatów.
31 APL: 39/221–29670, #555, p. 151, payment of 295 RM related to *Aktionen* in Złoczew; FGM, doc. 220, pp. 290–291, personal payment November, 1942, bank activity for the months of November and December 1942.
32 APL: 39/221–29667, costs of personnel for the deportations during mid-October, 1942; ŻIH: 205/412 payments for the personnel involved during the *Aktionen*; ŻIH: 205/413, personnel *Aktionen* for September.
33 APL: 39/221–29664, bank statement September 1, 1942, payment related to the liquidation of the Warta ghetto 670 RM.
34 APL: 39/221–29664, bank Statement September 2, 1942, payment for the liquidation of the Zduńska Wola ghetto 108,707 RM.
35 APL: 39/221–29664, bank statement September 5, 1942; APL: 39/221–29669, #429, expenses of the R. Fischer 479,40 RM.
36 Founded on 1936, il VoMi served mainly as a tool for National Socialist foreign policy, APL: 39/221–29644, bank statement September 5; APL: 39/221–29669, #432, bank movements between May and June 30, 1942.

Bibliography

Alberti, Michael. 2006. *Die Verfolgung und Vernichtung der Juden im Reichsgau Wartheland 1939–1945*. Harrasowitz Verlag.

Aly, Gotz. 2013. *Die Belasteten. "Euthanasie" 1939–1945. Eine Gesellschaftsgeschichte*. Frankfurt am Main: S. Fischer.

Aly, Gotz and Heim, Susanne. 1998. *Vordenker der Vernichtung*. München: L. Fischer.

Aly, Götz and Heim, Susanne. 2002. *Architects of Annihilation: Auschwitz and the Logic of Destruction*. Princeton: Princeton University Press.

Arad, Yitzak. 1989. *Belzec, Sobibor, Treblinka: The Operation Reinhardt Death Camps*. Bloomington: Indiana University Press.

Bajohr, Frank. 1997. *"Arisierung" in Hamburg: Die Verdrängung der jüdischen Unternehmer 1933–1945*. Hamburg: Christians.

Bajohr, Frank. 2005. "Holocaust and Corruption." In *Networks of Nazi Persecutions: Bureaucracy, Business and the Organization of the Holocaust*, edited by G.D. Feldman and W. Seibel, 119–125. New York: Berghan.

Barkai, Avraham. 1990. *Nazi Economics: Ideology, Theory and Policy*. New Heaven: Yale University Press.

Bednarz, Wladyslaw. 1946. "Chełmno." *Biuletyn Głównej Komisji Badania Zbrodni Niemieckich w Polsce*, n. 1.

Berger, Sara. 2013. *Experten der Vernichtung. Das T4 – Reinhardt – Netzwerk in den Lagern Belzec, Sobibor und Treblinka*. Hamburg: Hamburger Edition.

Boelcke, Willi. 1985. *Die Kosten von Hitlers Krieg*. Schöningh: Paderborn.

Böhler, Jochen. 2006. *Auftakt zum Vernichtungskrieg. Die Wehrmacht in Polen 1939*. Frankfurt am Main: S. Fischer.
Bräu, Ramona. 2016. "The Economic Consequences of the German Occupation Policy in Poland." In *Paying for Hitler's War: The Consequences of Nazi Hegemony for Europe*, edited by Jonas Scherner and Eugene N. White, 427–450. Cambridge: Cambridge University Press.
Browning, Christopher. 1992. *The Path to Genocide: Essays on Launching the Final Solution*. Cambridge: Cambridge University Press.
Browning, Christopher. 2003. *Collected Memories: Holocaust History and Postwar Testimony*. University of Wisconsin Press.
Browning, Christopher. 2004. "The Decision-Making Progress." In *The Historiography of the Holocaust*, edited by Dan Stone, 173–196. London: Palgrave Macmillian.
Buchheim, Christoph. 1994. "Zur Natur des Wirschaftsaufschwungs in der NS-Zeit." In *Zerrissene Zwischenkriegszeit. Wirtschaftshistorische Beiträge*, edited by Christoph Buchheim. Nomos: Baden-Baden.
Corni, Gustavo. 1998. "L'economia del Terzo Reich: un lascito storiografico della ex RDT." *Contemporanea*, n. 1 (2): 331–343.
Corni, Gustavo. 2017. "La storiografia della ex RDT fra dogmatismo e innovazione. Un tentativo di bilancio dopo il crollo." In *I muri della storia. Storici e storiografia dalle dittature alle democrazie, 1945–1990, Atti del convegno internazionale*, edited by Gustavo Corni. Trieste: Eut.
Custodis, Johann. 2016. "Employing the Enemy: The Economic Exploitation of POW and Foreign Labor from Occupied Territories by Nazi Germany." In *Paying for Hitler's War: The Consequences of Nazi Hegemony for Europe*, edited by Jonas Scherner and Eugene N. White, 67–101. Cambridge: Cambridge University Press.
Dąbrowska, Danuta and Wein, Abraham. 1976. *Pinkas ha-kehilot. Encyclopedia of Jewish Communities: Poland*, vol. 1. Jerusalem: Yad Vashem.
Dean, Martin. 2010. *Robbing the Jews: The Confiscation of Jewish Property in the Holocaust, 1933–1945*. Cambridge: Cambridge University Press.
Dingell, Jeanne. 2003. *Zur Tätigkeit der Haupttreuhandstelle Ost, Treuhandstelle Posen 1939 bis 1945*, Frankfurt am Main: Lang.
Eisenbach, Arthur. 1946. *Dokumenty i materiały do dziejów okupacji niemieckiej w Polsce: Getto łódzkie*, vol. 3. Warsaw: Centralna Żydowska Komisja Historyczna.
Epstein, Cathrine. 2011. *Model Nazi: Arthur Greiser and the Occupation of Western Poland*. Oxford: Oxford University Press.
Friedlander, Henry. 1997. *The Origins of the Final Solution: From Euthanasia to the Final Solution*. Chapel Hill: University of North Carolina Press.
Goschler, Constantin. 2013. "The Dispossession of the Jews and the Europeanization of the Holocaust." In *Business in the Age of Extremes: Essays in Modern German and Austrian Economic History*, edited by Hartmut Berghoff, Jürgen Kocka and Dieter Ziegler, 195. Cambridge: Cambridge University Press.
Goschler, Constantin and Lilteicher, Jurgen (eds.). 1998. *"Arisierung" und Restitution: die Rückerstattung jüdischen Eigentums in Deutschland und Österreich nach 1945 und 1989*, 61–89. Gottingen: Wallstein.
Gross, Stephen G. 2018. "The Nazi Economy." In *A Companion to Nazi Germany*, edited by Shelley Baranowski, Armin Nolzen and Claus-Christian W. Szejnmann, 263–279. London: Wiley Blackwell.
Głowacka-Penczyńska, Anetta. 2015. *The First to Be Destroyed: The Jewish Community of Kleczew and the Beginning of the Final Solution*. Boston: Academic Studies Press.
Hardach, Gerd. 1984. "Banking and Industry in Germany in the Interwar Period 1919–1939." *Journal of European Economic History*, Special issue 13: 203–234.
Henke, Klaus-Dietmar (ed.). 2006. *Die Dresdner Bank im Dritten Reich*. Berlin: De Gruyter.
Henning, Friedrich-Wilhelm. 1992. "Börsenkrisen und Börsengesetzgebung von 1914 bis 1945 in Deutschland." In *Deutsche Börsengeschichte*, edited by D. Pohl, 211–290. Hamburg-Frankfurt: Knapp.

Herbst, Rudolf and Thomas, Weihe (eds.). 2004. *Die Commerzbank und die Juden 1933–1945*. Munich: C. H. Beck.

Hilberg, Raul. 1961. *The Destruction of European Jews*, 1st Edition. New York: Quadrangle Books.

Hilberg, Raul. 1999. *La distruzione degli Ebrei d'Europa* (ed. Or. *The destruction of European Jews)*. Torino: Einaudi.

Kater, Michael. 1983. *The Nazi Party: A Social Profile of Members and Leaders 1919–1945*, 129. Cambridge: Harvard University Press.

Kershaw, Ian. 2000. *The Nazi Dictatorship: Problems and Perspectives of Interpretation*, 42–60. London-New York: Oxford University Press.

Klein, Peter. 2009. *Die "Gettoverwaltung Litzmannstadt" 1940–1944: Eine Dienststelle im Spannungsfeld von Kommunalbürokratie und staatlicher Verfolgungspolitik*. Hamburg: Harbuerger Edition.

Klemann, Hein and Kudryashov, Sergei. 2012. *Occupied Economies: An Economic History of Nazi-Occupied Europe, 1939–1945*. Berg Publisher.

Levi, Primo. 1981. *Lilith e altri racconti*. Torino: Einaudi.

Loose, Ingo. 2007. *Kredite Für Ns-Verbrechen: Die Deutschen Kreditinstitute in Polen und die Ausraubung der polnischen und jüdischen Bevölkerung*. Munchen: Oldenbourg.

Loose, Ingo. 2013. "Die Bedeutung der Ghettoarbeit für die nationalsozialistische Kriegswirtschaft." In *Arbeit in den nationalsozialistischen Ghettos*, edited by Hensel, Jürgen and Lehnstaedt, Stephan, 71–91. Gottingen: Fibre Verlag.

Megargee, Geoffrey P. and Dean, Martin (eds.). 2012. *Encyclopedia of Camps anf Ghettos*, vol. 2 *Ghettos in German-Occupied Eastern Europe*. Washington: Holocaust Memorial Museum.

Merlin, Sidney. 1943. "Trends in German Economics Control since 1933." *Quarterly Journal of Economics*, n. 62: 180–183.

Milward, Alan. 1980. *War, Economy and Society, 1939–1945*, 159. Berkley: University of California Press.

Mix, Andreas. 2017. *Zwangsarbeit von Juden im Reichsgau Wartheland und im Generalgouvernement*. https://www.historikerkommission-reichsarbeitsministerium.de/sites/default/files/inlinefiles/Working%20Paper%20UHK%20A1_Mix_1.pdf

Moehrle, René. 2014. *Judenverfolgung in Triest während Faschismus und Nationalsozialismus 1922–1945*. Berlin: Metropol.

Montague, Peter. 2012. *Chełmno and the Holocaust: The History of Hitler's First Death Camp*. Chapel Hill: University of North Carolina Press.

Overy, Richard. 1994. *War and Economy in the Third Reich*. Oxford: Clarendon Press.

Overy, Richard. 2012. *Goering: Hitler's Iron Knight*. London: Tauris.

Pobbe, Anna Veronica. 2023a. "Il business delle deportazioni: la soluzione finale nel Warthegau attraverso la lente di un conto bancario." *Rivista Storica Italiana*, n. 3: 989–1007.

Pobbe, Anna Veronica. 2023b. *Un Manager del Terzo Reich: il caso Hans Biebow*. Roma: Laterza.

Pohl, Dieter. 2004. "War, Occupation and the Holocaust in Poland." *Historiography of the Holocaust*, edited by D. Stone, 89–111. London: Springer.

Pohl, Dieter. 2008. *Verfolgung und Massenmord in der NS-Zeit 1933–1945*. Wissenschaftliche Buchgesellschaft.

Schnaus, Julia, Smolorz, Roman, Spoerer, Martin. 2017. "Die Rolle des Ghetto Litzmannstadt (Łódź) bei der Versorgung der Wehrmacht und der deutschen Privatwirtschaft mit Kleidung (1940 bis 1944)." *Zeitschrift für Unternehmensgeschichte*, n. 62 (1): 35–56.

Schweitzer, Arthur. 1946. "Profits Under Nazi Planning." *The Quarterly Journal of Economics*, n. 61 (1): 1–25.

Schweitzer, Arthur. 1964. *Big Businesses in the Third Reich*. Bloomington: Indiana University Press.

Simpson, Christopher. 1993. *The Splendid Blond Beast: Money, Law and Genocide in the Twentieth Century*, 70. New York: Grove Press.

Simpson, Christopher. 2002. *The War Crimes of the Deutsche Bank and the Dresden Bank: The OMGUS Report*. New York: Holmes & Meier.

Snyder, Timothy. 2015. *Black Earth: The Holocaust as History and Warning.* London: Penguin.

Spoerer, Mark. 1996a. "From Paper Profits to Armaments Boom: The Profitability of German Industrial Stock Corporations 1925–41." *German History*, n. 14 (2): 218–219. https://doi.org/10.1093/gh/14.2.218

Spoerer, Mark. 1996b. *Von Scheingewinnen zum Rüstungsboom. Die Eigenkapitalrentabilität der deutschen Industrieaktiengesellschaften 1925–1941.* Stuttgart: Franz Steiner Verlag.

Spoerer, Mark. 2000. "Industrial Profitability in the Nazi Economy." In *After the Slump: Industry and Politics in 1930s Britain and Germany*, edited by Christoph Buchheim and Redvers Garside. Bern: Peter Lang.

Stiefel, D. 2001. "The Economics of Discrimination." In *Die politische Ökonomie des Holocaust. Zur wirtschaftlichen Logik von Verfolgung und "Wiedergutmachung,"* edited by D. Stiefel, 9–28. Wien-München: Oldenburg.

Stone, Levi. 2019. "Quantifying the Holocaust: Hyperintense Kill Rates During the Nazi Genocide." *Science Advances*, n. 5. https://doi.org/10.1126/sciadv.aau7292.

Temin, Peter. 1991. "Soviet and Nazi Economic Planning in the 1930s." *Economic History Review*, n. 44 (4): 573–593.

8 More repression in a repressed world

The Spanish financial sector during the Franco regime, 1939–1975

Joaquim Cuevas, Elena Martínez-Ruiz, and Maria A. Pons

8.1 Introduction

In the second half of the 20th century, the regulation of banking and financial markets was reinforced in most European countries. Their governments implemented quantitative and qualitative restrictions such as reserve requirements, interest rate controls and compulsory investment requirements. As a result, most European countries adopted a regime of financial repression.[1] There is no single reason which explains these repressive systems. The public finance approach considers that governments implement financial repression to gain revenue. Financial repression produces a distortion in the domestic interest rate (which is below global interest rates) that affects (and benefits) public finances. As the costs of implementing other alternative forms of taxation are high, the governments made use of financial repression to tackle budgetary problems. Moreover, financial repression is a less transparent and less obvious system of taxation than other alternative forms of taxation. However, assuaging budgetary problems is not the only reason for implementing financial repression. There are countries with similar budgetary constraints but with very different financial regulation (Battilossi 2005). Other possible factors behind the implementation of financial repression measures should therefore be considered. For example, financial restrictions through interest rate controls and other complementary measures alter the allocation of resources; in this sense, governments could use financial repression as a mechanism for redistributing financial resources towards groups that support the government (capture theory) or with allocative purposes.

As Mullin (2021) pointed out, there has been growing interest in financial repression in recent years due to the cumulative effects of the 2007–2008 global financial crisis, the European debt crisis and the COVID-19 pandemic. The energy crisis fuelled by the Ukrainian war has only added to the storm. The 2007–2008 crisis led to an extraordinary increase in government debt and most banks in the eurozone more than doubled their holdings of government debt, encouraged by a regulatory framework (Basel III) that gave government debt preferential treatment when it came to satisfying capital requirements (Reinhart et al. 2011). To tackle the consequences of the pandemic, governments have adopted expansive fiscal policies and central banks have adapted their monetary

DOI: 10.4324/9781032656199-9

policy to support these fiscal measures. Finally, governments have introduced very costly support packages in response to the recent energy crisis. Interest rates had been kept low to facilitate deficit finance and high indebtedness. In this context, there were calls for a tighter monetary policy to prevent financial repression (Hoffman 2019; Mullin 2021). The recent upsurge in inflation led the Federal reserve, the European Central Bank and other central banks to raise interest rates in 2022. Thus, financial repression has come back on the agenda. In light of these recent financial trends, it is worth looking back at past experiences of financial repression and to evaluate the relationships between the government and the financial system in different circumstances.

The aim of this chapter is to analyse financial repression in Spain in the period 1939–1975 in order to answer the following questions: How was financial repression implemented? What tools were used? Was the state the main beneficiary of financial repression and, therefore, the party that had the greatest interest in maintaining tight controls over the sector? What was the impact of regulation? The first part of the paper examines the characteristics of Spanish banking regulation and the degree of financial repression in comparative terms. The second part of the paper studies the role played by stock market regulation and exchange controls in the context of an autarkic economic policy. Finally, in the conclusions, the costs and benefits of financial repression are assessed.

8.2 Characterization of financial repression in Francoist Spain

Most European countries strongly regulated their financial sectors in the years following the Second World War. The Spanish case has some unique features in comparison to other European countries. The first is its early implementation. In Spain, financial restrictions were introduced at the end of the civil war (1939), and several regulatory measures were passed around the same time and even slightly earlier (1938 and 1939). Barriers to entry were introduced (the Decree Law of 1939 ratified the so-called "status quo" by prohibiting the establishment of new banks prior to governmental approval); the *Orden Ministerial* of 1938 fixed interest rate controls; the Decree Law of December 13, 1941, controlled the distribution of cash dividends; and the Decree Laws of 1942 and 1945 regulated the opening of branches. Finally, in 1946, a new Banking Supervision Law (BSL) was passed, which established the main regulatory constraints of the Spanish financial sector. It was not modified until 1962, and then only partially. In this context, banking regulation, stock market restrictions, and exchange rate controls reinforced state interventionism and financial repression.

The second unique feature is the political regime. Spain, like Italy and Portugal, was a dictatorship. Consequently, financial repression was likely used as a mechanism not only to guarantee revenues for the government but also to reallocate financial resources to benefit the economic and political groups that supported the Franco regime. However, ideological constraints linked to the Francoist programme must not be underestimated when considering the impact of the political regime.

Thirdly, there is the intensity of the financial repression. Battilossi (2004, 2005) calculated an index of financial repression for the period 1950–1991 based on three dimensions of regulation (market structure, prices, and assets composition).[2] He found that from 1950 to 1979 financial repression in Spain was high but very near to the average index for 16 European countries. The UK, Greece, and Belgium, among others, had a financial repression index above the average, whereas the countries with the lowest financial repression index were Switzerland, Sweden, and Finland. Therefore, Battilossi's (2005) results do not indicate that Spain had a high degree of financial repression by international standards. However, it is important to note the difficulties in calculating an index that covers all the regulatory aspects. In fact, this index does not capture the consequences linked to either stock market restrictions or foreign exchange controls. For this reason, in this paper, we particularly focus on these two aspects that have received less attention in the literature.

Fourthly, in Spain, the financial repression seems to have lasted longer than in other European countries. In general, European countries were very slow in liberalizing their banking and financial markets. The length of the Franco dictatorship and the difficulties in the democratic transition, among other factors, delayed the process of liberalizing the banking and financial markets in Spain. According to Batilossi's index, in the period from 1980 to 1991, the repression index for Spain was above the average for the 16 European countries in the sample (only two countries had a higher index: Greece and Portugal). The Spanish repression index in this period was around 50, whereas 10 of the 16 European countries had an index of below 45. As Cuevas and Pons (2021) indicate, the liberalization process during the 1970s and 1980s entailed advances but also many setbacks. However, according to the data reported by Abiad et al. (2010), Spain's financial liberalization index in 1992 was similar to that of France and Germany, slightly lower than that of the UK, and much higher than that of Italy.

8.3 Financial repression and the banking sector in Spain

The two main pieces of regulation during the Franco regime (the laws of 1946 and 1962) corresponded to different stages of Spanish economic development (see Table 8.1). As mentioned, after the civil war (1936–1939), Franco's dictatorship introduced very restrictive legislation, in terms of both the operating conditions of the financial system and the control of credit conditions (Pons 2002, 2011). Regarding private banking, the 1946 BSL established barriers to entry into the sector, prohibiting the creation of new banks, the opening of new branches, and the entry of foreign banks without prior authorization. In addition, interest rates on loans and deposits were regulated, the term of loans was limited, profits were controlled, and banks were encouraged to buy public debt. However, unlike in other countries, in Spain there were no bank nationalizations – neither the Bank of Spain nor the sectoral official banks were nationalized – as the more interventionist and radical sectors of Francoism had intended (Tortella and García Ruiz 2003).

This regulation significantly limited the competition among banks and distorted bank investments, because the government reallocated banking resource

Table 8.1 Key Spanish Banking Regulation Acts in Franco regime

1946 Banking Supervision Law	Statist regulation: limits on competition, barriers to entry, interventionist interest rates, compulsory public debt investments. Consolidation of existing banks.
1962 Banking Law	Openness regulation, with limits. Relaxed control over entry barriers and opening of branches; authorization of long-term loans; specialization – industrial banking and merchant banking. Rise in preferential credits and growth of public banking.

Source: Pérez de Armiñán (1976), Pons (2002, 2011), Faus-Mompart (2001), and Tortella and García-Ruiz (2013). Produced by the authors.

towards some investments it considered strategic. The specific regulations for savings banks were even more interventionist, as these banks were forced to devote a large part of the savings collected to low-return investments (Comín 2016; Comín and Cuevas 2017). Finally, the 1946 law renewed the Bank of Spain's exclusive right to issue money, but it remained a private bank, with no powers relating to monetary policy or assistance to other banks. In practice, there were no bank bailouts during this period of the early Franco regime because the lack of competition was counterbalanced by the stability of the sector and the absence of crises. After the civil war, many banks with solvency problems ended up merging with solvent banks; indeed, this was the main solution to banking problems during the 1940s and 1950s. As noted later, there was also no real banking supervision during this time.

The last pre-modern regulation of Spanish banking was the 1962 Banking Law, which sought to put an end to the main problems of the banking system, such as the scarcity of long-term credit, the lack of competition, the absence of an active monetary policy, and the Bank of Spain's lack of power to regulate the entire credit system (Pons 2002, 2011). Probably the most important change associated with the 1962 Banking Law was the nationalization of the Bank of Spain, which ceased to be a private bank and thus lost its shareholding. Despite being nationalized, the Bank of Spain still could not be considered a true central bank, as it did not have adequate monetary policy instruments. It was assigned the task of inspecting and co-ordinating the banking sector, although not the entire financial sector: savings banks were inspected by a separate agency (the *Instituto de Crédito de las Cajas de Ahorros*, ICCA) until 1971, when they also came under the control of the Bank of Spain. The public banks were placed under the supervision of a specific agency, the *Instituto de Crédito a Medio y Largo Plazo* (Medium- and Long-Term Credit Institute). Both ultimately depended on the Treasury.

Despite the fact that one of the intended aims of the 1962 Banking Law was to reduce interventionism in the banking industry, some of the measures approved by the law contributed to continued financial repression, especially the maintenance of interest rate controls and the reinforcement of compulsory investments for banks and savings banks as part of the national industrialization strategy.

There was also an attempt to break away from the Spanish tradition of universal banking, with banking specialization being encouraged through the creation of *industrial* and *investment* banking as opposed to typical commercial banking. In addition, loan terms were increased to 18 months. In this regard, one of the distinctive features of the Spanish banking sector during the 1960s was its significant contribution to industrial growth, as evidenced by the data on corporate indebtedness to banks, which exceeded that of other advanced European countries. (García Ruiz 2019). In practice, the 1962 law ended up being much less liberalizing than it was intended to be. Regardless of the increase in competition between banks, Franco's financial policy in the 1960s continued to be shaped by the so-called "preferential credit circuits" (the sectors and companies considered strategic by the government). By the end of the 1960s, the preferential credit circuits accounted for 45% of the total resources of the credit system (Poveda 1980).[3]

Franco's banking regulation also had a direct impact on the distribution of credit through the control of official sectoral banks.[4] After the 1946 BSL, and especially since the 1958 Act and the 1962 Banking Law, official banks were subject to strong government control. Franco's policy on official credit had as its main objective the coordination and maximization of available financial resources to use them to implement the regime's economic policies. There were three main features of Francoist interventionism in official banking (Martín-Aceña et al. 2016): First, during the 1940s and 1950s, official banks were subject to strong intervention, both in their operations (the Ministry of Finance decided the conditions and terms of the operations, the interest rates, the commission policy, etc.) and in their internal functioning. This intervention reached an extreme in 1962, when the official banks were nationalized and became public banks. Second, public banks offered loans at discounted interest rates, lower than those available in the market. To do this, they obtained their resources through the issuance of securities (bonds for investments), which banks and savings banks compulsorily bought. These certificates had the guarantee of the state because they were considered public debt. Although they were issued at 4%, well below inflation, they were automatically pledgeable at the Bank of Spain. Banks and savings banks were the main purchasers of these issues since financial repression forced private entities to buy this type of public debt to meet compulsory investment coefficients. Third, the official banks were used repeatedly as part of the government's economic planning, especially during the 1960s and 1970s, when the public bank became a transmitter of the priorities of the so-called "development policy", channelling resources to the sectors and companies previously indicated by the government planning. In short, the Franco regime intervened in the credit market directly, significantly increasing the supply of credit at the service of productive activity and the public sector, which consolidated public credit as an essential development factor for the growth of the Spanish economy from the 1950s on. The cost of this policy was borne by private entities that had to make investments in low-yield public debt and bank clients, who saw the profitability of their investments diminish. It also had adverse impacts on the macroeconomic context, especially inflation.

There are several interpretations as to why the Franco government maintained this very restrictive banking regulatory framework (Lukauskas 1992; Perez 1997; Pons 2002). The traditional view interprets regulation in terms of "capture theory", positing that financial regulation was part of a strategy framed within what has been called the "*via nacionalista*" (nationalist path). According to this view, the Restoration period (1874–1923) marked the starting point of a path determined by the interests of the groups that held power at the time. They not only chose the institutional design that maximized their own rents but were able to perpetuate it over time (Muñoz 1969; Roldán et al. 1973; García Delgado 1985). Under such an interpretation, the term "state capture" defines a situation in which the Spanish state was at the mercy of the designs of a group or sector, in our case the banking sector, whose influence allowed it to bend the political and regulatory processes to its own advantage against the common good (Calomiris and Haber 2014).

Other interpretations emphasize the need for the state to use monetary and banking regulation to ensure easy and cheap access to financing that the inefficient fiscal system did not provide (Sardá 1970; Poveda 1972, 1981). It should be pointed out that this interpretation is more common among specialists and scholars of monetary policy and those who approach this type of problem from the perspective of the Public Treasury, and among those who have studied the evolution of the banking system from a political economy perspective. The latter include those who defend the idea of a "repressed" financial system, such as Lukauskas (1997) and Perez (1997).

Finally, these two approaches can be merged such that Spanish financial regulation is seen as the result of two pressures, as claimed by Pons (2002). On the one hand, the Franco government displayed a keen interest in engaging the banking sector in its industrialization program and obtaining cheap public financing.[5] On the other hand, the Franco government extended certain advantages to the banking sector and other economic groups to guarantee their support and collaboration; in particular, it closed the market, reduced competition, and eliminated uncertainty. Subsequent studies by Javier Pueyo (2003, 2006) further expanded this analysis to the inter-war period, where he presents a very nuanced interpretation in which the fiscal advantages offered by the state take centre stage, though the possibility of negotiations between banks and legislators is not entirely ruled out.

8.4 Financial repression, stock market regulation, and exchange rate controls

Banking regulation and the benefits obtained by the state through its monetary and financial policy have been the focus of many research studies, but the role of stock market and exchange rate controls has received less attention. However, these regulations were an integral part of a system of financial repression as they enabled the creation of a captive demand for the financial instruments favored by the state, whether for real balances and public securities or for the bonds and securities of firms in privileged sectors. Stock market regulation and exchange and capital controls hence served to prevent the erosion of the internal tax base of the implicit tax embodied in financial repression. This tax could be avoided by seeking greater profitability either in stock market operations or abroad.

With respect to stock market repression, during the early Franco regime in the 1940s and 1950s, the rigidity of monetary policy made it difficult for a bond (fixed-income) market to function, and this was compounded by the lack and asymmetry of information which influenced investors. Furthermore, the legal restrictions stemming from the autarkic policy ensured that the stock market played a limited role in the financial sector and that savings were channelled through the banking sector. Banks could use available funds to purchase private securities and to ensure they received the necessary financial resources from the private sector. It was therefore essential for the Franco government to control financial markets and non-bank financial institutions. All of this was compounded by the isolationist policy, which made it difficult for the stock market to increase its integration with international markets. Regulation on the stock market was restrictive, at least until the mid-1960s; consequently, the bond and stock market (the stock exchange) played an insignificant role in Spain. Although it is unlikely that its role would have been decisive in the absence of state intervention, it is true that Franco's regulation placed many obstacles in the way of its development.

For example, a 15% tax was imposed on income derived from stock market profits; and the obligation to inform the government of any investment in the stock market was established in contrast to the banking secrecy proclaimed in 1940. In 1946, the law on capital increases was approved, aiming at limiting speculation and setting a significantly burdensome premium on capital increases. The purpose of the law was to channel a greater amount of funds towards public debt as a central piece of economic policy. Furthermore, all attempts to modernize the markets or to create secondary markets were paralyzed; and, finally, bond yields were regulated, which meant that the Spanish financial system was not allowed to develop. Then, there was a clear reversal of the stock market after the civil war (Figure 8.1) and all attempts to modernize markets or create secondary markets were halted. In addition to the decline in stock market capitalization, the dominance of public debt was evident: in the 1950s, debt represented 60% of the total traded value on the Madrid Stock Exchange.

The economic policy associated with the liberalization of the 1959 Stabilization Plan led to an increase in investment, which was reflected in a growing number of issuances and capital increases. During the 1960s, there was an expansion of the stock market in Spain, as shown in Figure 8.1, driven by several factors. Firstly, there were the institutional and regulatory reforms that favoured investment, in terms of both fiscal benefits and information transparency. The combined effects of the 1962 Law, the earlier 1960 Law on the Dissemination of Securities Ownership, laws promoting collective investment in 1964, and the 1966 Law on Stock Savings Accounts, all contributed to a growth in investment that continued until 1974. Secondly, economic stabilization and expansion reduced the need for public sector issuances, making the private issuance market much more active (between 1959 and 1974, private issuances fluctuated between 2/3 and 3/4 of the total volume, unlike the autarkic period). Finally, it should be noted that foreign investment started to return (four decades on from the 1930s) through the first investment funds and portfolio firms, contributing to increased stock market capitalization from the late 1960s.

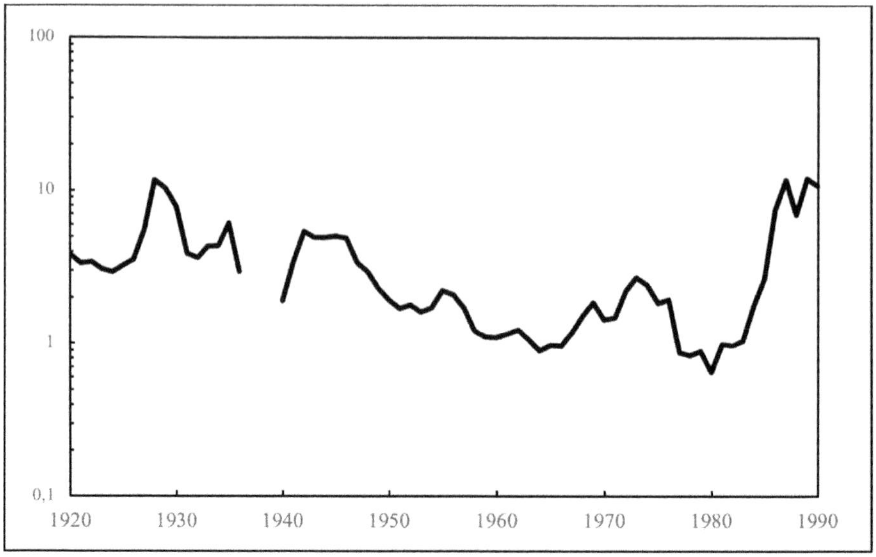

Figure 8.1 Stock market capitalization/GDP. Madrid Stock Exchange, 1920–1990.

Source: Stock market: Hoyo (2007) and Tafunell (2005); and GDP: Prados de la Escosura (2003)

Regarding exchange controls, these restrictions were originally conceived as an integral part of the state intervention apparatus, aimed at promoting the industrial development that allegedly private initiative had not been able to foster. In this sense, Franco regime was very similar to the fascist European countries and to the large South American countries. In addition to the totalitarian attempt to extend state control to all areas of the economy, balance-of-payments considerations were at the forefront of the minds of the economic leaders of the early Franco regime. Franco expressed his concern about the external balance on numerous occasions, placing the current account deficit among the main problems of the Spanish economy (Martínez-Ruiz 2000).

To ensure the reorientation of foreign relations, a vast apparatus of intervention was articulated, the basic pillars of which were exhaustive quantitative restrictions and rigorous exchange control. The exchange control system was characterized by the inconvertibility of both the internal and external peseta and the state monopoly on holding and trading foreign currency. Any transaction abroad, commercial or financial, required prior authorization from the authorities. Any foreign currency was supposed to be transferred to the authorities immediately. In the late 1940s, a complex system of multiple exchange rates was introduced. It made the system absurdly intricate and opened the door to opportunistic behaviour and arbitrary decisions.

With the Stabilization Plan of 1959 and the entry of Spain into the Bretton Woods institutions, exchange control was modified. The unification of the exchange rate and its fixation at a more realistic level, the liberalization of imports, the automatic granting of foreign currency for those countries with convertibility, and the opportunities provided to foreign investment, all radically changed the panorama of the foreign economic policy. In a few months, it moved to a somewhat more open system, where the external convertibility of the valuta was recognized and the state monopoly was relaxed. However, the internal convertibility of the currency was not declared. The general prohibition on payments abroad for any reason unless expressly authorized was maintained, and although numerous provisions gradually liberalized currency operations, progressively increasing the range and volume of permitted operations, capital controls remained in force until the end of the period.

8.5 Evaluating the impact of financial repression

It is not easy to evaluate the cost of Franco's financial regulation. Regarding banking regulation, two distinct aspects can be identified: the impact of regulation on banking performance and the fiscal impact of financial regulation. Regarding banking performance, Pons (2002) emphasizes several aspects. First, the lack of competition was the main reason why most of the very small banks survived. As a result, there was little growth in the average size of banks, negatively affecting banking efficiency. Second, the existence of barriers to entry limited the development of other alternative financial institutions such as savings institutions, insurance companies, or other financial markets such as the bond or equity markets, producing a relatively low diversification of the Spanish financial system and the dominance of banks. Finally, interest rate regulation and credit controls (in terms of maturity of loans, types of loans, sectors, and so on) affected banking strategy and the portfolio structure (with a clear predominance of public debt). The Franco regime tried to involve banks in their programme of industrialization by establishing a preferential interest rate for national interest industries and compulsory coefficients to finance these sectors. This explains the banks' strategy of increasing their participation in the industrial sector and their nature as mixed banks. Of course, it also explains the portfolio structure of the banking sector, with a clear predominance of public debt. As Comín and Cuevas (2017, 409) explain, "there were practically no non-financial investors in public debt, neither from Spain nor from abroad".

The impact of regulation changed throughout the period (1939–1975). As mentioned, in the 1940s and mid-1950s, regulation was very restrictive (in terms of restriction of entry, branch expansion, and mergers) but it allowed cartel agreements to fix banking conditions (García Ruiz 2002). The situation changed during the 1950s, and from 1952, there is no evidence of the existence of formal agreements, with banks attempting to compete not only through the price mechanism but through other mechanisms such as branch expansion (Pons 2002). Despite this, the regulatory framework and the lack of competition gave rise to problems of moral hazard and most banks adopted risky and even illegal banking practices. Moreover, banking supervision and inspection were non-existent during the 1940s, and when they started in the 1950s, the scope of inspections was very limited and centred on local and regional banks, focusing mainly on compliance with rules on interest rates, the number of branches, payment of dividends, etc. From the mid-1950s onwards, the number of inspections increased, and they highlighted the extraordinary level of credit risk concentration – especially surrounding credits for firms and individuals linked to the managers of banks – without the authorities imposing significant sanctions. Despite the increase in banking supervision during the 1960s (more controls on bank activity, an increase in the number of inspectors and inspections, the creation of specialized bodies, etc.) the Bank of Spain's capacity to control and sanction banking activity remained limited (Cuevas and Pons 2024). Therefore, the delicate financial situation of some banks was very evident when the financial sector started its liberalization process during the 1970s.

With respect to the fiscal impact of financial regulation, this regulation was used as a mechanism to avoid other reforms and secure resources for public finances. Banks and saving institutions were used as instruments of industrialization and to obtain cheap financing not only in the early stages but also in the later stages of the Franco era, with most of these mechanisms even being reinforced during the 1960s. However, the industrialist rhetoric of the economic leaders concealed the lack of resources devoted to promoting the country's economic development, which was the result of the entirely political decision not to tackle a tax reform (Comín 2003). The inadequate tax system, which especially benefited those groups that had supported Franco's uprising in 1936, made it impossible to increase state revenue, which led to the abandonment of facets of spending that were essential for the growth and development of the Spanish economy.

As can be seen in Figure 8.2, public deficit reached high levels between 1940 and 1948. This was partly due to the payments made to satisfy the arrears and credits derived from the civil war, but the lack of tax reform also curtailed public income, which barely grew during the 1940s. The fiscal pressure fell from 17% on

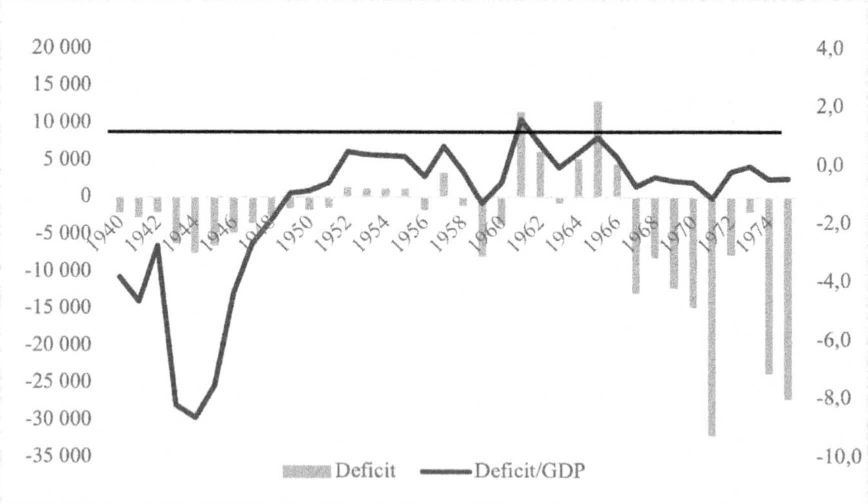

Figure 8.2 Public deficit (millions of Pesetas, left axis and %, right axis).

Source: Public deficit: Comín and Díaz (2005); and GDP: Prados de la Escosura (2003)

average in the first five years to 13% in the second half of the 1940s and 10% in the first five years of the 1950s. The public revenue crisis also worsened because the regulation of the foreign sector and the consequent drop in imports led to the collapse of customs revenues, and the failure to update quotas in an inflationary context also had a strongly negative effect on revenues of some other fundamental taxes. Figure 8.3 depicts the drop in customs revenues from 1940 onwards. As can be seen, exacerbated protectionism reduced the level of imports during the 1940s, which led to a drastic reduction in the share of customs revenues in the overall government revenue. The expansion of imports in the 1950s did little to improve the relative contribution of tariffs and it was not until the new tariffs were implemented following the Stabilization Plan that revenues from tariffs recovered their traditional importance in the Spanish tax system.

Although the budget balance was generally positive during the 1950s, the deficit of the autonomous bodies, which in 1958 numbered more than 800, meant that new securities had to be issued continuously, supplemented by direct recourse to the Bank of Spain. New debt was continuously issued during the autarkic period. The magnitude of credit drawn down at the Bank of Spain by banks (practically all of them), savings banks, public works, and private individuals with securities collateral, that is, debt securities pledged at the central bank, as shown in Table 8.2, meant that the banking sector had practically unlimited liquidity throughout the Francoist period. The acceleration of economic growth from 1950 onwards produced an increase in the demand for liquidity and credit, to which the banks responded with an increase in the pledging of securities, especially after the government attempted a contraction in 1957.

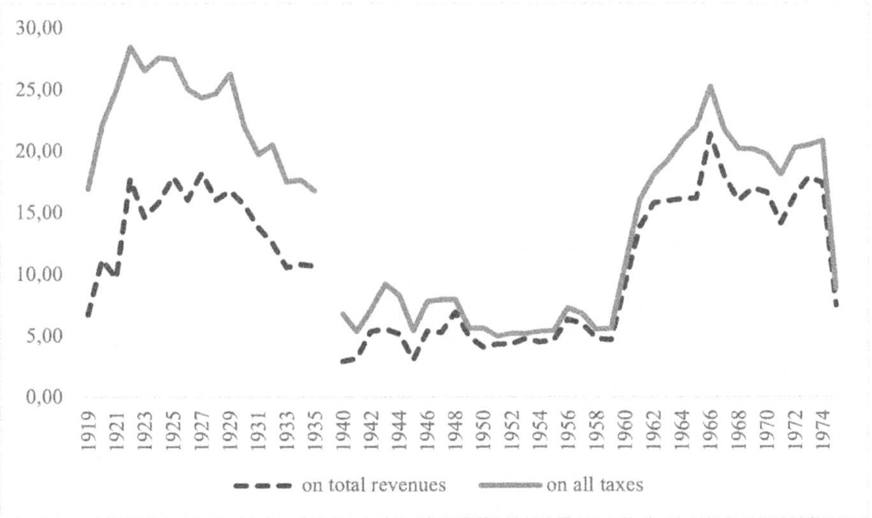

Figure 8.3 Custom revenues on total public revenues and on tax revenues.

Source: Comín and Díaz (2005)

Table 8.2 Issue and pledge of public sector debt (miles of millions *pesetas*)

	State and autonomous bodies	*Treasury loans – Bank of Spain*	*Pledged debt*
1950	2.6	5.6	2.8
1951	4.0	2.0	5.8
1952	4.4	6.0	3.9
1953	4.7	5.0	3.9
1954	4.3	5.9	7.4
1955	7.1	9.6	10.2
1956	12.1	7.9	11.7
1957	6.8	4.6	22.2
1958	8.1	–	30.7

Source: González (1979).

As a result, any attempt at implementing a real monetary policy was abandoned, prevented by the impetus provided by the issuance of pledgeable debt. The Bank of Spain limited itself to passively meeting the system's liquidity needs. Monetary aggregates reflect the lack of concern for monetary stability. Figure 8.4 illustrates the evolution of the money supply. Together with the rigidity of the agricultural supply and wage increases, the accumulation of pledgeable debt in the hands of banks appeared as an underlying factor in the inflation of the 1950s (González 1979).

As can be seen in the graph, there was uninterrupted growth in the money supply (M1) between 1941 and 1958, with two notable points of acceleration: the first in 1948 and the second from 1954 onwards. The growth of the monetary base was slower but also continued until 1958. During much of the period, the uncontrolled increase in the money supply exceeded the rate of economic growth, creating an "inflationary gap". Prices rose sharply. The wholesale price index rose sevenfold between 1940 and 1958, an increase of more than 30% per year.

Some authors argue that the Franco authorities were not conscious of the seriousness of inflationary problems. However, we can find plenty of evidence to contradict this claim. For example, a Bank of Spain Report of 1945 emphasized the grave effects of inflation on the Spanish economy and there was an interesting debate among the preeminent economists of that time – Paris Eguilaz, Olariaga, and Figueroa, among others – about whether or not inflation was a priority problem of the Spanish economy. Nevertheless, the official stance was that the top priority was the increase in production, especially industrial production, and inflation was the price that Spain had to pay for its industrialization (given the refusal to carry out a tax reform) (Pons 2002).

The situation improved slightly after the Stabilization Plan. In 1957, a minor fiscal adjustment was made aimed at boosting revenue without introducing new taxes. Tax names and collection methods were altered, yet the change marked a regression from previous efforts to equalize the tax system by broadening income tax. The plan to make income tax the principal tax was abandoned, and the revised collection

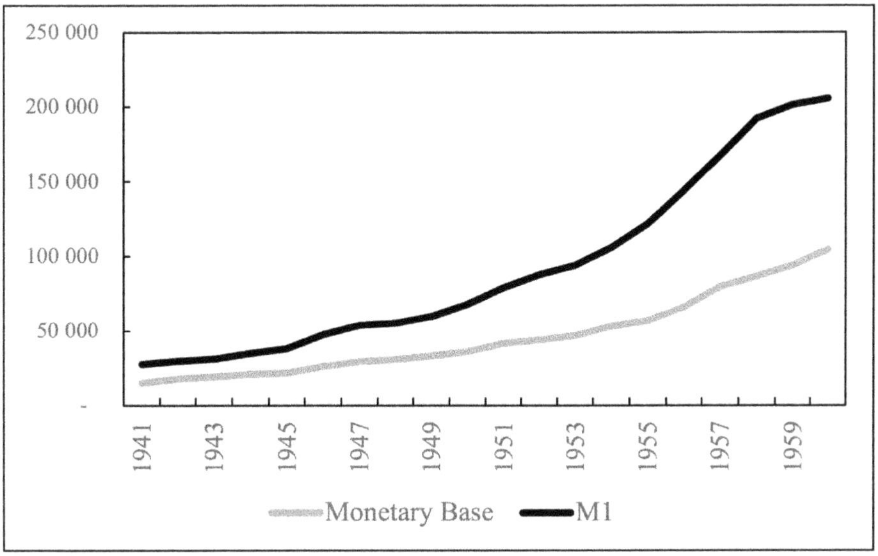

Figure 8.4 Evolution of money supply, 1940–1958.

Source: Martín Aceña (1988, 1989)

approaches perpetuated evasion and hindered the government's revenue-gathering abilities (Comín and Martorell 2013) In its initial year, the reform did raise revenue, but this was an illusory success; by 1959, the growth in taxpayer numbers and revenue plateaued (Comín and Vallejo 2012). Neither the 1957 reform nor the Stabilization Plan modified the antiquated tax structure that disproportionately taxed labour over capital, with indirect taxes making up most of the revenue. The tax system still heavily relied on indirect taxes, which grew from under half to nearly 60% of tax revenue by 1969. Tax evasion also plagued the system, with evasion rates at the end of the 1960s reaching over 40% of fiscal revenues. Such a fiscal system was characteristic of a less developed country, with dire implications for inequality and the scarcity of fiscal resources needed to foster economic development.

In sum, given the unwillingness to undertake reforms, it became essential to use other channels: monetary policy and the regulation of financial markets. Certain practices, which had become entrenched as pernicious habits of governments of all stripes in previous decades, were continued. In this sense, the Franco regime was heir to this tradition, typical of poor and outdated treasuries. However, the intensity and breadth of the regulatory measures taken by the successive governments of Franco and their very limited fiscal commitment point to a new phase in the history of the Spanish economy. In this way, the Franco regime was able to continue serving the interests of the groups that had supported it since the uprising, while at the same time attending to the minimal needs of the state and supporting its autarkic programme.

Martínez-Ruiz (2017) makes a series of estimations to assess state revenues from financial repression for the period (1946–1975) (see Figure 8.5).[6] Using

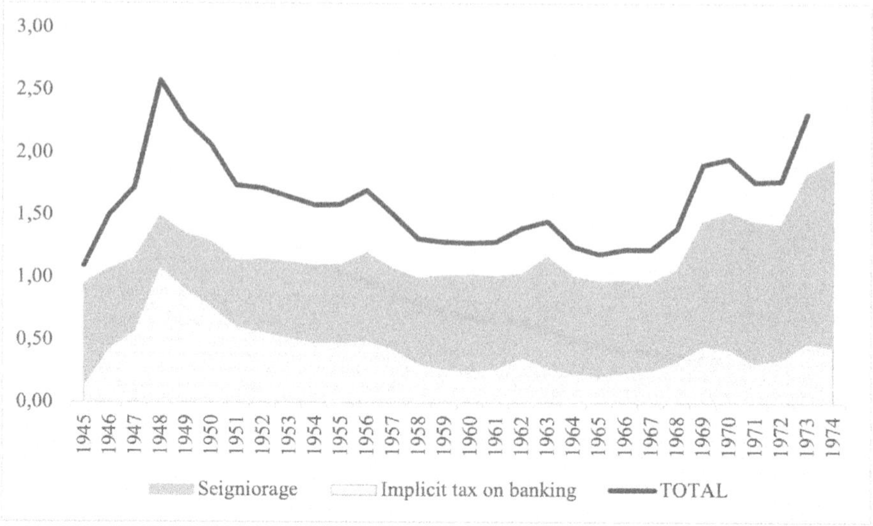

Figure 8.5 Implicit revenues on GDP, % (1946–1975).

Source: Martínez-Ruiz (2017)

the methodology proposed by Repullo (1992), which allows for a simultaneous and consistent estimation of the types of revenue from monetary and financial regulation in a single framework, she estimates that the average ratio of revenues from seigniorage and implicit tax to GDP was around 1.68% on average (very close to the average value of 1.7% calculated by Repullo (1992) for the period 1980–1990).[7] Seigniorage accounted for about a 1.2% share of GDP and the implicit taxes on the banking system amounted to around 0.7% on average over the analyzed period. Hence, the main source of revenue was money creation, averaging 11.7% of total state revenue during the autarky. In fact, seigniorage always accounted for around 70% of total state revenues from financial repression, while the regulation of the financial system contributed around 30%. It is worth mentioning though that the banking system was more heavily used as a source of income for the state at the beginning of the period, while the seigniorage revenues grew steadily in the last years of the regime. Martínez-Ruiz also uses the Giovannini and De Melo (1993) index, which focuses on the revenues due to the placement of public debt in the banking systems, to estimate the costs of financial repression. The ratio of financial repression tax revenues to GDP according to Martínez-Ruiz estimates is around 2%, almost identical to the estimate of Giovannini and De Melo (1993) for a sample of developing countries in the same period.[8]

Looking now at the ratio of the implicit tax of the financial repression to total fiscal revenue, we gain a better understanding of the importance of the implicit tax for the Francoist state.

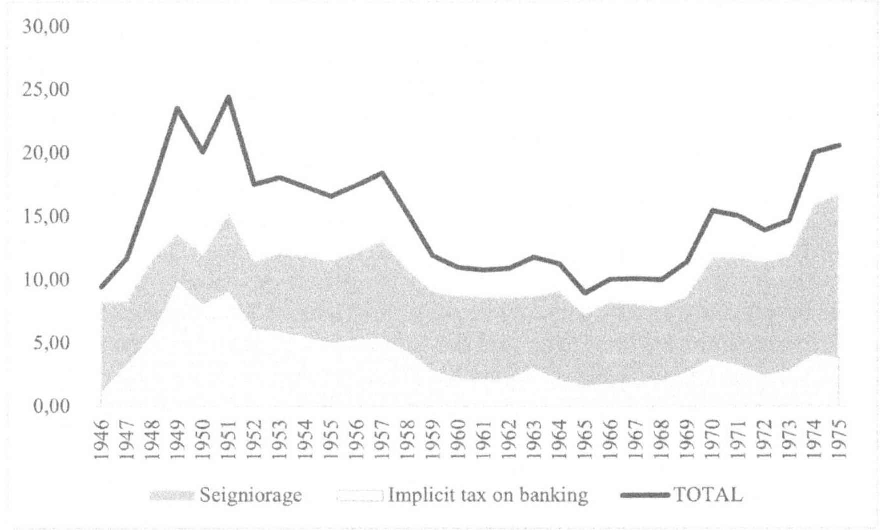

Figure 8.6 Implicit taxes as percentage of ordinary revenues (1946–1958).
Source: Martínez-Ruiz (2017)

As Figure 8.6 shows, revenues from financial repression amounted to around 1/5 of ordinary revenues from 1945 to 1958 and represented around 12% of total revenues. The highest tax revenues were obtained in the sub-period 1949–1951. Moreover, the ratio of financial repression tax revenues to total revenues was high, averaging 18% from 1945 to 1957, and even getting close to 25% in the sub-period 1949–1952. It then fell, before rising again from 1968 onwards. The fall in tax revenues due to banking regulation from 1959 onwards is most probably related to the limitations imposed on new public debt issuance. It should not be forgotten, however, that these financing channels were replaced by the so-called privileged financing circuits that directed capital towards the sectors considered a priority by the state.

In any case, the inflationary tax or seigniorage represented the most important revenue-raising channel. It is true that some of these forms of financing were not new in Spain, as the direct or indirect monetization of the deficit had a long tradition dating back to 1874. However, during the Franco period, the main and almost sole objective of monetary policy was to respond to the state's financial needs, with no attention paid to monetary stability. In this sense, it can be said that the authorities sacrificed the goal of controlling inflation to promote industrialization and growth. Although Spain was no different from some other European countries in this regard, Francoist authorities were less sensitive to the risks of inflation than other European governments, as shown by the massive use of inflationary methods of public financing and the passive monetary policy.

8.6 Conclusions

During the Francoist regime, the industrialist rhetoric of the economic leaders clashed with the lack of resources needed to promote the country's economic development. As the government decided, for strictly political reasons, not to tackle a tax reform, it became essential to use other channels: monetary policy and the regulation of financial markets. The impact of banking regulation on the financial sector and in macroeconomic terms has been widely studied in the literature. As this paper has shown, the main effects on the banking system were the lack of competition, the banking sector inefficiencies, distortions caused by privileged credit circuits, the price of bank investments, the Bank of Spain's lack of power to regulate the entire credit system, and the lack of a real banking supervision. The main approaches to banking regulation have also been discussed. From a monetary policy perspective, the use of financial repression had significant effects in terms of inflation.

Furthermore, less emphasis has been placed on other control mechanisms that were also essential for financial repression: stock market regulation and exchange rate controls. As mentioned, Franco's regulation presented innumerable obstacles to the development of the stock market, and its reversal after the civil war is clear. Stock market controls were conceived by the Franco government as an instrument to discourage alternative investment opportunities for the private sector (including the banks) and guarantee the necessary financial resources. This situation was especially marked during the years of the most autarkic policy, when the rigidity of monetary policy posed significant challenges for the functioning of the bond (fixed-income) market and international isolation prevented the integration of the Spanish stock market with the rest of Europe.

Exchange restrictions were also essential for the financial survival of the Franco regime, as they prevented private agents from evading the taxes implicit in the monetary and financial regulation put in place during the autarkic period. This financing strategy harmed the growth possibilities of the Spanish economy because the use of seigniorage and financial regulation as sources of revenue created distortions that prevented an efficient allocation of resources, delayed the formation of an efficient financial system, and reduced the formation of productive capital. Thus, the use of the inflationary tax during the Francoist period was complemented by other forms of regulation of the financial markets, which were also used to raise funds for the state and allowed the indefinite postponement of the increasingly necessary fiscal reform.

Notes

1 Financial repression can be defined as "a set of policies, laws, regulation, taxes, distortions, qualitative and quantitative restrictions, which do not allow financial intermediaries to operate at their full potential" (McKinnon, 1973).

2 The index goes from 0, indicating the minimum, to 100, indicating the maximum repression. It is based on the following variables: a) real reserve requirements (the ratio of bank reserves to total bank deposits), b) real interest rates, c) the level of financial

intermediation (M2/GDP ratio), d) government liabilities held by the banking sector, and e) size of the securities market (the ratio of securities annually issued in the domestic market to GDP).

3 This significant proportion encompasses not only commercial and savings banks but also credits offered by public banks (official banks) to firms considered strategic according to the Development Plans.

4 Spanish Mortgage Bank (BHE), Agrarian Credit Bank (BCA), Building Credit Bank (BCC), Industrial Credit Bank (BCI), Local Credit Bank (BCL), Fishing and Social Credit Bank (CSP), and Spanish Foreign Bank (BEX).

5 Although the main objective of some regulations was to protect the interest of traditional lobbies, government intervention also had a strong ideological motivation. The interest of the Franco government in involving the banking sector in their strategy of development explains why several measures did not benefit the banking system. For example, the branch expansion restrictions, the limits on dividends, or the monopolistic position of some public banks such as the Banco Exterior de España in foreign trade (because the bank was specifically authorized to conduct all banking operations in Spain connected with the interchange of goods, services, and capital between Spain and foreign countries). The serious criticisms of the Superior Banking Council and the Banco de Vizcaya (Bank of Spain Archives, *Informe sobre el Proyecto de Ley de Ordenación Bancaria de 1946*, unclassified) levelled at the *Proyecto de Ley de Ordenación Bancaria de 1946* (Bill of the 1946 BSL) and the opposition to some of the main amendments proposed by the Franco government is another example of this lack of alignment between banking and government interests.

6 The article includes estimations following different approaches proposed by Giovannini and de Melo (1993), Beim and Calomiris (2001), and Reinhart and Sbrancia (2011).

7 Repullo's methodology is based on an opportunity cost approach, in which it is possible to simultaneously measure the agents' opportunity cost of holding money or debt and – the relevant aspect from a fiscal point of view – the interest savings that the state obtains from its monopoly on money issuance and debt placement.

8 Using a different methodology, Battilossi (2005) estimates a similar index for Spain and Portugal for the period 1950–1998. According to his estimation, the revenues from financial repression would be lower, with a maximum of 0.08.

References

Abiad, A., Detragiache, E. and Tressel, T. A. (2010): "A New Database of Financial Reforms." *IMF Staff Papers*, vol. 57, No. 2, pp. 281–302. https://doi.org/10.1057/imfsp.2009.23.

Battilossi, S. (2004): "The Little Reversal: Capital Markets and Financial Repression in Western Europe in the Second Half of the 20th Century." http://hdl.handle.net/10016/5533.

Battilossi, S. (2005): "The Second Reversal: The Ebb and Flow of Financial Repression in Western Europe, 1960–91." http://hdl.handle.net/10016/5537.

Beim, D. O. and Calomiris, Ch. W. (2001): *Emerging Financial Markets*. New York: McGraw-Hill Irwin.

Calomiris, C. H. and Haber, S. (2014): *Fragile by Design*. Princeton: Princeton University Press.

Comín, F. (2003): "La Hacienda pública en el franquismo autárquico, 1940–1959," in C. Barciela (Cord.) *Autarquía y mercado negro: el fracaso económico del primer franquismo, 1939–1959*. Barcelona: Crítica, pp. 247–272.

Comín, F. (2016): *Las crisis de la deuda soberana en España (1500–2015)*. Madrid: Catarata.

Comín, F. and Cuevas, J. (2017): "The Deadly Embrace Between the Banks and the State in Spain, 1850–2015." *Revista de Historia Económica, Journal of Iberian and Latin American Economic History*, vol. 35, No. 3, pp. 387–414.

Comín, F. and Díaz, D. (2005): "Sector público administrativo y estado del bienestar," in *Estadísticas Históricas de España*. Bilbao: Fundación BBVA, pp. 873–964.

Comín, F. and Martorell, M. (2013): *La hacienda pública en el franquismo. La guerra y la autarquía (1936–1959)*. Madrid: Instituto de Estudios Fiscales.
Comín, F. and Vallejo, R. (2012): "La reforma tributaria de 1957 en las Cortes franquistas." *Investigaciones de Historia Económica*, vol. 8, No. 3, pp. 154–163.
Cuevas, J. and Pons, M. A. (2021): "1977: Hopes Fulfilled-Building Democracy in Turbulent Economic Times," in C. Betrán and M. A. Pons (Eds.) *Historical Turning Points in Spanish Economic Growth and Development, 1808–2008*. Palgrave Macmillan, pp. 159–194.
Cuevas, J. and Pons, M. A. (2024, forthcoming): *Historia de la supervisión bancaria en España*, Madrid: Banco de España-Estudios de Historia Económica.
Faus-Mompart, E. (2001): *Regulación y desregulación. Notas para la historia de la banca española*. Barcelona: Península.
García Delgado, J. L. (1985): "Nacionalismo económico e intervención estatal, 1900–1930," in N. Sánchez Albornoz (Ed.) *La modernización económica de España, 1830–1930*. Madrid: Alianza Ed.
García Ruiz, J. L. (2002): "Los arreglos interbancarios durante el Franquismo." *Revista de Historia Económica, Journal of Iberian and Latin American Economic History*, vol. 20, No. 2, pp. 365–386.
García Ruiz, J. L. (2019): "Las políticas industriales del Franquismo: una revisión," in J. L. García Ruiz (Coord.) *Políticas industriales en España. Pasado, presente y future*. Madrid: Paraninfo, pp. 33–75.
Giovannini, A. and De Melo, M. (1993): "Government Revenue from Financial Repression." *American Economic Review*, vol. 83, No. 4, pp. 953–963.
González, M. J. (1979): *La Economía Política del Franquismo (1940–1970): Dirigismo, mercado y planificación*. Madrid: Tecnos.
Hoffman, A. (2019): "Beware of Financial Repression: Lessons from History." *Intereconomics. Review of European Economic Policy*, vol. 54, No. 4, pp. 259–266.
Hoyo, A. (2007): *Economía y mercado de valores en la España contemporánea: la evolución de la Bolsa antes del big bang español, 1831–1988*. Santander: Universidad de Cantabria.
Lukauskas, A. J. (1997): *The Political Economy of Financial Deregulation: The Case of Spain*, Ann Harbor, MI: University of Michigan Press.
McKinnon, R. I. (1973): *Money and Capital in Economic Development*. Washington, DC: The Brookings Institution.
Martín-Aceña, P. (1988): *Una estimación de los principales agregados monetarios en España, 1940–1962*. Madrid: Banco de España.
Martín-Aceña, P. (1989): "Sector financiero" en A. Carreras (Coor.) *Estadísticas históricas de España, siglos XIX-XX*. Madrid: Fundación Banco Exterior, pp. 363–394.
Martín-Aceña, P., Blasco, Y. and Cuevas, J. (2016): *El Instituto de Crédito Oficial, 1971–2015*. Madrid: Dextra.
Martínez-Ruiz, E. (2000): *El control de cambios en la España franquista: el Instituto Español de Moneda Extranjera, 1939–1973*, PhD thesis, Universidad de Alcalá.
Martínez-Ruiz, E. (2017): *Represión financiera y liquidación de deuda pública en España (1899–1975)*. WP-17/03, Dep. Economía, Universidad de Alcalá.
Mullin, J. (2021): "A Look Back at Financial Repression." *Econ Focus*, first quarter 2021, pp. 22–25.
Muñoz, J. (1969): *El poder de la banca en España*. Madrid: Ed. Zero.
Perez, S. A. (1997): *Banking on Privilege: The Politics of Spanish Financial Reform*. Ithaca-London: Cornell University Press.
Pérez de Armiñán, G. (1976): *Legislación bancaria Española*. Madrid: Banco de España.
Pons, M. A. (2002): *Regulating Spanish banking, 1939–1975*. Aldershoot: Ashgate.
Pons, M. A. (2011): "The Main Reforms of the Spanish Financial System," in J. L. Malo de Molina and P. Martín-Aceña (Eds.) *The Spanish Financial System. Growth and Development Since 1900*. Bansigtoke: Palgrave Macmillan, pp. 71–98.
Poveda, R. (1972): *La creación de dinero en España, 1956–1970*. Madrid: Instituto de Estudios Fiscales.

Poveda, R. (1980): "Los circuitos privilegiados del sistema crediticio." *Papeles de economía española*, No. 3, pp. 114–135.

Poveda, R. (1981): "Política monetaria y financiera," en L. Gámir (Ed.) *Política económica en España*. Madrid: Alianza Editorial, pp. 71–132.

Prados de la Escosura, L. (2003): *El progreso económico de España (1850–2000)*. Bilbao: Fundación BBVA.

Pueyo, J. (2003). "Oligopolio y competencia en la banca española del siglo xx: concentración económica y movilidad intra-industrial, 1922–1995." *Revista de Historia Económica*, vol. 21, No. 1, pp. 147–198.

Pueyo, J. (2006): "El comportamiento de la gran banca en España (1921–1974)." *Estudios de historia económica*, No. 48, pp. 1–97.

Reinhart, C. and Sbrancia, B. (2011): *The Liquidation of Government Debt*. NBER Working Paper Series, No. 16893.

Reinhart, C. M., Kierkegaard, J. F. and Sbrancia M. B. (2011): "Financial Repression Redux." *Finance & Development*, vol. 48, No. 1, pp. 23–27.

Repullo, R. (1992): "Financing Budgeting Deficits by Seigniorage and Implicit Taxation: The Case of Spain and Portugal," en D. E. Fair y C. de Boossieu (Eds.) *Fiscal Policy, Taxation and the Financial System in an Increasingly Integrated Europe*. Boston, Dordrecht, London: Kluwer Academic Publishers, pp. 235–253.

Roldán, S., García Delgado, J. L. and Muñoz, J. (1973): *La consolidación del capitalismo en España*. Madrid: Confederación Española de Cajas de Ahorro.

Sardá, J. (1970): "El Banco de España 1931–1962," en VV.AA. *El Banco de España. Una historia económica*. Madrid: Banco de España.

Tafunell, X. (2005): "Empresa y bolsa," in *Estadísticas Históricas de España. Siglos XIX y XX*. Bilbao: Fundación BBVA.

Tortella, G. and García Ruiz, J. L. (2003): "Banca y política durante el primer franquismo," in G. Sánchez Recioand J. Tascón (Eds.) *Los empresarios de Franco. Política y economía en España, 1936–1957*. Barcelona: Crítica, pp. 67–99.

Tortella, G. and García Ruiz, J. L. (2013): *Spanish Money and Banking: A History*. Basingstoke: Palgrave Macmillan.

9 Dictatorial rule and macroeconomic management

Greece, 1967–1974

Michalis Psalidopoulos

9.1 Introduction

Greece, an independent country since 1830 and a constitutional monarchy since 1843, and up to 1974 (with a republican interval between 1923 and 1935), experienced political instability quite often in its history. During six months in 1926 and for four years between 1936 and 1940, dictatorial rule was imposed to control social tensions and economic dead ends. Then, after the Second World War and a civil war from 1946 to 1949 leading to the defeat of the communist camp, a good economic performance started brewing. At first British and later American financial assistance supported the healing of the wounds of World War II and civil war, followed by a successful currency devaluation in 1953. The political right ruled the country after the 1952 elections. The rates of growth were high and inflation was low for the next decade. The political climate however remained tense with the Center Union government winning the 1963 elections. Two years later, a clash between the Prime Minister and the King erupted, with the latter overstepping his jurisdiction and trying to impose a new political order in the country. This led political turbulence and instability to reach new heights that finally led to the imposition of a military dictatorship in April 1967. In October 1973, the junta attempted to transition to a controlled "democratic" regime with the consequence of internal fighting between military fractions and a change of dictatorial guards. The winners of this fight provoked six months later a political crisis in Cyprus that led to Turkey invading that island. In the wake of this crisis, the military regime collapsed in July 1974.

The Greek dictatorship was short-lived compared to Spain and Portugal, and its legacy, political and economic, is still being debated.[1] The purpose of this chapter is to assess macroeconomic management and development policy of the dictatorship with emphasis on the evolution of economic thought in Greece during that period and thus provide a different perspective from studies offering political explanations in the realm of East/West relations in times of the Cold War.

Economics in Greece was institutionalized as an academic discipline in 1920, and a generation of economists who either were mostly trained in interwar Germany, to a lesser degree in France, or had simply completed their PhDs in Greece and gone through a specific academic process, was dominant. This generation was

DOI: 10.4324/9781032656199-10

approaching retirement age during the dictatorship, and it was during the rule of the colonels that economics in Greece became internationalized and more extroverted.

Our narrative starts with a brief reference to international political economy after the Second World War, followed by economic developments and the state of economic thought and policy in Greece up to the imposition of the dictatorship. In a next subchapter, we acquaint ourselves with the economic administrators of the dictatorship trying to identify differences in approach and economic ideas between them and the older generation of policy makers. We revisit macroeconomic developments and trace the different expansionary roles played by the central bank and by specialized development banks during that period. We also take note of changing international economic conditions after the breakdown of the Bretton Woods Agreement in 1971 and investigate the economic policy of the dictatorship at times before and after the collapse of the fixed exchange rate system. In the final paragraph we draw our conclusions.

9.2 The international setting from 1945 up to the mid-1970s

The immediate post-Second World War global economic order to which Greece was a part was characterized by the Cold War and the gradual decolonization of the Third World countries that was completed in the early 1960s. The Bretton Woods conference in 1944 was a starting point[2] with the creation of institutions such as the IMF and the World Bank and the introduction of the dollar as main international currency. The need to safeguard free trade led to the creation of the General Agreement on Tariffs and Trade (GATT) in 1947. The West-European countries were led in the wake of the implementation of the Marshall Plan to cooperate in the Organization of European Economic Cooperation (OEEC), and later the Organization of Economic Cooperation and Development (OECD). This cooperation led to the creation of the European Economic Communities (EEC) in 1957. French "Planification" and German "Konzertierte Aktion" were two economic policy mixes that were in line and proved the validity of the "neoclassical synthesis" propagated after the Second World War by prominent academics such as Paul Samuelson. The quick rebound of the US economy under J.F. Kennedy's watch in 1962 through lower taxes combined with increases in state expenditure cemented the global belief that private initiative plus government intervention was a necessity for fast growth rates (Stein 1969; Bernstein 2001; Spulber 1990). Development economics as a subfield of the discipline rose to prominence and offered to less developed countries alternative strategies to growth (Arndt 1987; Rist 1997). Thus, from 1945 to 1971, a "golden era" in economic policy was internationally achieved: growth – price stability – (nearly) full employment. In certain countries, economic downturns due to either short-lived competitiveness losses or balance-of-payments deficits led to currency devaluations as in France (1959) and in the UK (1967). Under the existing global system, Germany and Japan accumulated huge current account surpluses and the United States was always in deficit, a situation that led eventually the fixed exchange rate system in a dead-end and to its demise in August 1971. In December 1971, the short-lived "Smithsonian Agreement" tried to control existing monetary fluctuations and stayed in place until May 1973. This agreement tried to support weaker economies, such as Greece, to cope with international exchanges, but could not withstand the occurrence of irregular capital movements. Then, the first oil crisis hit the global economy in October 1973 and less developed economies faced renewed adjustment challenges.

These events coincided with internal fighting among dictatorial fractions in Greece on the proper way to handle political life. The global economy entered a period of stagflation, which challenged the dominant economic paradigm of the neoclassical synthesis. Greece experienced an unprecedented inflation in 1973–1974 that provoked popular unrest. Monetarism, already known and popular, became after a transition period the basis of economic policy in the US and the UK, especially after the second oil crisis, in the early 1980s. The adoption of free market policies and the control of the money supply rose to superior fame as policy maxims in place of ad hoc fiscal and monetary "Keynesian", "neoclassical synthesis" policies. The slow but irreversible transition to this new situation coincided with the restoration of democracy in Greece.

9.3 Economic performance and economic thought in Greece up to 1967

Throughout the Greek economy's course towards higher income levels, successive governments since 1953 strived to transform the institutional framework with a view to encouraging private initiative, domestic and foreign, to invest in Greece. Despite the tense political environment of the times, Greece experienced an annual GDP growth rate of 6.6% between 1953 and 1967 with the inflation rate at 1.8%, starting however from a very low income level.

The economy remained heavily agricultural with the primary sector accounting for 30% of GDP in 1960. Manufacturing increased its share in GDP from 18% in 1960 to 30% in 1975, and services, including shipping and tourism, were expanding constantly. Industrial development was assisted by specialized development banks that provided targeted credit for big investment projects.

Despite the strong growth performance, the negative balance of payments was a serious problem and concern for policy makers. In fact, Greek economists defined a "balance of payments problem" as an obstacle to growth in Greece (Chalikias 1958). Exports of commodities were always less than imports since independence. The growing industrial sector imported most of its technological equipment due to the almost complete absence of home industrial units producing means of production. Although inflows from shipping and emigrant remittances covered this deficit partially, the balance of payments remained negative.

Laws inducing businesses to continue investing in the secondary sector and favouring foreign capital to invest in Greece were vehicles used but were not capable of solving the continuous government need for funds that would balance the external sector of the economy. In the late 1950s, faced with a reduction of US financial aid and a persistently growing trade deficit, the Greek economy sought a closer association with broader economic areas that were taking shape at the time. After the talks with the Economic Free Trade Association (EFTA) came to an impasse, Greece turned to negotiations with the EEC, applying for membership in July 1959. These led to the signing of an Association Agreement on 9 July 1961. This agreement envisaged the abolition of tariffs on Greek exports to the EEC countries over a period of 12 years, and a respective elimination of Greek tariffs on imports from the EEC in 22 years. It also provided access to European Investment Bank (EIB) financing for investment projects in Greece. EEC association provided a fresh impetus to economic growth in Greece and encouraged a reorientation of Greek exports towards EEC countries.

Economics in Greece was, as already mentioned, institutionalized since 1920 but the group of academics teaching the subject at various Greek universities was small. Academic economists needed to have next to a PhD a second monograph ("ifigessia") to be eligible in the future for a full professorial appointment. This degree was mostly granted by the Law School of the University of Athens, which thus controlled the reproduction of academic teaching in economics at all Greek universities until the late 1970s.[3]

Professor and Central Banker Xenophon Zolotas was the most influential economist of the period and due to his profile and personality he could count on a big following. According to Zolotas, the declared aim of economic policy ought to be monetary stability accompanied by fiscal prudence and this was the norm for successive governments until 1963. His approach foresaw an ordinary budget that should be always balanced. Next to it a separate budget for public investment existed and this could be in temporary deficit to be covered through grants and loans from abroad (Zolotas 1965).

The prominent politician Panagis Papaligouras, a philosopher turned economist, minister of the right-wing governments of the period, and close to Prime Minister Constantine Karamanlis, was implementing and supporting these policies. Papaligouras held Law and Economics degrees from the University of Athens and a PhD from the Advanced School of International Studies in Geneva. He adopted during his graduate studies the globalist agenda of the Geneva School (Slobodian 2018) and fused it with (German) ordoliberalism and social market economy views in line with his early philosophical thought that favoured social policy.

In the late 1950s/early 1960s, despite the satisfactory economic indicators, many intellectuals criticized the rejection of Keynesian-type expansionary policies by these Greek liberals. The main reason that sprung out of continued unemployment and underemployment led to massive emigration to Belgium and Germany. Between 1956 and 1966, almost 10% of the Greek labour force migrated to these countries.[4]

When, in 1963, the Centre Union came to power, Andreas Papandreou, a US-trained economics professor and politician, started rising to superior fame. Papandreou had returned to Greece to assist the efforts to modernize Greek economics. He advocated import substitution and structural changes in the footsteps of the ideas propagated in the ECLA, the OECD, and various academic circles about the need to accelerate economic growth in less developed countries. These ideas didn't emphasize monetary stability and sound public finance and led the Center Union government to expand expenditure for education and public health.

Papandreou founded the Center of Planning and Economic Research (KEPE) with American assistance in the early 1960s. KEPE started publishing monographs on current economic problems, undertook the drafting of indicative five-year plans, and invited foreign economists to give seminars to KEPE staff. Econometrics and mathematical techniques in economics became the new routine. KEPE staff was assisted with scholarships to pursue academic degrees in the USA or in the UK and return to the country. Thus, economics in Greece was internationalized and some members of this young generation of economists got appointments during the dictatorship. Others followed in the mid-1970s, and they all started conquering Greek academia. In 1971, the dictatorship introduced the autonomous degree in economics at all existing Greek universities and started the gradual process of filling academic positions on various subfields of the discipline. Membership in the Hellenic Association of Economic Science grew from approximately 80 members in the early 1960s to over 300 in 1973 when the Association hosted its last annual conference meeting.[5] The older generation members who had gone through the ifigessia process at the Law School of the University of Athens and were trained mostly in Germany and France were reaching the retirement age during that period. As we will see, some of the KEPE economists together with the selected members of the older generation provided their services to the dictatorship after 1967.

9.4 Economic developments, 1967–1974

The dictator Georgios Papadopoulos was an authoritarian leader who used in his speeches a bombastic rhetoric against individualism favoring the fulfillment of collective goals (Papadopoulos 1968–1972, vol. 2, 26). He appealed very early, on March 15, 1968, to the Greek bankers, comparing them with the special forces of the army on a night mission, demanding that they "avoid arteriosclerosis" from the past (Papadopoulos 1968–1972, vol. 2, 28) and provide liquidity for business activities.

One of the first measures of his government, and despite criticizing the populist, vote seeking, and corrupt, according to him, Greek political system, was to write off all debt of peasants to the Agricultural Bank of Greece (Papadopoulos 1968–1972, vol. 2, 90–96). The aim was to provide the restart of Greek agriculture without past burdens and to reap popular consent in place of abolished individual rights. In his many interventions, he advocated indicative planning for increased spending for research (Papadopoulos 1968–1972, vol 3, 41–46) and the need to impact economic performance for a better economic future for Greece (Papadopoulos 1968–1972, vol. 3, 52–53).

The specialists of the dictatorship on economic affairs included above all Nikolaos Makarezos who served as Economic Coordination Minister from 1967 to 1971 and as Deputy Prime Minister from 1971 to 1973. He held degrees in economics and politics from Greek universities, but he had no exposure to graduate studies. His ministerial team included Aristidis Dimopoulos, Ioannis Rodinos-Orlandos, Emmanuel Fthenakis, Ioulios Evlambios, and others. Another important administrator was Nikolaos Androutsopoulos, a lawyer who was Minister of Finance from 1967 to 1971, Minister of the Interior, and then Prime Minister and Finance Minister after 1973. Professor Ioannis Koulis, a public finance specialist and an academic of the old generation, was Finance Minister between 1971 and 1973.

Other important economists who became professors during the dictatorship and served it from ministerial positions after 1973 included Elias Balopoulos, Chairman of KEPE and Triantafyllos Eleftheriou from the same institution. From the old generation of economists, Prof. Georgios Coutsoumaris served as Minister of Agriculture in 1973, Sotirios Agapitidis as Vice Minister of Coordination from 1972 to 1973 and Dimitrios Delivanis as Chairman of KEPE after 1973. From this group, Balopoulos, Eleftheriou, and Koulis were suspended from public service for life after the restoration of democracy. Coutsoumaris was suspended for one year and Agapitidis for three years. Delivanis was not affected, as he retired due to age in 1974.

At the Central Bank, Deputy Governor Dimitrios Galanis became the new governor and served until 1973 followed by Kostas Papagiannis, whereas Efstathios Panas and Kostas Thanos served as vice governors, the latter until 1973, when he became vice minister. Panas and Thanos held Galanis in check, making sure that the economic policy goals of the dictatorship were accommodated.

The economists/administrators of the dictatorship did not commit to the ideas of the former generation. The slow anglo-saxonization of Greek economics after 1944 had penetrated the dominating German/French economic thought of the period and led during the dictatorship to a clear shift in the realm of ideas. After all those who got their degrees in the 1960s knew mathematical techniques. They also knew that the neoclassical synthesis as applied worldwide could assist performing good economic results.

Balopoulos who had a PhD from the UK and was considered an expert on active fiscal policy (Balopoulos 1967) mastered from KEPE the new policy-in-the-making, submitting proposals, and overseeing implementation. He was coordinating the former five-year plan and mastered the one covering 1968–1972. Galanis from the Bank of Greece oversaw the transition of the economy to a new paradigm in monetary policy. Makarezos as a practitioner was preoccupied with the positive depiction of the government's actions and called, like Papadopoulos, the approach of the junta as having "humanistic" instead of selfish aims (Makarezos 2006, 83). Planning for growth was hailed by him (Makarezos 2006, 104–121) and a comprehensive approach for sectoral growth was envisaged combined with a propaganda to prefer local rather than imported goods.

Efstathios Panas as co-governor of the Central Bank analyzed the policy of control of effective demand (Panas 1971a) and concluded that this was an important weapon for pursuing active policies in the economy. Only if authorities were slow in intervening in times of inflation would effective demand policy prove problematic (Panas 1971a, 74). In a follow-up publication, he outlined the government's planning for growth in positive terms (Panas 1971b).

A basic problem of the dictatorship consisted in the 1962 agreement with the EEC. Relations between the democratic EEC countries and the Greek authoritarian government froze. The tariff part of the agreement continued as scheduled but financing to Greece from European Investment Bank sources stopped. Therefore, the need to access liquidity and thus minimize pressure on the balance of payments was greater than ever.

The ultimate goal of economic policy during the dictatorship was economic development, with monetary stability coming second. On paper and in speeches government economists pleaded in favor of less regulation and sound monetary policy, in practice however, the programs of public investment, housing construction, and tourism became the vehicles for more growth. Tax rates for businesses were relaxed and the KEPE five-year plan 1968–1972 suggested an expansionary monetary policy. The Currency Committee at the Central Bank that monitored monetary stability became more forthcoming to financing economic activities without broader "quality type" considerations of the past. Being dependent from the central government, the Bank of Greece supported verbally this new approach towards more flexibility referring as we will see in the next section to similar policies pursued abroad. The new mantra was "the accelerated rhythm of economic development" and past regulations about the use of borrowed money were relaxed/abolished. Commercial banks became totally free to judge about private investment proposals as opposed to the period before 1967 and import substitution and a "prefer Greek products" strategy was introduced and implemented. The stirring of the economy brought as already mentioned initially positive results. Almost full employment, leading to immigrants appearing in the Greek labor market, was recorded in 1971, accompanied however by signs of overheating. The new situation after the collapse of the Bretton Woods system and the absence of political ties with European countries led to the drachma depreciating but not leading to increased exports.

An overall climate of uncertainty prevailed, in which the productive classes felt disoriented. The industrialists, in particular, who were recipients of credit and benefited from the reduction of European tariffs for their products started worrying for prospects. The Bank of Greece tightened its monetary policy in 1972, with a view to reducing liquidity in the economy: the minimum reserve ratio in the Bank of Greece was raised and credit to construction companies was suspended. In February 1972, when the US dollar lost another 10% of its value vis-à-vis gold, the drachma followed suit and depreciated again. As the situation was not improving the Central Bank increased in May 1973 interest rates on bank deposits, as well as the discount rate, in a new effort to limit liquidity. Soon afterwards in October 1973, the first oil shock occurred, and higher oil prices were passed through to domestic inflation. The Central Bank in an ultimate attempt to defend the drachma, decided to unpeg it from the US dollar and appreciate it by 10%, alongside a relaxation of price controls. These spontaneous actions without prior agreements with partners took place amid internal dictatorial fighting. Domestic economic activity slowed down, and growth stalled. The Greek economy experienced a hard landing, and inflation leaped to 35% year-on-year between August 1973 and August 1974. The drachma returned to its old parity of 30 drachmas per US dollar in the next few months, while the Central Bank pursued once again a disinflationary policy as the political crisis peeked following the events in Cyprus that led to the restoration of democracy.

9.5 Monetary policy expanding, 1967–1974

The orientation of economic policy, in particular credit policy, as practiced until 1967, was as already mentioned, drastically changed during the military dictatorship. The dictatorial regime promised verbally to free the economy of controls and restrictions and reduce state intervention. Emphasis was placed on galvanizing the economy by increasing public investment expenditure, supporting the construction and tourism industries, repealing tax provisions such as those regarding taxation of capital gains on immovable property, lowering tax rates and raising tax-free thresholds.[6]

During autumn 1967, the ceiling on the Central Bank's temporary facilities to the Greek State increased. Legislative Decree 513/1970 increased the share capital of the Bank of Greece by 25%, with a view to strengthening the Bank's capital position, but also stimulating the capital market through the public offering of the new shares.[7] Monetary and credit policy became expansionary and geared towards the goals of the Five-Year Economic Development Plan (1968–1972), while also having "a redistributive character" in terms of reallocation of the available credit resources.[8]

The Central Bank was allowed to discount medium-term loans extended by banks for investment in industry, construction, tourism, and shipyards. This measure was intended to encourage investment activities in the above four sectors on a more permanent basis. Furthermore, special low-cost credit in the form of discounts was granted for new categories of short-term financing, inter alia, to wheat merchants and public works contractors, while the long-term funding programmes for the specialized financial institutions, such as the Agricultural Bank, the Postal Savings Bank, the National Mortgage Bank, and the Consignment and Loan Fund, were expanded. A large-scale agricultural housing programme and an affordable workers' housing programme were launched, along with an expansion of the existing housing loan schemes of mortgage banks. In the tourist sector, a special programme for the financing of tourism facilities was launched, and the Greek National Tourism Organisation was supported by Bank of Greece funds for extending loans to tourism enterprises.

Credit regulations underwent fundamental changes: commercial banks were now allowed to extend medium-term financing for residential construction and investment in tourism. Credit to shipyards was expanded, the procedure for the financing of domestic trade was simplified, and a scheme was introduced for the short-term financing of wheat trade by commercial banks.

According to authorities, some of these changes related to "countercyclical policy" and other changes were aimed at establishing "a more liberal credit system" and restore banks' functional role in managing the available credit instruments.[9]

The changes represented "a transition from specific to general regulations" and to a "more flexible" credit control system, marking a first step towards a full abolition of qualitative controls on credit.[10]

The requirement on prospective borrowers to submit tax and social security contribution clearance certificates was abolished. Commercial banks were given a free hand to carry out lending operations at their own discretion, with almost no restriction as to the type of lending.[11] This marked a shift from qualitative to quantitative credit controls, therefore bank credit to private and public investments grew rapidly.

It is worth noting that the general guidelines provided by the Bank of Greece to commercial banks did not include restrictions, but only recommendations, for example, to avoid the overfinancing of enterprises. Thus, banks were "absolutely free to make decisions on the best part of their financial operations".[12]

Thus, the primary objective of currency stability was superseded by the pursuit of fast economic growth. To comply with the instructions of the military dictatorship, the Central Bank noted that monetary equilibrium was not the ultimate aim of economic policy, and that the role of the Bank of Greece was to promote the development process and implement the Five-Year Economic Development Plan. As was stated, "[M]onetary stability is not viewed by the Bank of Greece as an exclusive and independent goal. On the contrary, the central bank regards as its basic objective, mainly through its redistributive role, the rapid promotion of the country's economic development", adding that economic policy should be prepared for any adjustments needed to maintain monetary equilibrium and continue the economic development process without any interruption, which represented a national target and the point on which the efforts of the Greek people ought to be focused.[13]

This stance in support of the dictatorial regime's choices began to gradually change after August 1971, against the backdrop of the international monetary crisis and, subsequently, the emergence of strong inflationary pressures. Now critical words were articulated about monetary expansion. It was admitted that it "cannot be beneficial for the economy, as it leads to development-inhibiting asymmetry in the structure of production and the allocation of available resources".[14]

The international monetary crisis slowed Greek growth. There was an increase in invisible receipts and a rise in total liquidity, which however made the Greek economy more vulnerable to changes in sentiment and less responsive to short-term fiscal/monetary steering.

Galanis defended the policy choice to keep the drachma pegged to the devalued US dollar by invoking the country's long-term political orientation to the West. He pointed out to the expected beneficial effects of this peg on the Greek economy's competitiveness, and the certainty that the international monetary system would rebalance with a new exchange rate arrangement.

According to Galanis, the Smithsonian Agreement had not introduced an organic reform in the international monetary system but was able to restabilize the existing system at a new level of equilibrium. Although the Agreement provided no final solution, it ensured the conditions needed, in terms of time and psychological climate, for a more systematic and effective tackling of the problem in the future. Greece's handling of the situation had placed the economy in a position "reasonably in line with its present phase of development and the prospects of further growth".[15]

The international monetary crisis brought monetary stability back into policy focus, while at the same time prompting a revision of credit policy under operation. According to Galanis, the existing monetary conditions had favoured the implementation of an eased credit policy, which had served the economic development process satisfactorily. The rapid growth of all types of bank deposits had provided healthy resources for strong credit expansion. However, after August 1971, "credit measures were dictated . . . by international monetary developments and by the concomitant need to strengthen the country's balance of payments position".[16]

The discount rate of the Bank of Greece was kept at the high level of 6.5%, while bank deposit and lending rates remained unchanged. These interest rate changes were mainly aimed at attracting saving deposits in foreign currency by Greeks working abroad.

The problems with financing economic development involved the financing triangle: banks, enterprises, and the capital market. Excessive bank credit to businesses in the period 1967–1971 had not only reduced the funds available for new productive activities and investment but also slowed down; according to Galanis, "the transition from family businesses to genuine sociétés anonymes, which offer business activity a wider and firmer basis for growth".[17]

The rapid rise in deposits during that period reflected the underdevelopment of the capital market, with the result that Greek industrial enterprises heavily depended on bank credit. Thus, the functioning of the banking system was key to tackling the financing problem: "Therefore, it is ultimately up to the banking system itself to make full use of the opportunities offered by the new credit regulations for improving existing conditions".[18]

Banks were called on to play an active role in the development of the stock market since the measures taken earlier (including Emergency Laws 148 and 149 of October 1967) had yet to deliver visible results due to insufficient supply of securities "from healthy sources".[19] This supply could not be increased as long as banks continued to accommodate at a low cost the financing needs of enterprises, including those with access to the capital market: "The required institutional and organisational framework has been provided. The missing factor is the business world's interest and boldness and, mainly, the active cooperation of the banking system, which must develop vigorous activity to this end".[20]

This activity was provided through development banks, that is, the Hellenic Industrial Development Bank – ETBA (state-owned), the National Investment Bank for Industrial Development (ETEBA/NIBID), and the Investment Bank (subsidiaries of the National Bank and the Commercial Bank, respectively). These banks extended medium- to long-term loans to large corporations, with a view to supporting industrial development. Their main sources of funding were the Bank of Greece and loans from foreign banks. Throughout that period, along with the temporary advances it continued to extend to the Greek State,[21] the Bank of Greece was also involved in the management of Greek government bond issues on the domestic market (the so-called development bonds).[22,23,24]

According to the Annual Report of the Bank of Greece in 1971, the balance of payments was in surplus – partly due to higher invisible inflows – that led to a substantial increase in the country's foreign exchange reserves. The impact of the international monetary crisis manifested itself through abrupt and strong fluctuations in the trade balance, mainly imports. The decision to maintain the drachma/dollar exchange rate at the level set in 1953 (30 drachmas per dollar) implied that the drachma was less expensive than the currencies of the EEC countries and Japan and contributed to a rise of inflation in Greece. Regarding the structure of the Greek economy, a slowdown was observed in the rate of growth in agricultural income in favor of manufacturing, which from 1969 onwards had exceeded the agricultural sector in terms of relative size.

Developments in 1972 were marked by an overheating in certain sectors of the economy, most notably construction, along with a pick-up in inflation and import prices. In the labour market, conditions of nearly full employment prevailed. Industrial production increased, driven by buoyant building activity and higher public expenditure. The share of manufacturing in GDP rose from 16.5% in 1962 to 22.9% in 1972 (at 1958 prices), and that of the secondary sector was 33.5% of GDP in 1972. The Bank's Annual Report noted that "[r]apid industrial expansion is coupled with a commensurate increase in social cost owing to the strong and multiform incentives given to promote industrial development", and "industrial development and production are being promoted through disproportionately large and growing support from the banking system".[25] Moreover, after a long period of relative stagnation, prices were rising at accelerating rates (on average 6.5% in 1972, while the wholesale price index increased by 10.5%).

The economy faced much more adverse conditions in 1973, against the backdrop of the first oil shock: between the beginning and the end of the year, the Consumer Price Index (CPI) increased by 30.6%, being on average 15.5% higher than in 1972, and the rise in the wholesale price index (which is directly affected by international prices) came to 44.2%. At the same time, a slowdown in agricultural production was a cause of concern. The Bank of Greece pointed out a need for a review of agricultural policy and the relevant objectives, recalling that agriculture employed and secured income for 40% of the population and contributed about 15% to GDP. The slowdown in agricultural production was associated with urbanization and the excessive growth of the construction sector: during the 1969–1973 period, residential investment as a percentage of total gross fixed capital formation was 30%, which was much higher than that in comparable economies (Turkey 22%, Spain 18%, and Portugal 17%). The Report stressed that "the overexpansion of the building sector cannot be considered to be a favourable development in the long run, since it entails a lopsided structure of the productive mechanism".[26]

In conclusion, the exchange rate policy of the Bank of Greece after the collapse of the Bretton Woods system, as well as the overall policy of the military dictatorship, was erratic, complicated, and often contradictory. While the economic development process continued, the Bank of Greece allowed an overheating of the economy and took comfort in industrial expansion and the attainment of full employment. Pressures on the drachma became unsustainable, and no alternative strategy was in sight, as the dictatorial regime was by its nature averse to plurality of views. Even though the country's European prospect appeared too remote at the time, it was a fact that Europe was the chief destination for Greek exports, and this should normally not have been forgotten in exchange rate policy making. The – albeit short-lived – pegging of the drachma to the US dollar perhaps reflected contemporary political priorities, but these were not in line with the long-term interests of the Greek economy.[27]

9.6 Concluding remarks

The literature about the economic performance of the Greek military dictatorship is split with supporters and opponents stressing their beliefs in a partial reading of events and decisions. The fact is that growth continued in the short term and despite its oppressive character the regime remained politically unchallenged at least until 1971. What the dictatorial regime lacked was a long-term strategy for the Greek economy. The freezing of the relations with the EEC was negative for the economy not only in terms of possible resources but also in relation to potential allies in times of crisis. Therefore, economic growth met an impasse at times that demanded an alternative strategy for the management of the economy.

Economic policy is based on prescriptions derived from economic theory and best existing practices. The old generation of Greek economists mostly exposed to interwar German Historical Economics went into retirement and a new generation with an Anglo-Saxon graduate education emerged. Favoring monetary stability as the ultimate policy goal was overshadowed by the management of the money supply from a new generation of economists who saw monetary expansion, planning, and ad hoc intervention as keys for growth and popular support. Fiscal policy was used through incentives and exemptions rather than to monitor aggregate effective demand. These new economists shifted the priorities of Greek economic policy making based on post-Second World War international experiences with the neoclassical synthesis. At first and up to 1971 this paradigm switch seemed to be successful. However, the political isolation of the dictators led them to ignore international political economy cooperation and developments which proved fatal for economic performance, next to their grave missteps in national politics.

We conclude therefore that the dictatorship sought to accelerate economic growth through expansive fiscal and, to a far greater extent, monetary and credit policy, but it failed to consider the changing global economic system. The result was that inflation exploded in 1973, led to social unrest, internal differences of opinion among dictators, and, finally, to their collapse in 1974.

Notes

1 A positive assessment is given by the long-time economy minister of the junta and later Vice Prime Minister up to November 1973 by Makarezos (2006), a negative assessment is given by Zolotas (1975). See also Meletopoulos (2008) and Psalidopoulos (2016).
2 For the system, its functioning, and its many dysfunctions in the course of time, see Eichengreen (2008), Cesarano (2006), and Bordo and Eichengreen (1993).
3 For more details on that front, see Psalidopoulos (2024).

4 These statistics were calculated after ten years by the Bank of Greece and included in the *Annual Report for 1978*, 511.
5 The Association was dissolved after 1974 for having identified itself totally with the goals of the dictatorship.
6 *Annual Report for 1967*, 24–25.
7 See also Legislative Decree 889/1971 "Share capital increase of the Bank of Greece".
8 *Annual Report for 1970*, 107.
9 *Annual Report for 1967*, 96.
10 *Annual Report for 1967*, 97.
11 *Annual Report for 1968*, 105.
12 *Annual Report for 1970*, 105.
13 *Annual Report for 1970*, 24 and 118.
14 *Annual Report for 1971*, 16.
15 *Annual Report for 1971*, 29.
16 *Annual Report for 1971*, 120.
17 *Annual Report for 1971*, 126.
18 *Annual Report for 1971*, 128.
19 For the measures to support the capital market, see *Annual Report for 1968*, 96–99. Legislative Decree 608/1970 "Investment Trusts and Mutual Funds" aimed to promote a shareholder society.
20 *Annual Report for 1970*, 27. By Legislative Decree 827/1971 "Amending and supplementing the provisions on the Athens Stock Exchange, and regulating other relevant matters", the Athens Stock Exchange Rulebook was amended, and a special account was opened at the Bank of Greece for increasing the joint guarantee fund.
21 "Extension of temporary advance to the Greek State", General Council minutes, Vol. 76, meeting of 18/08/1971, 198.
22 "Domestic Economic Development Lottery Loan for 2,350,000,000 drachmas at 6.5%, 1971", General Council minutes, Vol. 76, meeting of 18/08/1971, 201–202.
23 "Extension of loans using as collateral bonds of the 1972 6.5% 3,000,000,000 drachmas Lottery Loan", General Council minutes, Vol. 81, meeting of 1/11/1972, 5.
24 "Appointment of the Bank of Greece as underwriter of a 260,000,000 drachmas tranche of the 6.5% 1972 Domestic Lottery Economic Development Bond Issue to be launched under Legislative Decree 1183/72", General Council minutes, Vol. 81, meeting of 1/11/1972, 6–9.
25 *Annual Report for the year 1972*, 16.
26 *Annual Report for the year 1973*, 21.
27 For more details on monetary policy, see Psalidopoulos (2018).

Bibliography

Arndt, H. W. (1987), *Economic development. The history of an idea*, Chicago: University of Chicago Press.
Balopoulos, E. (1967), *Fiscal policy models of the British economy*, Amsterdam: North Holland.
Bernstein, M. A. (2001), *A perilous progress. Economists and public purpose in 20th century America*, Princeton: Princeton University Press.
Bordo, M. and B. Eichengreen (1993), *A retrospective on the Bretton Woods system*, Chicago: University of Chicago Press.
Cesarano, E. (2006), *Monetary theory and Bretton Woods*, Cambridge: Cambridge University Press.
Chalikias, D. (1958), *The economic problem of Greece*, Athens: Bank of Greece (in Greek).
Eichengreen, B. (2008), *Globalizing capital. A history of the international monetary system,* Princeton: Princeton University Press.

Makarezos, N (2006), The *economy of Greece, 21/4/67 to 8/10/73,* Athens: Pelasgos (in Greek).
Makarezos, N. (2010), *How we ended up in the metapolitefsi, Nov 73-July 74*, Athens: Filipotis (in Greek).
Meletopoulos, M. (2008), *The dictatorship of the colonels. Society, ideology, economy*, Athens: Papazissis (in Greek).
Panas, E. (1971a), *Problems of policy control of aggregate demand,* Athens: Bank of Greece (in Greek).
Panas, E. (1971b), *Collected papers on economic planning*, Athens: Bank of Greece.
Papadopoulos, G. (1968–72), *Our credo*, 5 volumes, Athens: Press Directory (in Greek).
Psalidopoulos, M. (2016), "Dilemmas and priorities of economic policy: From the dictatorship to political changeover", in: *The dictatorship of the colonels and the restoration of democracy*, pp. 573–601, Athens: Foundation of the Hellenic Parliament (in Greek).
Psalidopoulos, M. (2018), *History of the Bank of Greece*, Athens: Bank of Greece.
Psalidopoulos, M. (2024), *A history of Modern Greek Economic Thought,* London: Routledge (forthcoming).
Rist, C. (1997), *The history of development*, London: Zed Books.
Slobodian, Q. (2018), *Globalists. The end of Empire and the birth of neoliberalism*, Cambridge: Harvard University Press.
Spulber, N. (1990), *Managing the American economy, from Roosevelt to Reagan*, Bloomington: Indiana University Press.
Stein, H. (1969), *The fiscal revolution in America*, Chicago: University of Chicago Press.
Zolotas, X. (1965), *Monetary equilibrium and economic development*, Princeton: Princeton University Press.
Zolotas, X. (1975), *Our economic problem*, Athens: Bank of Greece (in Greek).

10 The making of the transformation of Turkey between 1980 and 1983

Tayfun Mertan

10.1 Introduction

The year 1980 marked the beginning of Turkey's adoption of neoliberalization of the form of the state and relations of production. The minority government of the time, with the policy package called the January 24 Decisions, took the first step towards starting the process of neoliberalization. However, it was not in a hegemonic position that would provide it with the necessary political power needed to implement the Decisions. The bloody military coup of September 12, 1980, created the required socio-political environment, produced political power, and ensured the so-called "social peace" – or stability. From 1980, until the general elections of November 6, 1983, the three years under the junta rule laid the foundations for an intertwined political, social, and economic transformation that Turkey would experience in the following decades.

By employing a neo-Gramscian approach, this study will start with an analysis of the nature of the January 24 Decisions. This will be followed by the analysis of Turkey's relationship with the US, NATO, IMF, World Bank, and European Community regarding the internationalization of the country's economy and the reformation of the state structure during the junta rule. These relations will be examined to understand how the junta rule benefited from the economic and military material capabilities of these organizations, how it changed the legal and institutional basis of the socio-economic structure and the form of state in the country, and how it attempted to integrate Turkey into the neoliberal world order ideologically.

10.2 Theoretical and conceptual framework

Robert Cox's two seminal articles (1981 and 1983) not only filled an essential gap in international political economy literature but also provided a methodology for case studies based on the neo-Gramscian approach it established. Within this approach, the relations between states and international organizations, the expansion and functioning of the global capitalist system, and the processes of hegemony building have been critically examined and theorized. The impossibility of an in-depth theoretical discussion here is apparent. Instead, I prefer to discuss the concepts that will serve as tools and guides for me in the following sections. The first of these must be the state.

DOI: 10.4324/9781032656199-11

In his concept of hegemony, Gramsci merges civil society and the state. However, this does not mean that the state's role diminishes, or its power becomes irrelevant. As his famous description of classical liberalism states, laissez-faire was a "form of State 'regulation', introduced and enforced by legislative and coercive means" (Gramsci 1971, 160). It is not incorrect to argue that Cox and later neo-Gramscians were inspired to suggest that power resources essential for an attempt at hegemony that aims to permeate civil society and political structures cannot be acquired without the state.

According to Cox (1981), the three "categories of forces" operate in three "spheres of activity", namely, social relations of production, forms of state, and world orders, which are what the hegemonic project is built upon. He divides these categories of forces into three distinct groups: material capabilities, institutions, and ideas. Bieler and Morton formulate that the hegemony "appears as an expression of broadly based consent, manifested in the acceptance of ideas and supported by material resources and institutions" (Bieler and Morton 2006, 10–12).

In detailing these forces, Cox urges that each of these operate interactively and without dominating one another. The *material capabilities* involve not only productive resources but also destructive ones. These can be natural reserves, technological means, or military equipment. The *ideas* can be described as "shared notions of the nature of social relations" or "collective images of social order held by different groups of people". For the power bloc attempting to build hegemony, these definitions point to the goal of an ideological unity that the majority of society will not object to. At the same time, the necessity of ideological cohesion between capitalist international organizations and states is obvious. Last, the *institutions*, as Cox writes, are the "amalgams of ideas and material power", and they function to stabilize and maintain the order. This stabilization and maintenance unquestionably comes from the ability of institutions to influence ideas and material capabilities (Cox 1981, 136–137).

Cox's (1983) emphasis on the role of international organizations also guides this study. The international organizations, for him, are "the mechanisms of hegemony":

> They embody rules which facilitate the expansion of hegemonic world orders; are themselves the product of the hegemonic world order; ideologically legitimate the norms of the world order; co-opt the elites from peripheral countries and absorb counter-hegemonic ideas.
>
> (Cox 1983, 172)

In the face of the world order, where international organizations assume these roles, the state assumes one more function. It operates as a "transmission belt" in "adjusting national economic activities to the exigencies of the global economy" (Cox 1993, 260). However, this should not lead to thinking about the state as a mere tool that acts according to the top-down directions of global capitalism. Because, as it was mentioned earlier, the required "coherent conjunction or fit between a configuration of material power, the prevalent collective image of world order (including certain norms) and a set of institutions which administer the order with a certain semblance of universality" for the hegemonic project (Cox 1981, 139), can only be constituted with the state.

Similar to various examples in Latin America and some parts of the Middle East, it was the junta regime that took over the state and played a leading role in the inception of the neoliberal transformation in Turkey between 1980 and 1983, in accordance with international organizations and the US. It emerged precisely because of the failure of civil political actors and groups to achieve a hegemonic position. It took civil society and state under strict control and eliminated the social forces whose clash created the crisis of hegemony. By ending the crisis, it started the process of constructing hegemony.

In this chapter, I will take agreements, projects, and statements made by these organizations and Turkey, as well as legal and institutional changes – including the 1982 Constitution – and national newspapers as primary sources. I will consider legal changes as part of the *institutions* because the creation of institutions and the transformation of existing ones were executed through the adoption of laws and decrees. The resources of destructive material capabilities are obviously military resources. However, the resources of productive material capabilities are primarily economic rather than technological and natural ones. Therefore, I will examine economic aid, loans and credits, and other financial resources as resources of productive material capabilities. I will show the ideological coherence in the statements of state and government officials.

10.3 The January 24 decisions

According to the Central Bank of the Republic of Turkey (2002), the January 24, 1980 Decisions aimed "to curb inflation, to fill in the foreign financing gap, and to attain a more outward-oriented and market-based economic system". For this aim, the Bank reports that "export subsidies were granted and exchange rates were allowed to depreciate in real terms to make Turkish exports more competitive" (The Central Bank of the Republic of Turkey 2002, 5). On the 25th of January, Prime Minister Süleyman Demirel emphasized the IMF's endorsement of the decisions, which include "33 percent devaluation, devotion to restrained money growth, abolition of price controls and subsidies to state economic enterprises, and cessation of deficit spending – all to be monitored by the IMF" (Yalpat 1984). During the following decade "a deliberate contraction in real wages" and an increase in "producing an exportable surplus and enhancing export competitiveness through lower labor costs" were aimed according to the Central Bank (The Central Bank of the Republic of Turkey 2002, 19).

In the background of the January 24 Decisions "stabilization package", there were "several unsuccessful attempts in 1978–79 and two failed IMF programs" that could not manage to reform Turkey's economy according to an outward-oriented path (Arıcanlı and Rodrik 1990, 1344). In "close cooperation between the Turkish government and the Bretton Woods institutions", the January 24 Decisions started a new era that was characterized by flexible exchange rates, austerity and export drive, public enterprise reform and privatization, financial and import liberalization, and promotion of direct foreign investment (Altınörs 2017, 1344–46).

Owen and Pamuk wrote that the decisions aimed "to improve the balance of payments, to reduce the rate of inflation in the short term, and to create a market-based, export-oriented economy in the longer term" (Owen and Pamuk 1999, 118). Yet, the full implementation of the decisions was only possible after the junta took control of the state and suppressed any social force that would fight against the negative consequences that were certain to befall society. The reason for this was the fact that the minority government of the Justice Party (AP) was short on the political power required to enforce the decisions (Akça 2014, 14; Owen and Pamuk 1999, 117; Bedirhanoğlu and Yalman 2010, 110; Boratav 2015, 150). Turgut Özal, then Undersecretary of the Prime Ministry and Deputy Undersecretary of the State Planning Organization, and Prime Minister after 1983, stated in 1982 that the program would not have been successful if it had not been for the September 12, 1980, coup and that the junta administration embraced the program (Yalpat 1984). As the junta embraced the neoliberalization strategy, the US, NATO, IMF, World Bank, and EC embraced the junta.

10.4 Destructive and productive material capabilities

The resources for both productive and destructive powers were vitally required for the construction of a hegemonic structure after the 12 September coup d'état in Turkey. Turkey received resources primarily in the form of credits, loans, and military assets through IMF stand-by agreements, World Bank and EC projects and aids, and NATO and the US modernization and technology transfer programs. Surely, the provision of these resources was conditional on the neoliberalization of the economy in Turkey. Turkey received these resources in exchange for the further articulation of state military and economic power to the capitalist bloc.

The United States of America and Turkey signed the Defense and Economic Cooperation Agreement on March 29, 1980, more than five months before the coup. However, the US chose not to suspend the agreement after the coup. The agreement entered into force on December 18, 1980. This five-year agreement included the infamous Article 5, stating that "Turkey authorizes the US government to participate in joint defense measures at specified Turkish Armed Forces installations" (The United States of America and Turkey 1980, 3327). By opening the way for the US to utilize military facilities in Turkey (Bölme 2012, 301), the Article demonstrated the pre-coup civilian government and the junta's goal of further integration into the capitalist bloc. This agreement was supported by three supplementary agreements on defense support, defense industrial cooperation, and installations, respectively. The first agreement starts with the US government recognizing "the needs of the Turkish Armed Forces for a modernization and maintenance program". The US emphasizes that it "is committed . . . to provide defense support (defense materials, services, and training). . . on the best terms as may possible" with a five-year procurement program and the Joint Turkish–United States Defense Support Commission in Turkey's capital, Ankara (The United States of America and Turkey 1980, 3329).

The second supplementary agreement highlights the cooperation for the flow of technological know-how, the production, and the repair of equipment. Various projects regarding the production of anti-armor ammunition, fuses, explosives, rockets, and improvements of aircraft and tanks were also planned with this agreement (The United States of America and Turkey 1980, 3332–37). The last supplementary agreement specifies the cities and installations to be used by the US. The objectives listed were electromagnetic monitoring, radar warning, space monitoring, air operations, seismic data collection, and radio navigation (The United States of America and Turkey 1980, 3338). Later, on November 29, 1982, the "Memorandum of Understanding" was signed by the US and Turkey in Brussels. With this agreement, the US was burdened with the modernization of ten air bases and the construction of two new air bases in Eastern Turkey (Aydın et al. 2001, 253).

In its capacity as an international organization, NATO continued its relations with the junta mainly as a source of knowledge regarding material capabilities. A specific example of this support was the program called "Science for Stability". Before the North Atlantic Council convened in Ankara in June 1980, three months before the coup, the NATO Secretary General stated that a five-year program by the Science Committee was to be evaluated by ministers (NATO 1980a). This program aimed to help Greece and Portugal, as well as Turkey, to develop a national scientific and technological infrastructure. Another final communiqué, published after a ministerial meeting in 1987, stated that the program successfully earmarked nearly 80 percent of its funds (NATO 1987). Later, final communiqués during the junta rule continuously emphasized Turkey's economic problems and supported its efforts to overcome them. Additionally, the aid from the US, West Germany, and the Netherlands to Turkey was mentioned in these texts (NATO 1980b, 1981, 1982, 1983). It is also worth mentioning that according to SIPRI data, during the junta period and afterward throughout the 1980s, Turkey imported arms mainly from the US, West Germany, the UK, and the Netherlands.

Turkey's growing importance in the face of the Iranian Revolution and the USSR invasion of Afghanistan was one of the reasons behind the further military support. As Athanassopoulou wrote (2014), Turkey was "an extremely valuable ally". This was visible when Turkey and General Dynamics realized an agreement in 1983 to produce a total of 160 F-16 fighter jets in Turkey. The Turkish National Defense Ministry and General Dynamics established the Turkish Aerospace Industries, Inc. (TAI) in 1984 after the sale was approved by the US. The parties held 51 percent and 49 percent stakes, respectively (Aydın et al. 2001, 253; Athanassopoulou 2014, 37).

Regarding the productive material capabilities, the economic support of international organizations to Turkey continued throughout the junta rule. Three months before the coup, in June 1980, the first long-term stand-by agreement between Turkey and the IMF was signed based on a three-year program. The main aim of the agreement was clearly described as realizing the neoliberalization project that was embodied in the January 24 Decisions (IMF 1980a). According to the government's memorandum on its economic and financial policies, it was committed to significant structural adjustment policies such as "moving from detailed regulation to greater reliance on market forces", and "opening up the economy to external competition and foreign investment", (IMF 1980a, 6).

Four days after the coup, General Kenan Evren, as the head of the National Security Council, which was the highest governing body of the Junta rule, informed the IMF that they would honor all agreements and that the economic stabilization program would continue (IMF 1980b). This commitment was mentioned in the IMF staff reports when the government appointed by the junta requested a modification of the credit limits set by the stand-by agreement in October 1980. The IMF continued the stand-by program and did not fail to provide the productive material resources necessary for the neoliberalization of Turkey under the junta rule. On May 2, 1983, Turkey withdrew the last part of the loan opened under this agreement. Two weeks later, the government requested a new stand-by agreement for a year (IMF 1983a) "to carry through the program of stabilization and structural reform which was instituted in January 1980" (IMF 1983b, p. 5). Seeing no need to wait for the general elections in November 1983, and a civilian government to hold the office through a democratic process, the IMF approved this stand-by agreement request for about 300 million dollars (IMF 1983c).

Dagi wrote that "Americans helped to secure Turkey an IMF credit of US$92 million in 1980 and postponed US$350 million Turkish debts for the next year. American economic and military aid to Turkey . . . amounted to US$453 million in 1981, US$704 million in 1982 and US$688 million in 1983" (Dagi 1996, 127). Among these contributions to Turkey's productive material capabilities that came from the US, I must mention the three here. An agreement signed by the parties to "consolidation and rescheduling of debts owed to, guaranteed or insured by the US" in September 1981 (US Department of State 1988a, 1469). This agreement was based on the decision taken at the OECD meeting in July 1980 to alleviate Turkey's external debt (US Department of State 1988a, 1484). Towards the end of 1982, another agreement between the US and Turkey was signed. This one involved a 200 million USD grant to Turkey "for balance-of-payments financing to support and promote the financial stability and economic recovery" (US Department of State 1988b, 4715). Yet another agreement between these two countries was signed in April 1983 on a 45 million USD loan – a relatively small number – again to support Turkey's balance-of-payments financing (US Department of State 1992, 1191).

Indeed, the burden was not solely on the shoulders of the US and the IMF. The presence of junta rule in Turkey was not enough of an issue for the EC to cut resources and impose sanctions. Just a week after the coup, the EC–Turkey Association Council made two decisions on enhancing the cooperation between the parties. The first decision was to assist Turkey's agricultural, economic, and technical problems, as well as the free movement of products and workers. The second decision was directly on the economic support of the EC, which consisted of a grant of 75 million European units of account (Turkey–European Union Association Council 2001, 155–167). Even though the European Parliament adopted a resolution concerning the rights and safety of the detainees under the junta rule, the EC increased its "aid to Turkey by about 94 percent over the previous one to 600 million ECU" in June 1981 (Dagi 1996, 128–130).

The World Bank also played an essential role in providing resources to Turkey during the junta rule. The Bank's private and public sector-oriented projects in

Turkey date back to the 1950s. There are at least 20 loan agreements that were approved by the Bank between 1975 and 1980, totaling close to 1.3 billion dollars, aimed at financing agricultural, industrial, and infrastructural development projects. During the junta rule, the Bank approved 14 more loan agreements, totaling close to $1.1 billion, to finance agricultural, industrial, and infrastructural development projects. These included extension of irrigation facilities, animal health, village poultry production, establishment or modernization of the factories, financing of technical assistance, and workforce development and training. All of these projects continued under the junta rule, meaning that the disbursements were realized by the parties in Turkey.

Apart from these, there are four Structural Adjustment Loans worth $1.1 billion. The first of these was SALs, which was initiated in February 1980 and continued until September 1981. After the coup, in November 1980, the Bank supplemented the first loan with an additional $75 million (World Bank 1980a). The second SAL was implemented between May 1981 and November 1982, the third between May 1982 and December 1983, and the fourth between June 1983 and March 1985. All these agreements aimed to support Turkey's January 1980 structural adjustment program. The policies aiming at the neoliberalization of the economy in the country were highlighted through repetitive phrases such as "greater reliance on market forces and less on direct state intervention and control; increased export orientation; increased mobilization of domestic resources" (World Bank 1980b, 3), export promotion, and import liberalization; reforms aiming the marketization of state economic enterprises (World Bank 1981, 9), deregulation of interest rates, adoption of a realistic and flexible exchange rate (World Bank 1982, 3), and "rationalization of the public investment program" (World Bank 1983, 4). All of the SAL credits were to be used to finance imports of inputs for agricultural and industrial production.

10.5 Legal and institutional transformation

As the amalgams of ideas and material capabilities, according to Cox (1981), the institutions are both products of and mechanisms that maintain the hegemonic order. Here, I also emphasize the importance of legal basis and mechanisms that realize the same function. These mechanisms and basis provide the power bloc and its aimed order with legitimacy and the legality that regulates the relations of production and the form of state. Moreover, the realized changes made it possible for the post-coup power bloc to impose neoliberal transformation in a suitable socio-political environment with the required public organs. The social forces, such as trade unions, that were active and effective in political decision-making processes during the 1960s and 1970s were eliminated (Doğan 2014), and the bourgeois fractions obtained the support of the state. Since the junta rule achieved these through decrees, laws, and even a new constitution as well as through institutions, I see much benefit in dealing with the legal and institutional transformation together.

Even though it is a short period of three years, the junta rule managed to realize essential changes regarding the legal and institutional structure of the state and society in Turkey. Considering its importance for the state in Turkey, the IMF, and the World Bank, I prefer starting with the January 24 Decisions. The policies that were adopted as a result of these decisions were realized through several decrees. The main elements of the policies can be classified under five titles. First, regarding the exchange rate regime, the Turkish Lira was devalued by 100%, and 1 dollar was pegged from 35 liras to 70 lire, and it was decided that the Central Bank would adjust the cross rates. Second, to create incentives for export and foreign investments, the government allowed commercial banks to run accounts that would hold export earnings or worker remittances; the commercial banks were facilitated to provide export credits, term loans, and working capital. Third, the state economic enterprises, the institutions that are unacceptable to the neoliberal mindset, were reorganized to set prices for their products in accordance with the market, meaning significant increases in prices of products such as petroleum, cement, steel, sugar, coal, lignite, and printing paper. Moreover, the SEEs' access to Central Bank borrowings was terminated. Although one of the main objectives of the January decisions was to curb inflation, getting rid of the SEEs, which were seen as a burden on the state budget, took precedence. Fourth, concerning domestic resource mobilization, the government planned to introduce a new indirect tax. Accordingly, the value-added tax was introduced in 1984 and still applies to many goods, including basic necessities for citizens. Last, as administrative arrangements, the Money and Credit Committee, the Foreign Investment Department, and the Incentives/Implementation Department were established to coordinate and approve relevant policies under the Undersecretary in the Prime Ministry (World Bank 1980b, 35–38). The government also formed a Labor Contracts Coordination Committee that worked "to ensure that wage settlements should be in harmony with the basic stabilization policy measures", and "achieve work discipline" (IMF 1980a, 11).

These were the signs of the transformation that the form of state and relations of production were set to go through. The aims were to open the economy to the global market, reorganize the state's role as the facilitator that operates in favor of the capital and ensure that decisions concerning the management of the economy were taken by decision-making mechanisms isolated from the social opposition (Özden et al. 2017, 190). Particularly, these newly established public institutions assumed decision-making roles in practice, while formally, their role was limited to advisory work (Sönmez 2011; Önder 2016, 27). The State Planning Organization's shifting status was "the most dramatic case" according to Önder. The organization was on target because it symbolized the state's role in the management of the economy. It was "the principal agency for economic policy in the 1960s and 1970s" and now "relegated to a less important role during the 1980s. In 1991, it lost some of its most important functions and responsibilities to the Undersecretariat of Treasury and Foreign Trade" (Önder 2016, 29). Moreover, one month after he was elected the Prime Minister in November 1983, one of the first things that Özal did was to establish the Undersecretariat of Treasury and Foreign Trade. Reporting to the Prime Minister's Office, this body was authorized to decide on treasury and trade affairs. As the top executor of neoliberalization programs that were realized with the IMF and the World Bank (Sönmez 2011), it operated as "the headquarters of the prospective neoliberal revolution, charged with overseeing the implementation of structural adjustment . . . and the expansion and integration of the Turkish economy with the global networks" (Ünay 2006, 122). In general, these new state organs "assumed most critical powers and responsibilities in directing the restructuring of the Turkish economy towards an export-led form of accumulation in an open-market economy" (Önder 2016, 27).

Perhaps the most crucial step in the legal and institutional transformation of the form of state and socio-economic structure in Turkey was the enactment of the 1982 Constitution (Yalman 2009), which is still in force today, though with many amendments. Alongside the constitution, the junta rule enforced 535 laws and 91 decree-laws during this process (Önder 2016, 25). Faced with the impossibility of reviewing all legal provisions, I prefer to focus on the main text, the Constitution. It was drafted by the Advisory Parliament, in which all members were appointed by the National Security Council consisting of force commanders and the chief of staff. It was submitted to a referendum in an atmosphere where political parties were shut down, politicians were detained, and counterpropaganda was forbidden. With over 90 percent participation, the Constitution was adopted with 91 percent of the vote.

One of the most critical aspects of the Constitution is that it reinforced the executive against the legislation and judiciary. The bicameral system that was established in the 1961 Constitution was abolished on the grounds that it slowed down decision-making processes. Article 104 defines the president as the head of the executive and grants him the power to issue decrees. In addition, a 10 percent threshold was introduced in the elections, aiming to create as homogeneous a parliament as possible. Without a clear definition, the concept of National Security was included in the Constitution, paving the way for restricting fundamental rights and freedoms on the grounds of National Security.

Even though the preamble and Article 1 of the Constitution emphasized social justice and the social state, the rights granted in the previous constitution have been mostly removed. Following a ban on strikes immediately after the coup, the junta rule included lockout as a right in the Constitution to strengthen the hand of capitalist factions during the transition to civilian politics. Moreover, Articles 51, 52, 53, and 54 of the Constitution significantly restricted trade union rights. Membership of more than one trade union was banned. Trade unions were prohibited from pursuing political goals or supporting political parties or associations. Workers were required to carry out strikes within a certain period and to notify the employer in advance. The right of civil servants to form trade unions was not included in the new constitution. In addition, the requirement to be an active worker for ten years to become a trade union executive was introduced, making it more difficult to form a trade union. Trade unions were required to store their income in public banks and to be open to administrative and financial audits. Historical forms of working-class resistance, such as politically motivated strikes, workplace occupations, work slowdowns, and productivity reductions were banned.

Two laws introduced during the junta rule continued to restrict labor rights, making access to trade union rights more difficult. The Trade Union Act No. 2821 and the Collective Bargaining, Strike, and Lockout Law No. 2822 were enforced in May 1983. The former prohibited students, teachers in private institutions, private security guards, and workers whose jobs were related to religious activities from union membership. Also, Act No. 2821 introduced the practice of forming and being a member of a trade union if it was affiliated with a specific line of work, banned workplace and professional unionism, and made union membership and dissociation subject to notarization. Act No. 2822 made it difficult for a union to achieve collective bargaining authorization. Collective bargaining in one or more workplaces was possible, but national and line-of-work-scale bargaining was prevented. The conditions for authorization were very difficult: membership of at least 10 percent of the workers in the line of work and more than half of the workers in the workplace to the same union (DİSK-AR 2020).

The number of unionized workers and working days spent on strike before and after the coup can be compared to show how these legal and institutional arrangements tipped the balance of power in favor of capital. While in the first nine months of 1980, the number of workers participating in strikes was 70 thousand, it remained at 55 thousand for the seven years between 1984 and 1991. In the same period, the number of days on strike per worker dropped from 76 to 32 (DİSK-AR 2020, 34). As Yalman argues, this transformation aimed at the reconstitution of "the balance of class forces within society which is registered in the state itself" (Yalman 2009, 299; Altınörs 2017, 505–506).

10.6 Ideological transformation

The process of Turkey's ideological articulation with the neoliberal hegemony can be examined at two levels. The first is at the national level, in the political relationships within the country, and the second is between the country's political elites, the US, and international organizations. Before the September 12, 1980 coup d'état, it was obvious that there was an ideological conflict both among the political elites and at the social base. At the end of the 1970s, there were three main currents in Turkish politics. The major actor of the first current was the Republican People's Party (CHP), positioned on the center-left with its left populist strategy that could not manage to gain "the consent of the bourgeoisie or more radical fractions of the working class". The second current was embodied in the authoritarian populist strategy that was embraced by the center-right liberal-conservative Justice Party (AP), which could obtain "the support of important sections of the bourgeoisie" at the cost of the support of the dominated classes. The last was the revolutionary leftist movement supported by different small parties and organizations (Akça 2014, 15). In addition to these, it is worth mentioning right-wing extremist organizations, which increased their influence and became part of the political violence, especially towards the end of the 1970s (Gümrükçü 2023). Within this political atmosphere, Turkey's import-substituting industrialization strategy was in crisis. While the working classes embraced widely effective strikes as a response to deteriorating living conditions, in the face of this workers' organization, the bourgeois fractions targeted basic rights such as unionization and collective bargaining (Akça 2014, 14).

The steps to legitimize the targeted neoliberal transformation in the form of state and relations of production began even before the announcement of the January 24 Decisions. Three weeks before the January 24 Decisions, Prime Minister Süleyman Demirel wrote that the 1961 Constitution in force at the time was causing instability in the country, leading to a political and economic crisis (Demirel 1980). In the aftermath of the Decisions, to craft the discursive armor around the neoliberalization policies, Demirel further stated that the Decisions were "precaution to eradicate poverty" (Milliyet 1980a). In an interview, by adopting the classical liberal motto, he stated that they say, "Let it be done", and the government would benefit from the IMF's resources (Milliyet 1980b). Moreover, the reactions from bourgeois fractions were unsurprisingly positive. While the chairman of the Istanbul Chamber of Industry claimed that the devaluation of the Turkish Lira would support to stabilize the economy (Milliyet 1980c), the Turkish Industry and Business Association (TUSIAD) stated that opening the economy to the world market was imperative (Özuslu 1980).

The reaction of the working class intensified even more after the January 24 Decisions of the minority government led by Demirel. As Owen and Pamuk wrote, "strikes and other forms of labor unrest, often violent, became increasingly common in the summer of 1980" (1999, 118). Faced with the crisis of hegemony that reached its peak, no political actor was positioned to overcome this intertwined political, economic, and social crisis. Particularly, realizing the neoliberal transformation targeted by the bourgeois fractions and liberal political elites as a hegemonic project was impossible. The coup d'état ended this crisis. Parliament and political parties were dissolved, party leaders were detained, and MPs were stripped of their immunity. In his declaration published in the Official Gazette (Official Gazette 1980), Chief of General Staff Evren stated that they aimed to protect the integrity of the country, ensure national unity and solidarity, prevent civil war, re-establish state authority, and eliminate any obstacles to the functioning of the democratic order.

The Junta government's adherence to the capitalist bloc and the neoliberalization project prepared before the coup was rewarded by the bloc's international organizations and the US with political support alongside destructive and productive resources. Yilmaz Şener quotes from the Economist:

> On September 20, 1980, one week after the coup, The Economist published an article about the military coup in Turkey. According to the journal, the coup was "regrettable" for ". . . the Western alliance (which) draws strength from its democratic institutions and is morally weakened when the democratically elected government of a member country is forcibly overthrown. . . ." It was still hard, ". . . not to concede that Turkey's armed forces . . . acted as they had to when they took over power on September 12th.
>
> (Yilmaz Şener 2006, 14)

The public was comforted that the IMF had confidence in the new ruling. World Bank and IMF loans and US aid, which were high on the agenda before the coup, would continue to be granted and the country would not be isolated (Gören 1980). The newspapers in the country also claimed that the army's seizure of power was welcomed by the international community (Milliyet 1980d). Indeed, as Yalpat (1984) writes, this was how the Economist summarized the process on the first anniversary of the coup in 1981:

> The first step was an economic package announced on January 24, 1980. Designed by the government of Süleyman Demirel, it was the brainchild of his finance minister Turgut Özal. The second step was the freeing of interest rates on July 1, 1980. And the third was a series of measures introduced after the military takeover on September 12, 1980.

This was how the coup and the neoliberalization process were legitimized at the national level. At the international level, alongside the media coverage, international organizations and the US did not compromise on ideological unity. Before the coup, two final communiqués that were published by NATO after the Defense Planning Committee meetings in 1979 stated that Turkey was struggling to fulfill its commitments to the Alliance due to its economic constraints, and hence it needed urgent external assistance (NATO 1979a, 1979b). This issue took place in nearly every NATO communiqué during the 1980s. Strong ideological unity and support were also present in the US and Turkey's Defense and Economic Cooperation Agreement, which came into force after the coup. It was emphasized that the US would "exert maximum efforts to develop economic cooperation, including commercial, economic, industrial, scientific, and technological relations" to strengthen the Turkish economy (The United States of America & Turkey 1980, 3326). This and similar pledges were to strengthen and maintain the ideological unity between the states and further, to reinforce the position of the ruling in Turkey in the country's political context.

Not only NATO and the US but also the EC supported Turkey's neoliberalization process both before and after the coup. Alongside the aforementioned EC-Turkey Association Council decisions on the free movement of products and workers, the IMF's executive director de Groote's encouraging statements on the January 24 Decisions and the ideological unity between the parties must be highlighted here:

> The measures recently taken . . . aim at bringing the economy back on the right track after an initial correction . . .. The achievement of this objective is predicated on a major reorientation of the economy in the direction of liberalization. . . . the objectives of the stabilization program fully comply with the fundamental objectives and purposes of the Fund.
>
> (IMF 1980c)

Moreover, in 1981 and 1982, de Groote indicated that Turkey's economic problems were difficult, but its relationship with the IMF was cordial, and Turkish authorities were aware that a long process of recovery awaited them (IMF 1981) before the "ultimate objective of a self-sustaining economy with less reliance on official assistance" (IMF 1982, 3).

Turkey's relations with the World Bank carried similar expressions of ideological unity during the same period. Two weeks after the declaration of the January 24 Decisions, the brain behind the policies and the Prime Minister of the post-coup era, Turgut Özal, wrote a letter to Robert S. McNamara, the President of the World Bank. After explaining the Decisions' essence as part of the structural adjustment loan that Turkey requested from the Bank, Özal projected a four-year scheme:

> We are counting on the continued support of the international financial and commercial banking community, including the World Bank, both through project loans and additional program assistance. It is our hope that the World Bank would not only support these efforts through the provision of a second Program Loan in the coming weeks but also through other program assistance, as appropriate, during the 1979–1983 period.
>
> (World Bank 1980b, 43)

In a letter sent to the IMF director Jacques de Larosière on June 2, 1980, the Minister of Finance Sezgin stated the importance of the January 24 Decisions by promising that the policies would be adopted for the next two years in accordance with them (IMF 1980a, 4). In another letter regarding the second SAL, dated February 20, 1981, Özal wrote that "the new regime" of the junta rule "endorsed the January 1980 program" and even imposed new policies that furthered the January 24 Decisions: "A substantial liberalization of the import regime, abolishing entirely the quota list, and expanding the scope of the more liberalized list, . . . measures leading to more fundamental reforms of the SEE sector" (World Bank 1981, 78–79).

Despite its disregard for political and civil liberal values, the junta rule at the core of the inception of the neoliberalization process of the economy and the form of state in Turkey were not repressed by the capitalist bloc but instead supported by it. It should be recalled that the military Martial Law in Poland between 1981 and 1983 was condemned and sanctioned by the United States (Reagan 1981; Wasowski 2009).

10.7 Conclusion

On September 12, 1980, the junta took control of the state administration and officially remained in power for three years. Kenan Evren, who led the coup, remained the president until 1989. The Junta embraced the transformation initiated before the coup with the aim of neoliberalization of the economy and form of state in Turkey. By providing the hegemonic power that this transformation needed, it dominated domestic politics, initiated legal and institutional restructuring, prevented the emergence of ideological challenges, and kept the resources for the transformation flowing into the country by maintaining ideological unity with international organizations and the US.

In November 1983, under Özal's leadership, Turkey's first post-junta civilian government was elected. In 1989, Özal became the president, and his political alignments assumed the prime minister's office. After Özal's unexpected death in 1993, Demirel, the prime minister before the junta rule, became the president. The one-party governments Özal and his party enjoyed throughout the 1980s could not be achieved in the 1990s by other political parties. Under seven different coalition governments, the country went through two major economic crises. Neither the 1982 Constitution, nor numerous laws and decrees and structural adjustment and stand-by programs prevented Turkey from experiencing the 1994, 1999, and 2001 crises. The government's response to these crises was further neoliberalization.

Bibliography

Akça, İ. (2014). Hegemonic Projects in Post-1980 Turkey and the Changing Forms of Authoritarianism. In B. A. Özden, İ. Akça, & A. Bekmen (Eds.), *Turkey Reframed: Constituting Neoliberal Hegemony* (pp. 13–46). New York: Pluto Press.

Altınörs, G. (2017). The Role of International Monetary Fund as an Apparatus of Hegemonic World Order: A Gramscian/Coxian Approach to the Neoliberal Transformation of Turkey. *Bilecik Şeyh Edebali University Journal of Social Science, 2*(2), 493–514.

Arıcanlı, T., & Rodrik, D. (1990). An Overview of Turkey's Experience with Economic Liberalization and Structural Adjustment. *World Development, 18*(10), 1343–1350.

Athanassopoulou, E. (2014). *Strategic Relations Between the US and Turkey 1979–2000: Sleeping with a Tiger*. New York: Routledge.

Aydın, M., Erhan, Ç., & Erdem, G. (2001). Chronology of Turkish-American Relations. *The Turkish Yearbook of International Relations, XXXI*, 247–265.

Bedirhanoğlu, P., & Yalman, G. (2010). State, Class and the Discourse Reflections on the Neoliberal Transformation in Turkey. In A. Saad-Filho, & G. Yalman (Eds.), *Economic Transitions to Neoliberalism in Middle-income Countries Policy dilemmas, Economic Crises, Forms of Resistance* (pp. 107–127). London and New York: Routledge.

Bieler, A., & Morton, A. D. (2006). A Critical Theory Route to Hegemony, World Order and Historical Change Neo-Gramscian Perspectives in International Relations. In A. Bieler, W. Bonefeld, P. Burnham, & A. D. Morton (Eds.), *A Critical Theory Route to Hegemony, World Order and Historical Change Neo-Gramscian Perspectives in International Relations* (pp. 9–27). New York: Palgrave Macmillan.

Bölme, S. M. (2012). *İncirlik Üssü ABD'nin Üs Politikası ve Türkiye*. İstanbul: İletişim.

Boratav, K. (2015). *Türkiye İktisat Tarihi 1908–2008*. Ankara: İmge Kitabevi.

Cox, R. W. (1981). Social Forces, States and World Orders: Beyond International Relations. *Millennium, 10*(2), 126–155.

Cox, R. W. (1983). Gramsci, Hegemony and International Relations: An Essay in Method. *Millennium, 12*(2), 162–175.

Cox, R. W. (1993). Structural Issues of Global Governance: Implications for Europe. In S. Gill (Ed.), *Gramsci, Historical Materialism and International Relation* (pp. 259–289). Cambridge: Cambridge University Press.

Dagi, I. D. (1996). Democratic Transition in Turkey, 1980–83: The Impact of European Diplomacy. *Middle Eastern Studies, 32*(2), 124–141.

Demirel, S. (1980, January 3,). Bunalımın Köklerinde Neler Yatıyor? *Milliyet*, p. 2.

DİSK-AR. (2020). *40 Yıldır 12 Eylül Emeğe Karşı Sermaye Darbesi 12 Eylül İşçi Haklarını Nasıl Yok Etti?* İstanbul: DİSK. Retrieved from https://arastirma.disk.org.tr/wp-content/uploads/2020/09/D%C4%B0SK-AR-12-Eyl%C3%BCl-RAPOR.pdf

Doğan, M. G. (2014). The Deradicalisation of Organised Labour. In İ. Akça, A. Bekmen, & B. A. Özden (Eds.), *Turkey Reframed: Constituting Neoliberal Hegemony* (pp. 188–202). London: Pluto.

Gören, S. (1980, September 17). Dünya Bankası ve IMF Kredileri Sürdürecek. *MİlIiyet*, p. 3.

Gramsci, A. (1971). *Selections From the Prison Notebooks*. (Q. Hoare, G. N. Smith, Eds., Q. Hoare, & G. N. Smith, Trans.) New York: International Publishers.
Gümrükçü, S. B. (2023). Ideology, Discourse, and Alliance Structures: Explaining Far-Right Political Violence in Turkey in the 1970s. *Terrorism and Political Violence, 35*(1), 210–224.
IMF. (1980a, June 19). *Turkey – Stand-by Arrangement*. Retrieved from archivescatalog.imf.org: https://archivescatalog.imf.org/Details/archive/125019304
IMF. (1980b, September 17). *Turkey – National Security Council*. Retrieved from archivescatalog.imf.org: https://archivescatalog.imf.org/Details/archive/125018618 adresinden alındı
IMF. (1980c, February 20). *Statement by Mr. de Groote on Turkey – EBM (2/21/80)*. Retrieved from https://archivescatalog.imf.org/: https://archivescatalog.imf.org/Details/archive/125020208
IMF. (1981, September 8). *Statement by Mr. de Groote on Turkey – EBM/81/121 (9/9/81)*. Retrieved from https://archivescatalog.imf.org/: https://archivescatalog.imf.org/Details/archive/125003255
IMF. (1982, February 25). *Statement by Mr. de Groote on Turkey – EBM/82/25 (2/26/82)*. Retrieved from archivescatalog.imf.org: https://archivescatalog.imf.org/Details/archive/125002226
IMF. (1983a, May 20). *Turkey – Staff Report for the 1983 Article IV Consultation and Request for Stand-by Arrangement*. Retrieved from archivescatalog.imf.org: https://archivescatalog.imf.org/Details/archive/125068443
IMF. (1983b, June 27). *Turkey – Stand-by Arrangement*. Retrieved from archivescatalog.imf.org: https://archivescatalog.imf.org/Details/archive/125067913
IMF. (1983c, June 24). *Turkey – Stand-by Arrangement*. Retrieved from archivescatalog.imf.org: https://archivescatalog.imf.org/Details/archive/125067954
Milliyet. (1980a, January 25). *Demirel: "Yoklukları kaldırmak için önlem aldık"*, p. 1. Retrieved from http://gazetearsivi.milliyet.com.tr
Milliyet. (1980b, January 29). Demirel: "Bırakın Yapılsın Diyoruz". *Milliyet*, p. 6.
Milliyet. (1980c, January 26). İşadamları devalüasyonu genellikle olumlu karşıladı. *Milliyet*, p. 7.
Milliyet. (1980d, September 13). Ordunun yönetime gelmesi dışta olumlu karşılandı. *Milliyet*, p. 6.
NATO. (1979a, May 15–16). *Final Communiqué*. Retrieved from nato.int: https://www.nato.int/cps/en/natohq/official_texts_27036.htm?selectedLocale=en
NATO. (1979b, December 11–12). *Final Communiqué*. Retrieved from nato.int: https://www.nato.int/cps/en/natohq/official_texts_27042.htm?selectedLocale=en
NATO. (1980a, June 24). *Item STATEMENT SEC GEN 24/06/1980 – Preliminary Remarks to the Press by the Secretary General – Ankara 24th June1980*. Retrieved from https://archives.nato.int/: https://archives.nato.int/preliminary-remarks-to-press-by-secretary-general-ankara-24th-june-1980
NATO. (1980b, December 10). *Item M/DPC/2(80)27 – Final Communique – DPC in Ministerial Session 9th and 10th December 1980*. Retrieved from archives.nato.in: https://archives.nato.int/final-communique-dpc-in-ministerial-session-9th-and-10th-december-1980
NATO. (1981, May 5). *Item Press Communique M1(81)5-Annex – Extracts for Publication from the Minutes of the Ministerial Meeting of the Council 4th and 5th May 1981*. Retrieved from archives.nato.int: https://archives.nato.int/extracts-for-publication-from-minutes-of-ministerial-meeting-of-council-4th-and-5th-may-1981
NATO. (1982, December 1). *Item M/DPC/2(82)23 – Final Communique – DPC in Ministerial Session 1st and 2nd December 1982*. Retrieved from archives.nato.int: https://archives.nato.int/final-communique-dpc-in-ministerial-session-1st-and-2nd-december-1982
NATO. (1983, June 1). *Item M/DPC/1(83)8 – Final Communique – DPC in Ministerial Session 1st and 2nd June 1983*. Retrieved from archives.nato.int: https://archives.nato.int/final-communique-dpc-in-ministerial-session-1st-and-2nd-june-1983

NATO. (1987, 12 11). *Final Communiqué*. Retrieved from nato.int: https://www.nato.int/cps/en/natohq/official_texts_23395.htm?selectedLocale=en

Official Gazette. (1980, September 12). *Genelkurmay ve Millî Güvenlik Konseyi Başkanı Orgeneral Kenan Evren'in Türk Milleti'ne Açıklaması*. Retrieved from resmigazete.gov.tr: https://www.resmigazete.gov.tr/arsiv/17103_1.pdf

Önder, N. (2016). *The Economic Transformation of Turkey: Neoliberalism and State Intervention*. London and New York: I.B. Tauris.

Owen, R., & Pamuk, Ş. (1999). *A History of Middle East Economies in the Twentieth Century*. Cambridge: Harvard University Press.

Özden, B. A., Akça, İ., & Bekmen, A. (2017). Antinomies of Authoritarian Neoliberalism in Turkey The Justice and Development Party Era. In C. B. Tansel (Ed.), *States of Discipline Authoritarian Neoliberalism and the Contested Reproduction of Capitalist Order* (pp. 189–209). London and New York: Rowman & Littlefield International.

Özuslu, S. (1980, January 26). TÜSİAD: "Yeni önlemler kesin ve sürekli olmalıdır". *Milliyet*, p. 9.

Reagan, R. (1981, December 23). *Address to the Nation About Christmas and the Situation in Poland*. Retrieved from reaganlibrary.gov: https://www.reaganlibrary.gov/archives/speech/address-nation-about-christmas-and-situation-poland

Sönmez, Ü. (2011). *Piyasanın İdaresi Neoliberalizm ve Bağımsız Düzenleyici Kurumların Anatomisi*. İstanbul: İletişim Yayınları.

The Central Bank of the Republic of Turkey. (2002). *The Impact of Globalization on the Turkish Economy*. Ankara: The Central Bank of the Republic of Turkey.

The United States of America & Turkey. (1980). *Agreement for Cooperation on Defense and Economy*. Washington: Dept. of State.

Turkey–European Union Assosiation Council. (2001). *Turkey–European Union Association Council Decisions 1964–2000 (Vol. 2)*. Ankara: Prime Ministry State Planning Organisation.

Ünay, S. (2006). *Neo-liberal Globalization and Institutional Reform: The Political Economy of Development Planning in Turkey*. New York: Nova Science.

US Department of State. (1988a). *United States Treaties and Other International Agreements*. Washington: U.S. Government Printing Office.

US Department of State. (1988b). *United States Treaties and Other International Agreements*. Washington: U.S. Government Printing Office.

US Department of State. (1992). *United State Treaties and Other International Agreements*. Washington: U.S. Government Printing Office.

Wasowski, S. S. (2009). U.S. Sanctions Against Poland. *The Washington Quarterly, 9*(2), 167–184.

World Bank. (1980a). *Announcement of World Bank Provides Seventy-Five Million Dollars Supplementary Loan to Turkey for Structural Adjustment on November 26, 1980 (English)*. Washington: World Bank Group. Retrieved from http://documents.worldbank.org/curated/en/099041209202225677/IDU075573cbf0df65043340a5b007f9cb7ed2723

World Bank. (1980b). *Turkey – Structural Adjustment Loan Project (English)*. Washington: World Bank. Retrieved from http://documents.worldbank.org/curated/en/542791468760499743/Turkey-Structural-Adjustment-Loan-Project

World Bank. (1981). *Turkey – Second Structural Adjustment Loan Project (English)*. Washington: World Bank. Retrieved from http://documents.worldbank.org/curated/en/546011468779159115/Turkey-Second-Structural-Adjustment-Loan-Project

World Bank. (1982). *Turkey – Third Structural Adjustment Loan Project (English)*. Washington: World Bank. Retrieved from http://documents.worldbank.org/curated/en/442121468778214662/Turkey-Third-Structural-Adjustment-Loan-Project

World Bank. (1983). *Turkey – Fourth Structural Adjustment Loan Project (English)*. Washington: World Bank Group. Retrieved from http://documents.worldbank.org/curated/en/602491468338415101/Turkey-Fourth-Structural-Adjustment-Loan-Project

Yalman, G. (2009). *Transition to Neoliberalism: The Case of Turkey in 1980's*. Istanbul: İstanbul Bilgi Üniversitesi Yayınları.
Yalpat, A. (1984). Turkey's Economy Under the Generals. *Middle East Report*, p. 122.
Yılmaz Şener, M. (2006). *The Relationship Between Neoliberalism and Authoritarian States: The Case of Turkey*. Retrieved from https://www.rrojasdatabank.info: https://www.rrojas-databank.info/neolibstate/meltemyilmazsener.pdf

Index

Note: Page numbers in *italic* indicate a figure and page numbers in **bold** indicate a table on the corresponding page.

For Product Safety Concerns and Information please contact our EU
representative GPSR@taylorandfrancis.com
Taylor & Francis Verlag GmbH, Kaufingerstraße 24, 80331 München, Germany

www.ingramcontent.com/pod-product-compliance
Ingram Content Group UK Ltd.
Pitfield, Milton Keynes, MK11 3LW, UK
UKHW022042061126
477531UK00009B/497
9781032656175